汉英双语版

# 去学校化社会
**Deschooling Society**

[美] 伊万·伊利奇 著

吴康宁 译

中国轻工业出版社

**图书在版编目（CIP）数据**

去学校化社会：汉英双语版／（美）伊万·伊利奇
（Ivan Illich）著；吴康宁译. —北京：中国轻工业出
版社，2017.9（2024.8重印）
ISBN 978-7-5184-1430-7

Ⅰ. ①去… Ⅱ. ①伊… ②吴… Ⅲ. ①教育思想—美国　Ⅳ. ①G40-097.12

中国版本图书馆CIP数据核字（2017）第137058号

**版权声明**

© Ivan Illich 1970
Copyright owner: Valentina Borremans
First published in English by Calder & Boyars Publishers, London. 1971
(*Deschooling Society*) Published by Marion Boyars Publishers, London
All rights reserved

责任编辑：吴　红　王慧超　　责任终审：张乃柬
策划编辑：吴　红　　　　　　责任校对：刘志颖　　责任监印：吴维斌

出版发行：中国轻工业出版社（北京鲁谷东街5号，邮编：100040）
印　　刷：三河市鑫金马印装有限公司
经　　销：各地新华书店
版　　次：2024年8月第1版第5次印刷
开　　本：710×1000　1/16　印张：18
字　　数：240千字
书　　号：ISBN 978-7-5184-1430-7　定价：58.00元

读者热线：010-65181109
发行电话：010-85119832　010-85119912
网　　址：http://www.chlip.com.cn　http://www.wqedu.com
电子信箱：1012305542@qq.com
版权所有　侵权必究
如发现图书残缺请拨打读者热线联系调换
241120Y1C105ZYW

# 译 者 导 读

本书作者伊万·伊利奇（Ivan Illich, 1926—2002）是当代世界著名社会批评家、教育思想家，"去学校化社会"思想的创始人。其一生特立独行，著述甚丰，本书便是其主要代表作之一。

## 一、作者生平

本书作为伊利奇的个人作品，乃是本书出版前伊利奇的个人生活史、受教育史以及工作史综合作用的结晶。而伊利奇的个人生活史是复杂的，受教育史是丰富的，工作史是战斗的。

1926年伊利奇出生于奥地利的维也纳，父亲是南斯拉夫的天主教神父，母亲是德籍西班牙裔犹太人。童年期的伊利奇有时和居住在奥地利的祖父母生活在一起，有时和居住在南斯拉夫的外祖父母生活在一起。因为母亲的犹太血统，1941年伊利奇被迫离开奥地利，随父母去意大利生活。"国际化"的家庭生活背景，加上过人的天赋，使伊利奇得以通晓多种语言。除了英语、德语、西班牙语、意大利语和法语外，伊利奇还会使用克罗地亚语、古希腊语、拉丁语、葡萄牙语、北印度语以及其他一些语言。

伊利奇在教会学校接受了初等教育。他兴趣广泛，大学阶段先在意大利佛罗伦萨大学研习人体组织学和矿物晶体学，后来在意大利罗马教皇大学攻读哲学和神学，在奥地利萨尔茨堡大学攻读中世纪史并获历史学博士学位。多学科的教育背景使得伊利奇学养深厚，文理兼通。就人文与社会学科而言，伊利奇谙熟哲学、神学、历史学、社会学、经济学、人类学、政治学、法学、文学等诸多领域。这也是读过本书的人多为伊利奇的渊博学识与深刻洞察力所折服的原因。

1951年，伊利奇被罗马天主教会授命为神父后即迁居美国，在纽约最贫困的社区"华盛顿高地（Washington Heights）"，也是波多黎各人和爱尔兰人的教区担任签约神父。由此，伊利奇了解到美国少数民族及底层民众的生活状况和价值观念，致力于改善处境不利人群的社会福利。

1956年，30岁的伊利奇成为波多黎各庞塞天主教大学副校长，直至1960年。在此期间，伊利奇目睹了帝国主义经济与文化对贫困国家的侵略、穷人的生活疾苦，激发了他充当摧毁旧制度、建立新制度的代言人的强烈责任感。与此同时，伊利奇结识了后来成为美国激进主义教育学代表人物之一的赖默（Everett Reimer），并在其影响下开始关注并研究教育问题。1959—1961年，伊利奇担任波多黎各高等教育和公共福利顾问委员会委员。因对传统的天主教会活动深为不满、猛烈抨击，伊利奇与波多黎各天主教会产生严重分歧，遂于1960年离开波多黎各。自此，伊利奇拒绝被人称为神父。

1961年，伊利奇在墨西哥的库埃纳瓦卡（Cuernavaca）创建了跨文化文献中心（Center for Intercultural Documentation），旨在改善拉丁美洲各国的社会文化状况，探讨事关人类命运与出路的全球性问题。该中心除了培训神职人员之外，还为拉丁美洲各国民间机构培训了2000多名教师、护士、技术人员以及社会工作者。

从1967年开始，伊利奇和赖默定期在跨文化文献中心见面，交流并探讨拉丁美洲的教育和社会问题。在此过程中，伊利奇形成了自己的"去学校化社会"思想。1969年，伊利奇在《星期六评论》（*The Saturday Review*）上发表了《无用的拉丁美洲学校教育》（*The Futility of Schooling in Latin American*）一文，公开阐述其"去学校化社会"思想。1970年春夏期间，伊利奇每周向跨文化文献中心提供本书不同章节的内容，供研究项目的参与者们讨论。这些参与者来自美国、奥地利、比利时、巴西、波多黎各、智利等不同国家，有哲学家、社会学家、历史学家、社会评论家、作家、诗人、媒体人以及游戏设计师等，其中包括美国著名社会学家伯格（Peter Berger）、巴西著名教育家弗莱雷（Paulo Freire）等人。1970年，伊利奇将相关论文结集为本书，出版后立即在西方国家引起强烈震撼，出版第三年（1972年）便连续印刷3次，截至2015年已印刷15次。1971—1973年，伊利奇和赖默在跨文化文献中心举办"教育中的抉择"研讨班，研究与探讨教育改革的出路等问题，使"去学校化社会"思想得到更广泛的传播。

从20世纪80年代起，伊利奇先后在墨西哥、美国和德国等地的大学任教。2002年12月2日，伊利奇在德国不莱梅去世，享年76岁。

除本书之外，伊利奇的重要著作还有《觉醒的庆典》（*Celebration of Awareness*，1969）、《欢乐的工具》（*Tools for Conviviality*，1973）、《能源与公正》（*Energy and Equity*，1974）、《无能化的职业》（*Disabling Professions*，1977）、《影子工作》（*Shadow Work*，1981）等。

## 二、时代背景

本书问世于20世纪70年代初。恩格斯在谈到文艺复兴时曾经说过："这是一个需要巨人而且产生了巨人——在思维能力、热情和性格方面，在多才多艺和学识渊博方面的巨人——的时代。"套用一下这个句式，也可以说20世纪60年代至70年代初正是一个需要伊利奇及本书，而且产生了伊利奇及本书的年代。因为在那个年代，西方国家经过20多年的战后发展，教育与社会一方面成就巨大，另一方面却又陷入困境。此时需要有人挺身而出，扮演改造教育与社会的代言人的角色。于是，伊利奇横空出世，本书应运而生。作为催生本书的社会因素，那个年代至少呈现出以下三个重要特征。

其一，日益加深的社会矛盾导致社会冲突此起彼伏。第二次世界大战结束后直至整个20世纪50年代，西方国家的总体状况是平和的、平稳的。

但到了20世纪60年代，不同阶层、不同种族、不同性别之间的种种矛盾逐渐凸显出来，并呈日趋普遍、尖锐之势，以致社会冲突时有发生，甚至酿成爆发性社会事件。1963年8月28日在美国发生的25万黑人群众（也包括部分白人）参加的旨在争取平等与自由权利的大规模示威活动，便是最具代表性的一例。

其二，现代科技的迅猛发展让人的欲望不断膨胀。许多人觉得，借助现代科技，没有生产不出的东西，没有实现不了的愿望，人类几乎无所不能。尤其是在1969年美国宇航员成功登月后，人们的这种感觉愈发强烈。于是，永恒的进步成为追求，无节制的消费成为时尚，无限制的生产成为必然，无所不及的制度性安排成为日常。与之伴随的则是自然资源大量消耗，环境污染日益严重，社会结构两极分化，人的心理虚弱无能。

其三，人们对于学校教育的作用开始产生怀疑。第二次世界大战结束后至整个20世纪50年代，西方国家对于学校教育的作用普遍抱有热切的期待与乐观的预期，认为学校教育将会助益经济发展与政治进步，促进社会平等。为此，政府与民间对学校教育都有大量投入，但结果相当不如人意。在基础教育方面，以美国为例，詹姆斯·科尔曼（James Coleman）领导的研究小组1966年向美国国会递交的《关于教育机会平等的报告》用大量数据表明，学校在帮助"处境不利儿童"的学习方面成效甚微，影响学生学业成绩差异的主要因素还是家庭。美国政府在1965—1968年耗费逾30亿美元，对学校中的600万名处境不利儿童予以补偿，却"以彻底失败而告终"。在高等教育方面，20世纪60年代中期爆发了几乎席卷所有西方发达国家的大学危机。其中尤以美国和法国为甚。美国的"学潮"开启了这一时期西方国家学生运动的序幕，并同黑人民权运动、反越战运动紧密结合；1968年，法国突然爆发的"五月风暴"则使大学生对于大学教育制度的强烈不满，同民众对于社会现实的各种不满连为一体，全国范围的罢课与罢工活动相互推波助澜。一时间，社会陷入混乱，政府不知所措。

本书就是在这样的时代背景下问世的。

## 三、主要思想

本书共七章,第一章"我们为什么必须废除学校"阐述了"对一个学校化了的社会进行去学校化意味着什么";第二章"学校现象学"批驳了"关于学校与教育之关系的某些假设";第三章"仪式化了的进步"剖析了学校编造与灌输的一系列"神话";第四章"制度光谱"揭露了"虚假的公用事业"和"作为虚假公用事业的学校";第五章"荒谬的一致性"反思了"非个人自主的规定性学习"的观念本身;第六章"学习网络"提出了创建一种"新的正规教育制度"的若干构想;第七章"'厄庇米修斯式的人'的再生"则描绘了去学校化社会中"人的形象"。

"学校化社会"与"去学校化社会"是本书中反复出现的一对基本概念。伊利奇并未对这两个概念专门予以界定,但其基本含义则淋漓尽致地体现在他对"学校化社会"的猛烈批判和对"去学校化社会"的倾情构想之中,而批判与建构正是本书的两大基本内容。

### (一)对"学校化社会"的批判

从逻辑上看,本书对"学校化社会"的批判包括三个方面,即对现代学校的批判、对学校与社会关系的批判、对现代社会的批判。

#### 1. 对现代学校的批判

伊利奇将现代学校界定为"与教师有关的、要求特定年龄段的人全日制地学习必修课程的过程""是基于学是教的结果这一信条而建立起来的一种制度"。在他眼中,现代学校的制度与过程荒谬无比、背离人性。

其一,设立学校所依据的一组假设荒谬至极。这组假设声称:"人生万事皆存秘密;人的生活质量高低取决于是否知晓人生秘密;唯有经过按部就班的连续过程,才能掌握人生秘密;唯有教师才能正确揭示人生秘密。"

同样，学校对儿童进行教育所基于的三个前提也荒谬透顶，即所谓"儿童隶属于学校、儿童在学校中学习、儿童只能在学校中接受教育"。尽管这三个前提已然成"制度性常识"，但伊利奇一语道破："这种制度性常识本身是学校的产物。"他毫不客气地驳斥道："我们所知道的大部分东西都是在学校之外学到的。学生的大部分学习都是教师不在场时自己进行的；即使教师在场，学生也经常是自己进行学习的。"

其二，学校垄断了教育的权利与资源。伊利奇愤愤不平地指出，"学校不仅盗用了可用于教育的财力、人力以及人们对教育的良好愿望，而且阻碍了其他机构承担教育任务""辍学者则没有代替学校的其他教育途径可以选择……法律不强求任何人开车，却强迫每一个人上学"。如此，学校便对社会进行着相当霸道的世俗二分："强制性学校的存在本身便把任何社会都划分为两个领域，即：有些时段、有些过程、有些安排、有些职业是'学术的'或'教育的'，其他的则不是。这样，学校便具有了划分社会现实的无穷力量：教育成了非世俗领域，而世俗世界则成了非教育领域。"

其三，学校编造并灌输着社会神话。伊利奇直言不讳地揭露道："今天的学校行使着有史以来那些权力巨大的教会所共有的三重功能。它既是社会神话的收藏者，又是将社会神话所含的种种矛盾加以制度化的专业机构，同时还是日常仪式的实施场所，这些日常仪式再生产出并掩饰着社会神话与社会现实之间的矛盾。""在当今世界，没有任何一种制度能像学校，更为巧妙地对其成员掩饰社会原则与社会现实之间的深刻矛盾。"伊利奇还进一步揭露道，学校制度及学校中包括教学在内的各种仪式化活动本身都充斥着"隐性课程"，这些隐性课程诉说着四种神话，即"制度化价值观的神话""价值观测量的神话""套装价值观的神话""永恒进步的神话"。通过这些仪式，通过这些隐性课程，通过这些神话，学校也就成了"一个广告商，它让你相信你需要这个现存社会"，它把学生"诱入一个以增长为取向的消费社会之中"。

其四，学校剥夺了学生自主学习的权利、欲望和能力。伊利奇指责学校哄骗学生相信"有价值的学习是上学的结果""学是教的产物";指责学校"不是把相关品质或能力与角色相关联,而是把所设想的获取这些品质或能力所需的过程与角色相关联";指责学校中套装化了的价值观与课程、仪式化了的教学及各种活动导致学生变得一味"依赖于制度安排",误以为"安排越多,结果越佳;或拾级而上,则必至成功"。伊利奇痛心地说:"他们在扮演儿童角色时毫无快乐可言……这种角色是社会在其学龄时段强加给他们的。"于是,"聪明的学生也好,愚钝的学生也罢,其学习都是或因鞭棍所逼,或为理想职业所诱,他们总是靠死记硬背、阅读以及临场机智来应付各种考试。"伊利奇甚至认为,学校对人的伤害要甚于战争,因为"即便是战争制造者,所杀害的也只是人的躯体;而学校则通过使人放弃对于自己成长的责任,而导致许多人走向一种精神自杀"。

其五,学校使人早早异化。伊利奇对此明察秋毫:"在年轻人进入社会之前,学校就已经通过把他们与社会相隔离而将他们预先异化了。他们自认为既是自己所掌握的知识的消费者,同时也是这种知识的生产者,但实际上这些知识不过是学校这一市场中所出售的一种商品。学校使这种异化成为年轻人适应生活所做的准备,这就剥夺了教育的现实性与工作的创造性。"

其六,学校使大多数人成为失败者。伊利奇认为,学校教育最适合的对象"只是那些按照社会控制既定要求的那样去亦步亦趋学习的人","学校只对那些想要不断获得更高层次的文凭的人开放",而这就使得"大多数人都中了学校的圈套,即是说,接受学校教育的结果,使得他们在比自己受到更好的学校教育的人面前感到自卑"。

因此,伊利奇断言,"学校教育既不可能推动学习,也不可能促进正义",非但如此,"学校已成为一个社会问题,它正陷于四面楚歌之中"。

## 2. 对学校与社会关系的批判

伊利奇认为,现代社会中学校的社会属性已发生根本变化,学校与社会的关系也与过去迥然相异。伊利奇在这方面的观点或许最有自己的特点。

其一，学校已成为一种产业，而且是制造人们需要的一种主要产业。伊利奇提醒人们，在如今的"公司式国家"中，学校已成为"继行会、工厂以及公司之后出现的最典型的新型企业"；进一步来看，"假如我们把参与全日制教和学的人数加在一起，那么便会发现学校这个所谓的上层建筑已成为社会中的主要雇主"；更重要的是，"在今天，大多数人都从事着各种需要的生产，能够满足这些需要的是集约使用资本的产业。而在这当中，学校扮演着最主要的角色"。

其二，学校已成为一种自变量，即严重影响社会变革的自变量。伊利奇告诫说："我们已习惯认为学校是依附于政治与经济结构的一个变量，"然而，这"既低估了对学校教育制度的有效挑战中所蕴含的政治潜能，也低估了学校教育制度自身所具有的基本的政治属性与经济属性……将学校视为社会变革的因变量的主张都是不切实际的幻想"。事实上，学校已成为社会危机的一个根源，因为"学校成了把人诱入其自身所设陷阱的主要工具"。

其三，学校已成为一种模板，即社会的过程与机制的模板。在伊利奇眼中，与其说学校是社会的缩影，不如说社会是学校的延伸。充斥于现实社会中的制度性安排的全面操控、圣俗有别的截然二分、供给与消费的基本关系以及人的严重异化等，其实都肇始于学校，是学校中的那些基本关系、机制和过程的翻版。正所谓，"人们一旦承认学校的必要性，那么也就容易成为其他制度的俘虏。青少年一旦听任课程教学形塑自己的想象，那么也就会习惯于接受任何一种制度性计划。""人们一旦在学校的训导下形成了价值观可以被生产出来且可以被加以测量这一观念，往往便会认可所有类型的等级划分。"所以，伊利奇说："现在，不只是教育，社会现实本身也已经学校化了。"

### 3. 对现代社会的批判

既然学校如上所述满眼荒谬，既然社会已经全盘学校化了，那么，社会也必然问题丛生、危机深重。对此，伊利奇的批判同样毫不留情。

其一，现代社会已毫无教育可言。伊利奇伤感地写道，在一个学校化社会中，其他所有社会领域，包括"工作、闲暇、政治、城市生活甚至家庭生活等，其自身都已不再成为教育手段，而是依赖于从学校学习预先设定的习惯和知识"，而"如果人进行劳动的最大成果应当是他从中所受的教育以及劳动赋予其主动教育他人的机会，那么，现代社会在教育学意义上的异化甚至比在经济学意义上的异化还要严重"。

其二，现代社会已毫无惊奇可言。让伊利奇很难接受的是，现代社会中的一切都是制度安排的产物，都是预先设定的结果，"就连行道树所在的位置也是由园林部门决定的""在这个世界中，人与人之间以及人与世界之间的所有接触都是预见与操控的产物"。

其三，现代社会已毫无人道而言。伊利奇悲愤地说，现代社会把人最宝贵的"批判的独立精神""剥夺得荡然无存"，使人"愈发会成为广布于整个社会中的教学与操控的有效过程的牺牲品"。伊利奇怒斥道："世界已失去其人道的层面，再度回到被必然性与命运支配的状况中，而这曾是原始时代的特征。"与未开化时代不同的是，现代社会借助"人的计划安排"，使人"成了科学家、工程师以及计划制订者们的玩物"。

其四，现代社会已毫无希望可言。伊利奇十分不屑地说："由于人无法想象有什么东西是制度不能为他提供的，因此便形成了什么都想要的难填欲壑。人处于他自己制造出来的无所不能的种种工具的包围之中，结果降格为这些工具的工具。"现代社会中的各种制度"已紧紧扣牢这个世界之灵柩的顶盖"，"它们制造需要的速度要快于它们能使需要得以满足的速度；它们在试图让它们所制造的各种需要得到满足的过程中吞噬着地球"。如此循环往复，无休无止，结果导致"物品的生产污染了海水和空气，毁坏了不可替代的资源……"，"这些资源已经被破坏到近乎枯竭的地步。无论走到哪里，都可看到大自然满目疮痍，社会毫无人道，人的精神生活遭到侵犯，个人职业难以为继"。"现实世界已被我们自己制造的工具所产生的烟雾搅得天昏地暗，转瞬之间，我们发现已掉进自己设下的陷阱之中，伸手不见五指。"

总之,现代学校荒谬无比,现代社会已经学校化了,这种学校化社会让"人类自身正濒临危境"——这就是本书所做的全部批判的基本要义。

## (二)"去学校化社会"的构想

建构一个去学校化社会是伊利奇梦寐以求的目标。对此,伊利奇有如下构想。

### 1. 强化自我解放意识

伊利奇认为:"除非我们现在就把自己从教育傲慢中解放出来,从人能够为上帝所不能为这一信念中解放出来,也即从人可以为了拯救他人而操控他人这一信念中解放出来,否则,具有全面破坏作用而又持续加剧的强制性教育便会实现它的最终逻辑。"原因就在于,"如果今天的人们不将自身从强制性的学校中解放出来,那么也就无法从不断升级的消费中解放出来"。所以,伊利奇提出:"我们首先必须建立这样一个社会,在这个社会中,个人成为他自己将重新获得比制造物品与操控他人更为重要的价值。"他强调,不只是社会中的各种制度,而且还有社会的精神,都应当是"去学校化的"。

### 2. 改变生活道路选择

伊利奇语重心长地说,我们不能选择"消费的生活"取向,而是要选择"行动的生活"取向;不能选择"只会让我们走向耗竭资源与污染环境的末路""制造与毁灭、生产与消费的生活方式",而是要选择"能使我们具有自发性、自主性而又相互联系的生活方式"。

### 3. 更新政治评估标准

伊利奇意识到,建构去学校化社会这件事必须同制定政治纲领挂钩。

他断然指出,"一个没有明确认识到去学校化之必要性的政治纲领不是革命性纲领",提出应当把建构去学校化社会的努力作为对政治改革进行评估的标准,他直截了当地说:"对于20世纪70年代中任何一项重要的政治改革纲领,都应进行如下评估:它在多大程度上清楚地阐明了去学校化的必要性?并且,它在多大程度上提供了实现它所提出的改善社会的教育品质这一目标的指导方针?"

### 4. 创立全新教育制度

这是伊利奇在谈论去学校化社会的构想时着墨最多之处。伊利奇反复强调,建构去学校化社会,绝不是在维持现行学校制度不变的前提下进行一些技术性革新,包括增加新的教育渠道、建造新的教育设施、探究新的教育方法等,而是要进行教育制度的彻底变革,是要"打破学校的法定垄断地位,并由此而废除将偏见与歧视结为一体并将之合法化的制度",是要提升"所有社会制度的教育品质",通过"彻底改变教育结构来解放所有社会的重要意义",是要"创造出人与环境之间的新型教育关系","借助于真正的沟通互联网"形成"通体透明的世界"。这种新的教育制度,至少应包括以下三个基本要素。

其一,自由的教育理念。伊利奇认为,"学习是他人操控越少越好的一种活动""不应强迫学习者去学习某门必修课程",而应"把学习的主动权与责任感还给学习者或者他的最直接的指导教师"。因此,"建立新的教育制度的计划不应起始于确定校长的管理目标、专业教育者的教学目标或设想中的任何特定阶级的人群的学习目标";新的学习计划"一定不能起始于'某些人应当学习什么'的问题,而应起始于'学习者为了学习想要接触什么样的人和事'的问题";一定要改变教育者与受教育者之间的"供给者与消费者的关系"。

其二,平等的教育机会。伊利奇认为:"一个好的教育制度应当具有三个目标:第一,向所有希望学习的人提供其一生中任何时候均可使用的学习资源；第二，让所有希望与他人分享自己的知识的人都能找到想从他们那里学到这些知识的人；第三，向所有希望公开提出争议的人提供表达机会。"换言之，所谓平等的教育机会实际上包括三项内容，即平等地获取学习资源的机会、平等地自由分享知识的机会、平等地公开表达意见的机会。

其三，开放的教育网络。伊利奇提出，应当建立一种"易为公众所用且旨在扩大学与教之平等机会的新型网络"，这样一种"机会互联网"可以由四种"学习通道"或者获得教育资源的途径构成。换言之，这种教育网络（本书中"教育网络"与"学习网络"不时交替使用，含义相同）包括四个子网络：一是"教育物品查询服务"网。伊利奇认为："在一个好的教育制度中，学习者应可随意使用各种物品"，为此，可通过各种方法乃至通过立法来释放蕴含于各种社会机构与场所的设施设备之中的教育潜能。二是"技能交换"网。伊利奇呼吁，应当鼓励、吸引具有某项技能的人向那些想要学习这些技能的人进行演示和指导，包括"必须通过法律来保证所有人均享有技能交换的自由"。三是"伙伴选配"网。伊利奇主张，"一个理想的教育制度将会让每个人都有适合于自己的活动，并为之而选择学习伙伴""这种网络或服务将为每个人提供能与他人探讨共同关心的问题的平等机会"。四是"广义教育者查询服务"网。在伊利奇看来，广义教育者可以是专业人员，也可以是准专业人员或自由职业者，"他们既有实践智慧，又乐意帮助进入教育探索领域的新人""去学校化教育应当促进——而不是阻碍——我们去发现这样一些人"。

伊利奇对于实现去学校化社会的主张信心满满，他想借此来改变教育、改变社会、改变世界。他说："社会的去学校化必将使经济、教育和政治之间的界限变得模糊起来，而这些界限正是现今国际秩序与国家稳定的基石。"他认为社会的去学校化不仅是必要的，而且是可能的，因为"学校尚未像一个民族国家那样，或者甚至尚未像一个大公司那样在自我保护方面组织得卓有成效。从学校的支配下解放出来可以是不流血的"。

## 四、简要评价

本书虽非严格意义上的学术专著,但它是价值非凡的思想珍品;若从篇幅计,本书或许只能算作"小册子",但从思想贡献看,它堪称巨著。正因为如此,本书问世后便好评如潮。譬如,库佐尔(J. Kuzuoer)就认为,本书"可能是美国自20世纪50年代以来出版的著作中最重要的一部","凭着《去学校化社会》一书和那些不同凡响的论文,伊利奇一跃成为整个西方世界主张彻底改革学校的核心人物"。联合国教科文组织在1979年为汉堡教育研究所编辑的《国际教育评论》复刊25周年而出版的纪念专集中也指出:"从联合国教科文组织所开展的成人识字运动到伊利奇等人所提出的脱离学校教育论,实际上形成了一股巨大的潮流,给过去25年的世界教育以重大影响。"其后,联合国教科文组织的教育季刊《教育展望》(*Education Prospects*)在1993—1994年各期连续刊文,介绍世界各国最负盛名的教育思想家,伊利奇也因本书集中阐述的"去学校化社会"思想而当仁不让位列其中。弗兰克·M. 弗拉纳根(Frank M. Flanagan)在其2006年所著《史上最伟大的教育家》(*The Greatest Educators Ever*)一书中总共只介绍了自苏格拉底以来18位最伟大的教育家,伊利奇同样因本书的贡献而赫然位列其中。

当然,如同对于任何具有"革命"意义的著作的评价一样,对本书的批评声音也不绝于耳。归纳起来不外乎两点:一是伊利奇的批判过于片面、偏激,认为他只是以极端方式对学校和社会存在的问题进行了言过其实的批判,缺乏全面、辩证的分析;二是伊利奇的构想过于理想、浪漫,认为他提出的关于去学校化社会的种种主张不切实际,并非行之有效。

笔者以为,"译者导读"有别于书评,其主要任务不是要对原著评头论足,而应是交代、介绍与梳理,即交代相关背景、介绍主要思想、梳理基本逻辑,以便为读者自己的阅读与评价提供必要信息。为此,笔者这里只从"为我所用"出发，简要述及本书对于研究和改进我国当今教育与社会所具有的重要意义。

其一，本书为我们深入反思学校存在的问题提供了丰富的思想启迪。虽然本书写于将近半个世纪前，但阅读之后你会发现，伊利奇批判现代学校的大部分观点同样适用于当今中国。尤为让人叹服的是，伊利奇的视野十分开阔，他不是就学校谈学校，而是从个人的成长出发，从人类社会的历史、现状和未来出发去加以审视，这就使他比其他许多人看得更广、更深、更远。

其二，本书为我们全面认识学校与社会的关系提供了独特的方法引领。本书没有一味因循"学校受制于社会"这一近乎教条的主流观点，没有沿袭将学校只是看成社会的政治、经济结构的依存性因变量这一思维惯性，而是反其道而行之，去考察现代学校对于社会的前所未见的深刻影响，揭示学校已成为导致社会与人类濒临危境的重要根源这一值得注意的方面。尽管看起来似乎走向了另一个极端，甚至多少带有一点"学校决定论"之嫌，但客观地讲，如果有意回避或无意忽视现代社会中日益凸显的学校与社会相互嵌入、学校深刻影响社会这一日常事实，那么，我们对于学校与社会的真实关系也不可能做出全面、辩证的解释。

其三，本书为我们着力建设学习化社会提供了有益的参考路径。虽然伊利奇关于创建与现行学校制度完全不同的一套全新教育制度的构想多少有乌托邦之嫌，但这一构想的基本思路对于建设学习化社会的借鉴意义不可低估，因为建设学习化社会就必须要有自由的教育理念、平等的教育机会、开放的教育网络。尽管废除学校并无可能，也无必要，但改造学校自身、打破学校在整个教育体系中的垄断地位、挖掘并发挥整个社会的教育潜能、最大限度地保证所有社会成员在其"人生时时刻刻都可以进行学习、分享及关怀"，乃是我们正在努力建设的所谓学习化社会的题中应有之义。在这个意义上，本书提出的一些创构全新教育制度的理念、目标乃至具体途径就很有参考价值了，读者不妨细细品味。事实上，随着自由、平等、分享的理念逐渐深入人心，随着信息技术的飞速进步以及各种各样的互联与移动通信网络的迅猛发展，学习化社会正在不可抗拒地、一步一步地从理想走向现实，尽管完全实现这一理想不会一蹴而就。

或许是因本书并非严格意义上的学术专著的缘故，或许是受激情影响所致，伊利奇在本书中对于个别观点的表达、个别概念的使用不太讲究，存有逻辑上的瑕疵。譬如，伊利奇一方面反复呼吁要"废除学校"，另一方面又说要"打破学校的法定垄断地位""寻求学与教的更多途径"，"我们对于学校的专门化的全日制教学的依赖将会减少"。若按前一种说法，因为要"废除"，所以学校将不复存在；而按后一种说法，因为只是把学校从教育体系中的"垄断"位置上拉下来，只是寻求"更多"途径，只是"减少"依赖，所以学校将依然存在。再如，既然要废除"学校"，建立"教育网络"，那么在阐述教育网络时，严格来讲就不宜再使用与"学校教育制度"相依为命的诸如"教师""学生"之类的概念，而是有必要使用同"去学校化教育"相吻合的诸如"指导者""学习者"之类的概念。可伊利奇不管这些，他不时混用这两种不同性质的概念。这些，都是读者需要留意的。

有兴趣的读者若是比较一下本导读与20多年前拙译中文繁体本《非学校化社会》的"译序"，当不难发现笔者对于伊利奇的"废除学校"这一思想的理解已有所不同。毕竟速变速朽的四分之一个世纪过去了，教育与社会的现实都已发生了巨大变化，译者的认知和体验也与过去有诸多不同，而不变的只是伊利奇的这本"小册子"巨著以及蕴藏于其中的杰出思想。

吴康宁

2017年2月7日于金陵天地居

# 目　录

译者导读 ························································· I
　　一、作者生平 ················································ I
　　二、时代背景 ················································ III
　　三、主要思想 ················································ V
　　四、简要评价 ················································ XIII

## 去学校化社会（中文版）／ 1

作者序 ··························································· 3
第一章　我们为什么必须废除学校 ······························ 7
第二章　学校现象学 ············································· 33
　　一、年龄 ···················································· 34
　　二、教师与学生 ············································· 37
　　三、全日制就学 ············································· 38
第三章　仪式化了的进步 ········································ 43
　　一、制度化价值观的神话 ··································· 47
　　二、价值观测量的神话 ····································· 49
　　三、套装价值观的神话 ····································· 50
　　四、永恒进步的神话 ········································ 51
　　五、仪式游戏与新的世界宗教 ······························ 52
　　六、未来王国：普遍抱有的期待 ···························· 54

|  |  |  |
|---|---|---|
|  | 七、新的异化 | 56 |
|  | 八、去学校化的革命潜力 | 57 |
| 第四章 | 制度光谱 | 63 |
|  | 一、虚假的公用事业 | 69 |
|  | 二、作为虚假公用事业的学校 | 71 |
| 第五章 | 荒谬的一致性 | 77 |
| 第六章 | 学习网络 | 85 |
|  | 一、一种异议：当下无处可通的桥梁对谁有用 | 86 |
|  | 二、新的正规教育制度的一般特征 | 88 |
|  | 三、四种网络 | 90 |
|  | 四、教育物品查询服务 | 92 |
|  | 五、技能交换 | 100 |
|  | 六、伙伴选配 | 105 |
|  | 七、专业教育者 | 110 |
| 第七章 | "厄庇米修斯式的人"的再生 | 119 |

译后记 ································································· 133

## 去学校化社会（英文版）／139

| | |
|---|---|
| Introduction | 141 |
| 1. Why We Must Disestablish School | 143 |
| 2. Phenomenology of School | 167 |
| 3. Ritualization of Progress | 177 |
|     The Myth of Institutionalized Values | 181 |
|     The Myth of Measurement of Values | 182 |
|     The Myth of Packaging Values | 183 |
|     The Myth of Self-Perpetuating Progress | 184 |

  Ritual Game and the New World Religion ················ 185
  The Coming Kingdom: The Universalization of Expectations ····· 187
  The New Alienation ················································· 188
  The Revolutionary Potential of Deschooling ··············· 189
4. Institutional Spectrum ················································· 195
  False Public Utilities ················································ 200
  Schools as False Public Utilities ································· 203
5. Irrational Consistencies ················································ 209
6. Learning Webs ························································· 217
  An Objection: Who Can Be Served by Bridges to Nowhere? ······ 218
  General Characteristics of New Formal Educational Institutions ···· 220
  Four Networks ······················································ 222
  Reference Services to Educational Objects ··················· 224
  Skill Exchanges ····················································· 232
  Peer-Matching ······················································ 236
  Professional Educators ············································ 241
7. Rebirth of Epimethean Man ········································· 249

# 去学校化社会

（中文版）

Deschooling Society

【美】伊万·伊利奇　著

吴康宁　译

# 作 者 序

我对公共教育产生兴趣要归功于赖默[1]。我们于1958年在波多黎各（Puerto Rico）初次见面，在此之前，我对延长义务教育年限的价值从未产生过怀疑。而现在我们两人都认识到，义务就学剥夺了大多数人的学习权利。我提交给跨文化文献中心[2]的论文及本书所收的论文，是在我与赖默的讨论记录基础上形成的。我们的讨论进行于1970年，那是我和赖默开始对话的第十三个年头。本书最后一章则包括了我在与弗洛姆[3]对巴霍芬[4]的《母权论》进行讨论之后的一些思考。

自1967年以来，我和赖默在墨西哥库埃纳瓦卡（Cuernavaca）的跨文化文献中心定期见面。该中心主任博勒曼[5]也加入了我们的对话，并一直敦促我们对照拉丁美洲和非洲的现实来检视我们的思考。本书也反映了她的信念，即：不只是社会中的各种制度，而且还有社会的精神，都应当是"去学校化的（deschooled）"。

---

[1] 赖默（Everett Reimer, 1922—1998），美国教育学者，激进主义教育学代表人物之一。著有《学校已经死亡》（*School is Dead*）、《社会规划》（*Social Planning*）等。——译者注

[2] 跨文化文献中心，1961年由伊利奇等人在墨西哥的库埃纳瓦卡创建。——译者注

[3] 弗洛姆（Erich Fromm, 1900—1980），美籍德裔哲学家、心理学家，新精神分析学代表人物之一，人本主义心理学先驱。著有《逃避自由》（*Escape from Freedom*）、《健全的社会》（*The Sane Society*）等。——译者注

[4] 巴霍芬（Johann Jakob Bachofen, 1815—1887），瑞士法学家、人类学家、历史学家，进化学派代表人物之一。著有《母权论》（*Mutterrecht*）等。——译者注

[5] 博勒曼（Valentina Borremans, 1930—  ），比利时人，主要负责伊利奇等人创建的跨文化文献中心的运营。1967—1971年，与伊利奇及赖默三人在该中心定期研讨拉丁美洲教育现实问题。著有《欢乐工具参考指南》（*Reference Guide to Convivial Tools*）。——译者注

普及教育不可能通过学校来实现。即便尝试用其他机构取而代之，但只要这些机构依然因袭现今学校的模式，也同样无法实现普及教育。改变教师对学生的态度也罢，添置教育的硬件或软件（教室中的或宿舍里的）也罢，或者最终尝试将教师的教育责任延展至学生的整个生涯也罢，都无济于事。我们必须把目前对于种种新的教育渠道的探索转变为对与之完全不同的制度的探索，即：探索能增加每个人的学习机会的各种教育网络，使得人生时时刻刻都可以进行学习、分享及关怀。我们希望本书能为对教育进行这种根本性研究的人们——同时也为正在寻求其他用以代替现存服务性行业之途径的人们——贡献一些必要的概念。

在1970年春夏期间，我每周三上午都要向位于库埃纳瓦卡的跨文化文献中心的研究项目的参与者们提供本书的不同部分。其中有数十位参与者提出了建议或批评。他们中的许多人将会在本书中找到自己的观点，特别是弗莱雷[1]、伯格[2]、布尔内斯[3]，还有菲茨帕特里克[4]、霍尔特[5]、昆

---

[1] 弗莱雷（Paulo Freire, 1921—1997），巴西教育家，批判教育学代表人物之一。著有《被压迫者教育学》(*Pedagogy of the Oppressed*)、《教育政治学：文化、权力与解放》(*The Politics of Education: Culture, Power, and Liberation*)、《作为文化工作者的教师：致那些敢于教书的人的信》(*Teachers as Cultural Workers: Letters to Those Who Dare Teach*) 等。——译者注

[2] 伯格（Peter Berger, 1929—2017），美国社会学家，现象社会学代表人物之一。著有《社会学的邀请：人文主义的视角》(*Invitation to Sociology: A Humanistic Perspective*)、《现实的社会建构：知识社会学论文集》(*The Social Construction of Reality: A Treatise in the Sociology of Knowledge*) 等。——译者注

[3] 布尔内斯（José María Bulnes, 1931—2012），智利作家、哲学家。著有《瓦尔帕莱索：天主教大学1967年6月至8月的危机》(*Valparaíso: Crisis of Catholic University, June-August 1967*) 等。——译者注

[4] 菲茨帕特里克（Joseph Fitzpatrick, 1913—1995），美国社会学家，拉丁美洲和波多黎各移民问题专家。著有《波多黎各裔美国人：移民到美国本土的意义》(*Puerto Rican Americans: The Meaning of Migration to the Mainland*)、《一个教会，多种文化》(*One Church, Many Cultures*) 等。——译者注

[5] 霍尔特（John Holt, 1923—1985），美国作家、教育家。著有《教育你自己：约翰·霍尔特家庭学校教育手册》(*Teach Your Own: The John Holt Book of Homeschooling*)、《儿童如何学习》(*How Children Learn*) 等。——译者注

特罗[1]、艾伦[2]、古德曼[3]、拉德纳[4]、皮韦托[5]、斯普林[6]、邦迪[7]以及萨利文[8]。在这些批评者中，保罗·古德曼[9]的意见最为尖锐，他迫使我改变了自己的思考。西尔弗斯[10]则对本书第一、三、六章的编辑工作给予了卓有成效的帮助，这几章内容已刊登于《纽约书评》（*The New York Review of Books*）。

赖默和我决定各自公开发表我们在合作研究中的见解。他正在撰写一本内容全面、资料翔实的介绍性著作，预计将用几个月时间进一步征求批评意见后，于1971年晚些时候由双日公司（Doubleday & Company）出

---

[1] 昆特罗（Angel Quintero, 1916—1992），波多黎各教育家、散文家。曾于1961—1964年担任波多黎各教育部副部长，1965—1968年担任波多黎各教育部部长。——译者注

[2] 艾伦（Layman Allen, 1927— ），美国数理逻辑学家、游戏设计师。伊利奇在本书第六章第四节"教育物品查询服务"中提到的名为"Wff'n证明（Wff'n Proof）"的游戏便由其设计。——译者注

[3] 古德曼（Fred Goodman, 1932— ），美国大学教授。对体验式教育与教育游戏有诸多研究，强调与他人合作学习。20世纪60年代，曾任美国联邦教育总署对教育资源信息中心进行分散设计方面的首席顾问。著有《理论中的实践》（*Practice in Theory*）、《关于游戏的某些用途的思考》（*Speculations Concerning Some Uses of Gaming*）等。——译者注

[4] 拉德纳（Gerhard Ladner, 1905—1993），奥地利历史学家。著有《改革的理念：其对基督教思想和行为的影响》（*The Idea of Reform: Its Impact on Christian Thought and Action in the Age of the Fathers*）等。——译者注

[5] 皮韦托（Didier Piveteau, 1924—1986），比利时教育家，支持宗教教育改革，致力于教学计划与教学方法革新。著有《从一所精英学校到一种生活文化》（*From an Elitist School to a Living Culture*）等。——译者注

[6] 斯普林（Joel Spring, 1940— ），美国学者。著有《教育全球化导论》（*Globalization of Education: An Introduction*）、《美国学校：从清教徒到不让一个孩子掉队》（*The American School: From the Puritans to No Child Left Behind*）等。——译者注

[7] 邦迪（Augusto Salazar Bondy, 1925—1974），美国哲学家、教育家、社会学家。著有《我们美国的哲学还存在吗？》（*There is a Philosophy of Our America?*）、《新人类的教育：秘鲁教育改革》（*Education of the New Man: Peruvian Educational Reform*）、《教育与文化》（*Education and Culture*）等。——译者注

[8] 萨利文（Dennis Sullivan），美国媒体人。曾任美国国家广播公司节目制片人。——译者注

[9] 古德曼（Paul Goodman, 1911—1972），美国诗人、作家、社会评论家。著有《荒谬的成长：组织体制中的青年问题》（*Growing Up Absurd: Problems of Youth in the Organized System*）、《强制的反教育和学者团体》（*Compulsory Mis-Education and the Community of Scholars*）等。——译者注

[10] 西尔弗斯（Robert Silvers, 1929— ），美国《纽约书评》编辑。——译者注

版。萨利文在赖默和我会面讨论期间担任秘书,他正在为将于1972年春季出版的一本书做准备,该书将把我的观点置于美国当前正在进行的关于公共学校教育的辩论这一背景之中。我现在出版这本论文集,则是希望在拟于1972年和1973年在库埃纳瓦卡跨文化文献中心举办的"教育中的抉择"研讨班期间听到更多的批评意见。

我的目的是想讨论一旦我们接受了社会可以去学校化这一假设之后将会面临的一些疑难问题;是想寻求一些标准,这些标准有助于我们辨识能促进去学校化环境中的学习的值得发展的一些制度;是想阐明一些个体目标,这些个体目标将会促进闲暇时代的到来,这一时代将与服务业在经济结构中占支配地位的当下时代迥然相异。

*伊万·伊利奇*
*1970年11月于墨西哥*
*库埃纳瓦卡跨文化文献中心*

# 第一章　我们为什么必须废除学校

许多学生，尤其是穷学生，都能直觉到学校在为他们做些什么。学校训导他们混淆过程与实质。而一旦这两者之间的区别变得模糊不清，那么便会出现一种新的逻辑，即：安排越多，结果越佳；或拾级而上，则必至成功。于是，学校"训导"的结果，导致学生把教与学、升级与教育、文凭与能力、语言流畅与叙述新事物的能力混为一谈；导致学生的想象不是基于应有的价值，而是根据所受的服务；导致学生误将药物治疗等同于卫生保健，将社会工作等同于社区生活的改善，将警察保护等同于人身安全，将军事防备等同于国家安全，将激烈竞争等同于工作效率。健康、学习、尊严、独立以及创造性努力，被说成几乎完全是声称为这些目标服务的各种制度发挥作用的结果，而这些目标的更好实现则有赖于社会将更多资源配用于这里所说的医院、学校及其他各种机构的管理运行。

在本书所收论文中，我将说明为什么价值观的制度化必将导致自然环境的污染、社会的两极分化以及人的心理虚弱无能，这是全球性恶化与现代化灾难的进程所产生的三方面问题。我将阐明，当非物质需求被转换为商品需求时，当健康、教育、个体流动、社会福利或心理康复被说成是各种服务或"安排"的结果时，上述损毁过程是如何得以加速的。之所以这样做，是因为我确信，如今正在进行的关于未来趋势的研究都在鼓吹进一步推动价值观的制度化，我们必须指明与之截然相反的趋势得以出现的各种条件。我们需要研究技术的可能用途，以便创造出一些制度——这些制度将有助于个人之间进行创造性与自主性的互动，有助于形成不会被技术专家们实际控制的各种价值观。我们需要进行与目前的未来学迥然相异的研究。

我想提出一个具有普遍意义的问题，即：如何使人的本质与赋予我们的世界观及语言以特征的现代制度的本质相互界定？为此，我选择学校作为分析范例，而对于这个公司式国家[1]中的其他科层机构，比如作为消费单位的家庭、政党、教会、传媒等，只会间接述及。我对学校的隐性课程的分析应可表明，公共教育将从社会的去学校化过程中获益，恰如家庭生活、政治、安全、信仰以及交往将从类似过程中获益一样。

在这一章中，我将首先尝试分析并说明对一个学校化了的社会进行去学校化意味着什么。在此基础上，应会容易理解我为何要在其后各章选择与去学校化过程有关的五个具体方面加以论述。

现在，不只是教育，社会现实本身也已经学校化了。为使所有学生都依附于现存制度，花在富裕学生身上的费用与花在贫困学生身上的费用大致相同。在美国二十个城市中的任何一个城市，贫民区与富裕家庭集中居住的郊区的学生人均年度教育费用处于同一水准，且有时贫困学生的数额更高。[2] 富裕学生与贫困学生同样都离不开学校和医院，学校和医院指导他们的生活，形塑他们的世界观，并告诉他们何为合法、何为不合法。他们都认为个人自行诊治是不负责任的，个人自学是不可靠的，并且都认为未得到行政当局资助的社区组织具有攻击性和破坏性。他们都依赖于制度安排，都对自主行动投以怀疑的目光。在个人自主与社区自主日益欠缺方面，维斯特切斯特[3]甚至比巴西东北部地区更为典型。因此，不论在什么地方，不只是教育本身，整个社会都需要"去学校化"。

---

[1] 公司式国家，源自1970年美国的赖克（Charels A. Reich）的著作《绿化美国》（*The Greening of America*），书中认为国家是一台巨大的机器，完全不受人的控制，并置人的价值观于不顾。——译者注

[2] 杰克逊，《初等教育与中等教育费用的趋势：1965—1968年中心城市与郊区的比较》，美国联邦教育总署规划与计划评估办公室，1969年6月。（Penrose B. Jackson, *Trends in Elementary and Secondary Education Expenditures: Central City and Suburban Comparisons 1965 to 1968*, U.S. Office of Education, Office of Program and Planning Evaluation, June 1969.）——作者注

[3] 维斯特切斯特（Westchester），美国纽约州的一个县，境内有工业城市和高级住宅区。——译者注

福利机构制定了对价值和可行性予以判断的各种标准，以图在专业、政治和财政方面都支配人们的社会想象。这种支配是导致贫困现代化的根源。任何一种对于简单需求的制度性解决办法，都将导致新的贫困阶级的产生以及对贫困的新定义。在十年前的墨西哥，人生于家中、死于家中并由其朋友安葬是很平常的事情，唯有照料灵魂之事才托付给制度性的教会。而在今天，生于家中、死于家中已成为贫穷或特权的标志。临终与死亡已被置于医生与殡仪人员的制度性管理之下。

一旦社会将人的基本需要解释为对于科学地生产出来的各种商品的需求，那么，技术专家们便会按照由其随意改变的标准来界定贫困。于是，所谓贫困者，便是指在某些重要方面落后于社会所宣扬的消费观念的那些人。在墨西哥，所谓穷人是指所受学校教育不足三年者；而在纽约，所谓穷人则是指所受学校教育不足十二年者。

穷人在社会中总是无能为力的。而对于制度性照管的日益依赖使他们产生了新的无能为力，即：心理无能、无力自我谋生。居住于安第斯高原[1]的农民们遭受着地主与商人的剥削，而一旦他们在利马[2]生活，则还得依附于政治首领，并因缺少学校教育而变得无能为力。现代化贫困使得人对于环境控制的无能为力与个人潜力的减损紧密相连。这种贫困的现代化是一种全球现象，是当今时代存在欠发达现象的根本原因。当然，这在富国与穷国被饰以不同的伪装。

对这一现象感受最为强烈的大概要数美国城市，世界其他任何地方都不及美国城市在对付贫困方面花费之巨。世界其他任何地方都未像美国城市这样，对于解决贫困问题的制度安排反而导致贫困者出现如此之多的依赖、愤怒、挫败感以及对制度安排的更为强烈的需求。而且，世界其他任何地方都未像美国城市这样清楚地表明，贫困，一旦成为现代化贫困，便会抵抗仅仅仰仗于金钱的制度安排，并且需要一场制度革命。

---

[1] 安第斯高原（high plateau of the Andes），位于南美洲加勒比海与太平洋沿岸。——译者注
[2] 利马（Lima），秘鲁首都。——译者注

如今在美国，黑人乃至移民都可望享受到两代人之前的时代无法想象的专业化安排，这些安排对于第三世界国家的大多数人来说，近乎天方夜谭。比如，美国的穷人可以向劝学员[1]求助，将其未满17岁的逃学子女送回学校；也可以向医生求助，让其孩子入住每天需支付60美元的病房——这相当于世界上大多数人三个月的收入。但这些只会使穷人更加依赖于安排，使他们日益丧失利用自身经验与社区资源来组织自己生活的能力。

美国穷人正处于一种独特的可称之为"困境"的状态，这也让正处于现代化进程中的世界上的所有穷人都担惊受怕。他们发现，一旦各层各级福利机构的技术官僚们使社会相信这些机构提供的服务具有道义上的必要性，那么，无论花多少钱也不能消除这些福利机构所固有的破坏性。居住于美国城市中心地带的穷人可以用其自身体验来证明"学校化"社会中的立法基础之荒谬。

联邦最高法院的法官道格拉斯（William O. Douglas）认为："建立一种制度的唯一途径是向它提供资金。"据此做如下推论也是正确的，即：只有停止向现今的这些与卫生、教育以及福利有关的各种制度提供财源，才能阻止其产生让穷人无能为力的副作用并因此而导致穷人更贫穷。

我们在评价联邦政府救助项目时必须牢记上述这一观点。美国学校在1965—1968年耗费逾30亿美元对学校中的600万名处境不利儿童予以补偿，便是一个恰当的例子。这个项目以"第一标题（Title One）"而著称，是此前任何国家均未曾尝试过的花费最多的补偿教育项目。然而，这些"处境不利"的儿童在学习方面并未见有任何显著进步。与那些来自中等收入家庭的同学相比，他们之间的差距比以前更大。而且，在实施这一项目的过程中，专家们发现，除此之外还有1000万名儿童艰难生存于经济与教育的不利境况之中。于是，要求联邦政府提供更多补偿经费的理由便可轻易提出。

尽管改善穷人教育的努力耗资甚巨，但以彻底失败而告终，对此可有

---

[1] 劝学员（truant officer），美国地方教育行政人员的一种，负责检查学生旷课、逃学等情况。——译者注

以下三种解释：

第一，30亿美元的资金尚不足以使600万名儿童的学业成绩提高到可测试出来的程度；

第二，经费使用不当，即是说，应当设置不同课程，改善管理，将补偿经费集中用于贫困儿童身上，并对此进行更多的研究，这样才可望获得成功；

第三，教育处境不利的问题不可能靠学校中的教育来解决。

只要补偿经费是通过学校预算来使用的，那么，上述第一种解释无疑便可成立。补偿经费确已拨给那些收有大部分处境不利儿童的学校，但这些经费并未花在贫困儿童本人身上。在已将补偿经费纳入本校预算的学校中，因此而受惠的贫困学生大约只占全部贫困学生的一半。这样，补偿经费除了用于教育之外，还被用于对学生的监护、灌输以及各种社会角色的选拔上。而所有这些功能都同学校中的设施、课程、教师、管理者以及其他要素不可分离地交织在一起。因此，所有这些费用也都包括在学校预算中。

这些增加的经费使得学校能更多地满足那些相对富裕的儿童的需求，这些富裕儿童不得不与贫困儿童同校学习，因而也成了所谓的"处境不利者"。这样，经由学校预算，原本打算用于改善贫困儿童学习处境不利的补助经费，充其量只有很小一部分最终能用在他们身上。

经费使用不当或许完全属实。然而，即便是异乎寻常地使用不当，也不会比学校教育制度自身的问题更加糟糕。受自身特有结构的影响，学校反对把优惠集中于贫穷儿童身上，尽管这些儿童若无特殊帮助便会处境不利。为贫困儿童设置特殊的课程、隔离班级或者延长学时，只会花更多的钱并导致更多的歧视。

纳税者们还不习惯于容忍美国卫生、教育与福利部（HEW）像五角大楼那样，将30亿美元转眼花得一干二净。政府管理机构或许会认为它能够承受来自教育者的强烈不满。假如缩减教育补偿项目，美国中产阶级不会损失什么，而贫穷的父母们则认为他们会遭受损失。而且，他们会要求对用于其子女的补偿经费加以管控。于是,既可削减财政预算、又可增加穷人子女受惠程度的一个合乎逻辑的途径,便是建立一种譬如像弗里德曼[1]和其他一些人建议的助学金制度。这样,补偿经费便可到达受惠者手中,他们便可用来购买一份自己所选择的学校教育。然而,假如这些经费仅限于用来学习学校的课程,那么,尽管这会提供更平等的安排,但并不会因此就能增加社会权利的平等。

显然,即使不同学校在质量上处于同等水平,穷人子女的学习也很难赶上富人子女。尽管他们在相同年龄进入同等学校,但穷人子女也缺少中产阶级子女可随意享受的大部分教育机会。从家庭中的谈话与藏书,到假期旅行与自我意识,对于乐于享用的中产阶级儿童来说,这些都是有利的条件,将有助于他们在校内与校外的生活。因此,如果贫困学生只有依赖于学校才能发展或学习,那么他们通常会落在后面。穷人需要补偿经费,是为了使自己能够进行学习,而不是为了得到针对其所谓的严重缺陷做出安排的证明。

不论在穷国还是在富国,所有这些都是真实的状况,只不过表现形态有所不同。在穷国,现代化贫困的影响范围更广、更为明显,但就目前来看也更为浅表。在拉丁美洲,三分之二的儿童未念完小学五年级便中途退学。不过,倘若这些"辍学者"在美国,其境遇也并不会因此而变得更糟。

今天已很少有哪个国家仍然是传统贫困的受害者。这种传统贫困较为稳定,且很少会使人无能为力。大部分拉丁美洲国家正处于经济发展与竞争性消费的"起飞点"[2]上,并因此而开始走向现代化贫困,即:这些国家

---

[1] 弗里德曼(Milton Friedman, 1912—2006),美国经济学家,货币学派代表人物。1976年获诺贝尔经济学奖。著有《资本主义与自由》(*Capitalism and Freedom*)、《选择的自由:个人的立场》(*Free to Choose: A Personal Statement*)等。——译者注

[2] 起飞点,即美国经济学家罗斯托(Walt Rostow, 1916—2003)所说的经济成长第三阶段。罗斯托在其《经济成长的阶段》(*The Stages of Economic Growth*)一书中提出,人类社会的经济成长分为六个阶段,即:传统社会阶段、起飞前夕阶段、起飞阶段、趋向成熟阶段、高度消费阶段和追求生活质量阶段。——译者注

的国民尽管依然生活于贫困之中，但他们已经学会向往富裕生活。这些国家的法律规定，实行6~10年的义务教育。不光在阿根廷，而且在墨西哥或巴西，普通国民都是根据北美国家的标准来界定何为足够程度的教育，尽管只有极少数人能有机会享受这种长期的学校教育。在这些国家，大多数人都中了学校的圈套，即是说，接受学校教育的结果，使得他们在比自己受到更好的学校教育的人面前感到自卑。对于学校的盲信导致他们有可能遭受双重剥夺，即：越来越多的公共资金被用于少数人的教育；与此同时，许多人则越来越顺从于社会控制。

具有讽刺意味的是，对于绝对需要普及教育这一点最为深信不疑的，是那些迄今只有且今后也将只有极少数人才能受到学校教育的国家。然而，在拉丁美洲国家，大多数家长与儿童还是可以通过其他不同途径接受教育的。在这些国家，国民储蓄用于学校与教师方面的比例或许还高于富裕国家，但这些投入完全不足以对大多数国民实施哪怕只有四年的小学教育。当卡斯特罗[1]承诺，到1980年，古巴人的所有生活都将成为一种教育体验，因而可望解散大学时，他似乎要朝去学校化的方向迈进。然而，在初中与高中阶段，古巴与其他所有拉丁美洲国家一样，似乎仍然将所有人在"学龄期"都能接受学校教育作为一个毋庸置疑的目标，并把推迟实现这一目标的原因仅仅归咎于暂缺资源。

日益增多的安排——如同美国业已提供、拉丁美洲国家只是承诺的那样——导致产生了两个孪生的、相辅相成的欺骗性结果。北美国家的穷人由于接受了12年学校教育而变得无能为力，而南美国家的穷人则因未能享受到同样的教育而被视为不可救药的愚民。无论在北美国家，还是在拉丁美洲国家，穷人都没有从强制性的学校教育中获得社会平等。不但如此，无论在哪个国家，学校的存在本身都导致穷人丧失了掌控自己学习的勇气与能力。从世界范围来看，学校对社会都具有一种反教育影响，即：学校

---

[1] 卡斯特罗（Fider Castro，1926—2016），古巴前领导人。——译者注

被视为专门的教育机构,学校教育的失败被许多人用来证明教育乃是耗费极巨、复杂无比、总是神秘莫测且常常近乎不可能完成的任务。

学校不仅盗用了可用于教育的财力、人力以及人们对教育的良好愿望,而且阻碍了其他机构承担教育任务。工作、闲暇、政治、城市生活甚至家庭生活等,其自身都已不再成为教育手段,而是依赖于从学校学习预先设定的习惯和知识。结果,学校以及依赖学校提供服务的其他机构都因收费过高而失去市场。

在美国,人均学校教育费用的增速几乎已经赶上医疗费用的增速。然而,虽然医生与教师提供的安排日益增多,医疗与教育的效果却每况愈下。在过去40年中,集中消耗在45岁以上患者身上的医疗费用已经翻了几倍,但人均寿命只延长了百分之三。教育经费增长的效果更是不可思议,否则,尼克松[1]总统今年春天也不至冲动到做出要在短期内使每个儿童毕业前都获得"阅读权(Right to Read)"的许诺。

在美国,若要向所有初中生与高中生提供教育者们认为的平等的教育服务,则每年需要花费800亿美元。这个数字要比现在每年花费360亿美元的双倍还要高出许多。美国卫生、教育与福利部和佛罗里达大学(University of Florida)各自进行的费用预测研究指出,按可比价格计算,到1974年,美国教育费用将从目前计划的每年450亿美元增加到每年1070亿美元,这个数字甚至还完全不包括需求增长更快的所谓"高等教育"的巨额费用。对于在1969年已经支付包括越南战争费用在内近800亿美元国防经费的美国来说,显然已捉襟见肘,以致无法再提供平等的学校教育。总统学校财政研究委员会所需探讨的,不是如何维持或削减这一日益增长的费用,而是如何避免这些费用的发生。

必须认识到,平等的义务教育至少在经济上无法实施。在拉丁美洲,用于大学生的人均公共经费是用于"中层市民"(即生活水准介于最穷与

---

[1] 尼克松(Richard Milhous Nixon,1913—1994),曾于1969—1974年担任美国总统。——译者注

最富之间的市民）的350倍到1500倍。在美国，这一差距虽然较小，但教育不公平的现象更为严重。约占人口总数10%的最富有的父母能供其子女接受私立教育，并帮助他们获得基金会资助。而且，这些富家子弟所获人均公共经费的数额是占总数10%的最贫困家庭的儿童的10倍。其主要原因在于，富家子弟就学时间较长，且在大学学习一年的费用远高于在高中学习一年的费用。再者，大部分私立大学都是依靠——起码是间接依靠——源自税收的经费来维持的。

义务教育必然会使社会两极分化，并且把世界各国按照一种国际种姓制度分成各种等级。所有国家都像种姓制度[1]那样被加以排序，其教育的国际地位的高低取决于国民接受学校教育的平均年限。这种等级划分同人均国民生产总值密切相关，又远比基于人均国民生产总值的等级划分更令人感到痛苦。

学校的这种悖论显而易明：不论是美国还是其他国家，学校费用的增加都将强化其破坏作用。必须将这一悖论作为公共议题。现在，人们已普遍认识到，如果不扭转如今只顾物品生产的倾向，那么，我们的自然环境将很快会毁于生化污染。我们同样应当认识到，我们的社会生活与个人生活也同样受到卫生、教育与福利部的污染的威胁，这是社会福利的强制性与竞争性消费的必然恶果。

扩充学校教育与扩充军备同样具有破坏性，只是前者不如后者那样易为世人所察。无论是哪个国家，学校经费的增长都快于入学人数与国民生产总值的增长，却又远低于家长、教师以及学生的期待。这种状况使得世界各国都没有勇气制订非学校化学习（nonschooled learning）的大规模计划，并从财政上给予其支持。美国的状况向世界表明，没有任何一个国家富裕到足以供养得起一个因其自身存在便会产生各种需要的学校系统。因为，一个成功的学校系统会使家长与学生们认为，一个更高层级的学校系

---

[1] 种姓制度，印度的社会等级制度。按照规定，种姓之间界限森严，不得通婚、交往，甚至不能共食、并坐。印度独立后虽对这一制度予以废止，但实际上仍有很大的影响。——译者注

统具有更大的价值,随着更高层级的教育因供不应求而变得稀缺,学校教育经费也将大幅增加。

我们必须认识到,与其说平等的学校教育只是暂无可能实现,不如说从经济角度来看,平等的学校教育的尝试基本上是荒谬的。这种尝试会导致人们才智枯竭,导致社会两极分化,并使人们失去对推动这一尝试的政治系统的信任。义务教育的观念在逻辑上全无限制。关于这一点,白宫最近提供了一个很好的例子。在尼克松先生被提名为总统候选人之前,曾为其服务的"精神病学家"赫茨切纳克(Hutschnecker)博士向总统建议,应对所有6~8岁的儿童进行专门检查,以甄别出那些具有"破坏倾向"的儿童,并对他们进行强制性治疗,必要时应将他们送进专门机构进行再教育。总统已将这一建议交由卫生、教育与福利部加以评估。说实话,建立预防少年犯罪的集中营倒是学校教育制度发展的一种合乎逻辑的结果。

平等的教育机会的确是一个既理想又可行的目标,但把它等同于义务教育则无异于将拯救灵魂与教会组织混为一谈。学校已成为现代无产者的一种世界宗教(world religion),它凭空许诺要拯救技术时代的穷人。民族国家[1]通过学校来实施教育,驱使所有国民都循序渐进地学习与拾级而上的各种文凭相对应的课程,这同昔日的成人仪式及僧侣晋升过程并无二致。现代国家以为自己有责任通过那些并无恶意的劝学员以及各种入职资格规定,而将教育者的主张强加给国民,这同昔日的西班牙国王们通过征服者与宗教法庭而将神学家们的主张强加给被征服民族的做法如出一辙。

两个世纪之前,美国曾在打破单一宗教垄断的运动中走在世界前列。现在,我们需要打破学校的法定垄断地位,并由此而废除将偏见与歧视结为一体并将之合法化的制度。对于一个现代的、人道主义社会来说,其人

---

[1] 民族国家,近代以来通过资产阶级革命或民族独立运动建立起来的、以一个或几个民族为国民主体的国家。它是一种独立自主的政治实体,是政府体制的一种形式。民族是其共同体的认同概念,其来源可以是共享的制度、文化或族群。——译者注

权法案第一条就应与美国宪法第一修正案[1]相呼应，即"国家不得制定有关教育的任何法律"，不应进行强制所有人参与的任何例行活动。

为了有效打破学校的垄断地位，我们需要制定一部法律，以禁止在雇佣、选举或者准许进入学习中心（centers of learning）方面出现因学历而异的歧视。它并不排斥对履行某种职责或承担某种角色的能力进行考查，但将去除现在的荒谬而不公平的做法。这种做法仅仅有利于耗费最大部分的公用经费去学习特定技能者，或同样耗费这些公用经费而可获得文凭者，而这些文凭同任何有用的技能或工作之间都毫无关系。只有国民在其职业生涯中不再因任何学校经历方面的缘故而被剥夺资格，合乎宪法地废除学校才会产生心理效果。

由于教育者执意把套装式教学与文凭捆绑在一起，因此，学校教育既不可能推动学习，也不可能促进正义。学习与社会角色分配已被融入学校教育之中。然而，学习意味着习得一种新的技能或者获得新的见识，而社会晋升则取决于他人已有的观念。虽然学常常是教的结果，但在劳动市场中，对于应聘者适合担任的职场角色或工作类别的判断却越来越取决于其受教育年限的长短。

教学是对有利于学习的环境的选择。学校通过课程来进行角色分配，这些课程根据学生升级所需符合的各项条件而设置。学校把教——而不是把学——与所要分配的这些角色联系在一起，这既不合理，也不开明。之所以说不合理，是因为它不是把相关品质或能力与角色相关联，而是把所设想的获取这些品质或能力所需的过程与角色相关联；之所以说不开明，或者说不具有教育意义，是因为学校教学的对象只是那些按照社会控制既定要求的那样去亦步亦趋学习的人。

履力一直被作为分配社会地位的依据。这种分配有时会在人出生之前，

---

[1] 美国宪法第一修正案（First Amendment to the U.S. Constitution），美国权利法案的一部分，1791年12月15日获得通过。该修正案禁止美国国会制定任何法律来确立国教、妨碍宗教信仰自由、剥夺言论自由、侵犯新闻自由与集会自由、干扰或禁止向政府请愿的权利等。——译者注

比如，因世袭的缘故而被划入某一种姓，或者因血统而成为贵族。获得履历的方式，可以是参加某种例行活动，可以是参加拾级而上的各种圣职授予仪式，也可以是在战争或狩猎中所取功绩的积累。若是更高层次的晋升，则要凭借业已荣受的君王的恩宠。普及学校教育本来是要把角色分配同个人的生活史脱钩，即赋予每个人谋求任何职业的平等机会。但直到今天，仍有许多人错误地相信，学校能够确保公众根据相关学业成绩对学生加以判断。然而，学校教育制度并未使机会平等，而是垄断了机会的分配。

要使能力判断同履历脱钩，就必须像禁止调查个人的政治身份、宗教活动、血统、性生活习惯或种族背景一样禁止询问个人的学习经历。应当制定关于禁止学历歧视的法律。当然，法律无法根除社会对未受学校教育者的歧视，也不会强迫任何人与自学者通婚，但是法律可以阻止不公正的歧视。

人们的第二个主要错觉是：大部分的学都是教的结果。这一错觉是学校制度赖以生存的基础。诚然，在某些情况下，教确实可能有助于某些类型的学。但是，大多数人都是在学校之外获得他们的大部分知识的。迄今为止只有在少数富裕国家，人的知识主要是在学校中获得的，因为其一生被束缚在校园里的时间越来越多。

大多数学习都是自然而然发生的，即便是目的性最强的学习，大多也并非有计划的教学的结果。正常儿童是在不知不觉的过程中学习母语的，尽管父母对其予以关注他们会学得更快些。第二语言学得好的人大多并非按部就班的教的结果，而是独特语言环境影响的产物。他们或者是同祖父母一起生活，或者是去国外旅行，或者是因为爱上了一个外国人。同样，流畅阅读多半也是此类课余活动的结果。虽然大多数乐于广泛阅读者都把自己的阅读仅仅归功于学校，但若就此向他们提出质疑，那么他们也很容易抛弃这种错觉。

然而，时至今日大量的学习似乎仍然是自然而然地发生的，并且是工作或闲暇活动的副产品，这一事实并不意味着有计划的学就不能从有计划的教当中受益，也不意味着两者均无须改进。面对掌握新的复杂技能的任务，那些学习动机强烈的学生或许可以从训练中获益甚多。"训练"这个词现在会让人联想到讲授阅读、希伯来语、教义问答或死记硬背乘法运算表的那些老古董式教师。学校现在很少进行操练式教学，并对之予以差评。但一个动机强烈且心智正常的学生仍可通过这种传统教学方式在几个月内掌握诸多技能，如无线电密码的转译、第二及第三语言的阅读与写作；或者特殊语言的使用技能，如代数、计算机程序设计、化学分析之类；或者手工操作技能，如打字、钟表制作、管道铺设、线路安装、电视机修理之类；或者舞蹈、驾驶、跳水那样的技能。

在某些情况下，习得某种特殊技能可能要以其他一些技能中所蕴含的能力为前提，但这当然不应根据有无经过前提性技能的专门学习过程来加以判断。所谓前提性技能，譬如，修理电视机需要能阅读文字和进行某些计算，跳水需要有良好的游泳技能，而驾驶车辆则对这两者几乎都不需要。

技能学习的进步是可以测量的，一个有学习欲望的普通成人学习技能需花费的合适时间与合适材料也是容易估算的。在美国，把作为外语的一门西欧语言教到能流畅对话的高级水准所需费用在400～600美元，而教会一门东方语言所需的时间或许要翻倍。但这和在纽约接受12年学校教育（此为卫生署录用工人的一个条件）所需费用——近15000美元——相比，仍然是微乎其微。毋庸置疑，不光是教师，印刷工人与药剂师也会利用他们所受的技能训练费用十分高昂这一错觉来保护其行业利益。

如今，学校预先占用了大部分教育经费。操练式教学所需费用低于同层次的学校教育，但它现在成了富有到不进学校也能接受所需教育，以及由军队或大企业送来接受在职培训的人的一种特权。在不断推进美国教育去学校化这一计划的过程中，可用于操练式教学的资源一开始将会是有限的，但最终必将是任何人在其人生任何时候都可从由公共经费支付的数百种可加以界定的技能教学中进行选择性学习。

我们现在便可向所有人——不只是穷人——提供在任何技能中心均可使用的一定限额的教育贷款。我想，这种贷款可采取在每个人出生时便可向其提供的"教育护照（educational passport）"或"教育贷款证（edu-credit card）"的形式。为了有利于那些可能不会在其人生早期阶段就使用年度补助金的穷人，可在发放他们的教育"补助凭证（entitlement）"时将年度补助金的利息累加计入，并在他们日后使用时一并补发。这些教育贷款可使大多数人以比学校中的学习更方便、更有效、更快捷、更低廉且副作用更少的方式，去学习自己最需要的技能。

潜在的技能教师绝不会长期短缺。因为，一方面只有当某种技能在社区中得以有效运用时，对于这种技能的需求才会增加；另一方面，具有某种技能的人也能传授这种技能。然而在今天，尽管社会需要某些技能，而且期盼有人传授这些技能，但掌握这些技能的人缺少与他人分享的热情。之所以会出现这种状况，或者是因为教师垄断着执教许可证，或者是因为各种工会要保护其行业利益。与之不同，技能中心将会让光顾者们不是根据中心所雇员工的状况或技能传授的过程，而是根据技能传授的效果来对中心进行评价。技能中心将向人们，甚至向那些如今被视为不能受雇者[1]提供诸多意想不到的工作机会。事实上，没有理由认为工作场所本身就不能成为这样的技能中心。在工作场所中，雇主及其员工团队可以既向那些选择以这种方式使用其教育贷款者提供工作机会，同时又为他们提供技能教学。

1956年，纽约大主教管区（New York Archdiocess）需要在短期内教会数百名教师、社会工作者以及神父掌握西班牙语，以使他们能同波多黎各人进行交流。我的朋友莫里斯（G. Morris）通过一家西班牙语电台征聘母语为西班牙语的哈莱姆[2]区居民。翌日，约有200名青少年在其办公室门前排队应聘。莫里斯从中挑选了48名，这当中不少人都是辍学者。莫里斯使用美国海外服务机构（U. S. Foreign Service Institute）的西班牙语手册对他们进行培训，这些手册是语言学家为培训研究生而编写的。不到一个

---

[1] 不能受雇者，主要指因年龄、身体或精神缺陷等不能被雇用的人。——译者注
[2] 哈莱姆（Harlem），美国纽约市曼哈顿的一个黑人居住区，曾为20世纪美国黑人文化与商业中心，被誉为"黑人首府"。——译者注

星期，这些青少年就已经开始独立任教，每人负责教4个想学会说西班牙语的纽约居民；不到6个月，他们便完成了教学任务。红衣主教斯佩尔曼（Spellman）于是宣称，他所管辖的127个教区中，每个教区都至少有3名教职人员能用西班牙语进行交流。没有任何一项学校教学计划能够达到这样的效果。

技能教师短缺的原因在于人们笃信文凭的价值。资格认证成为控制教师市场的一种方式，而这种方式也只是在有着学校化心态的人看来是合理的。现在，大多数工艺类与商科的教师在技能熟练程度、创造性及语言交流能力方面都不如优秀的工匠与商人。大部分高中的西班牙语或法语教师的口语水平都不如经过半年充分训练的他们的学生。昆特罗在波多黎各所做的实验表明，只要给予适当的鼓励、安排合适的计划并提供可使用的工具，许多青少年在引导其伙伴对植物、星球和物质等进行科学探究，以及发现发动机与收音机的工作机制和工作原理方面，要强于大多数教师。

如果我们开放教师市场，那么，技能学习的机会便会大幅增加。这有赖于合适的教师遇到合适的学生，这些学生不受学校课程的束缚，并能够被富有挑战性的技能学习计划深深吸引。

在正统教育者看来，自由竞争的操练式教学具有破坏性，是对教育的彻底亵渎。他们认为，学校将技能的习得与"人文"教育合为一体，而操练式教学则使两者相分离。这样，操练式教学便既会助推结果难料的未经许可的教，也会怂恿未经许可的学。

最近公布的一份提案初看起来似乎很有价值。它受经济机会局（Office of Economic Opportunity）赞助，由公共政策研究中心[1]的詹克斯[2]提出。这份提案主张把教育"补助凭证"或助学金发放到家长和学生手中，以供他们支付在自己选择的学校中学习的费用。向个人发放这种补助确实朝正确

---

[1] 公共政策研究中心（Center for the Study of Public Policy），美国哈佛大学的研究机构。——译者注
[2] 詹克斯（Christopher Jencks, 1936— ），美国公共政策研究中心研究员。——译者注

的方向迈出了重要的一步，我们需要保证每个国民都有平等享用来自税收的教育资源的权利，都有核实自己是否得到平等享受的权利，都有一旦遭到拒绝便可提出申诉的权利。这是确保不受累退税[1]影响的方式之一。

然而，詹克斯提案的起始部分却令人失望："保守主义者、自由主义者以及激进主义者都曾在不同时期抱怨美国的教育系统给予专业教育者的鼓励太少，以至他们未能向大多数儿童提供优质的教育。"这份提案主张设立助学金，但同时又规定只能用于学校教育，这就陷入了自相矛盾的境地。

这就好比将一副拐杖送给一个瘸子，但同时又限定他只有把拐杖的两端捆在一起才能使用。如果按照这份提案主张的那样设立助学金，那不仅会中专业教育者的圈套，而且也会中种族主义者、教会学校支持者以及对社会分裂感兴趣的其他一些人的圈套。最重要的是，这种仅限于在学校中使用的教育补助，将有利于所有希望在这样一种社会中继续生存下去的人，即：在这种社会中，个人的社会晋升不是取决于有无实打实的知识，而是取决于有无事先设定的所需的学习经历。这种有利于学校的差别对待支配着詹克斯关于募集教育资金的讨论，它无视教育改革最需遵循的一个重要原则，即：把学习的主动权与责任感还给学习者或者他的最直接的指导教师。

社会的去学校化意味着承认学习的双重属性。仅仅强调技能操练可能会导致严重的后果，必须同样重视其他类型的学习。但是，如果学校并非学习技能的合适场所，那也就更非接受教育的合适场所。学校在完成这两种任务方面的效果都很差，部分归因于学校未能将这两者加以区别。学校之所以在技能教学方面没有成效，是因为技能在学校被当成了一门课程。在大多数学校中，旨在提高某种技能的学习计划总是同另一项不相干的任务拴在一起。比如，学好历史课被作为进一步接受数学技能训练的先决条件，而能否到操场上玩耍则取决于上课的出勤情况。

---

[1] 累退税，累进税的对称，纳税人的负担随课税对象数额的增加而递减的税。累退税的课税对象数额越大，负担率越低；反之，则负担率越高。——译者注

学校在对于激励学生不受限制地、探索性地运用所习得的技能的环境安排方面更是几无成效。为此，我得保留使用"自由教育（liberal education）"这个概念。造成这种状况的主要原因在于学校是强制性的，并且是为学校教育而学校教育，它强迫儿童处于教师的陪伴之下，结果又导致对于这种令人生疑的陪伴特权的更多需求。恰如技能教学必须摆脱课程的束缚一样，自由教育也必须同义务就学脱钩。技能学习与旨在培养发明创造行为的教育都可借助于制度性安排，但两者所需各不相同，且常常完全相背。

由于技能的习得意味着可界定、可预见的行为的熟练化，因此，大多数技能都可通过操练而习得并得以提高。这样，技能教学便可借助于模拟运用技能的环境来进行。然而，需要对多种技能进行探索性、创造性运用的教育，则无法依靠操练来进行。教育可以是教学的结果，但这种教学与操练完全不同，它有赖于对社区文化库藏的一些奥秘了如指掌的教育者与学习者之间的关系；有赖于所有能创造性地利用这些文化库藏的人的批判意识；有赖于人们对意想不到的问题的惊奇——这些问题向探究者及其伙伴敞开了通向文化库藏的一扇新的大门。

技能教师通过环境设置来让学习者形成标准反应，而教育引导者或导师的工作则是帮助学习者选配合适的伙伴，以使学习得以发生。他把这些从自身待解决的问题开始学习的个体选配到一起。他顶多只是帮助学习者清楚地陈述其困惑之处，因为只有清楚地陈述，学习者才会获得动力去寻找同他一样想要探究相同境况中的相同问题的伙伴。

为教育目的服务的伙伴选配在其初始阶段似乎比寻找技能教师和游戏伙伴更加超乎想象的困难。原因之一便在于学校已经在我们心中埋下了一种深深的恐惧，这种恐惧导致我们吹毛求疵。在人们看来，未经许可的技能交换（exchange of skills）——甚至是那些不受欢迎的技能交换——也比向那些想要解决同样问题的人们——他们认为这些问题对于他们当下的社会处境、心智活动以及情感生活都具有重要的意义——无休止地提供见面相识的机会在效果上更易预测，失败的危险也因此而似乎更小。

巴西教师弗莱雷从其经验中知晓这一点的重要性。他发现,如果成年人最初辨认的词汇带有政治含义,那么,任何成年人都可以用不到40个小时的时间学会阅读。弗莱雷培训了一些教师,让他们到一个村庄去找一些指称现实生活中的重要问题的词汇,比如"水井使用权"或"向债主借款的复利[1]"等。到了晚上,便把村民们聚集在一起,讨论这些重要词汇。村民们开始意识到,即使读音消失了,每一个词也还在黑板上。这些词不断揭示着现实问题,并指明可以解决问题的途径。我屡次亲眼看到参加讨论的村民们如何随着学会阅读,而在社会意识方面迅速觉醒并采取政治行动。看来,他们一旦能用文字表达现实,便可把握现实。

我回想起那个抱怨铅笔重量太轻的男人。他觉得铅笔难以摆弄,因为它不像铁锹那样有分量。我还记得另一个男人,他在去上工的路上和他的同伴停下来,用锄头在地上写下了一个他们正在讨论的"水(agua)"字。自1962年以来,我的朋友弗莱雷屡屡背井离乡,主要因为他拒绝围绕那些由正规教育者们预先选定的词汇去授课,而宁愿围绕他的讨论者们带到课堂中的那些词语进行讨论。

在已经被成功地学校化了的人当中进行具有教育意义的伙伴选配,则是一项性质不同的任务。不需要这种帮助的人为数甚少,即便在那些严肃刊物的读者中也同样如此。当然,我们不可能、也不应当把他们当中的大多数人召集起来讨论一句口号、一个词语或者一幅画。但是,这样一种观念依然是正确的,即:他们应当能够聚集到一起,讨论他们自己主动选择的并予以界定的某个问题。要想进行创造性的、探索性的学习,就必须要有正被同样的概念或问题困扰的伙伴。一些规模较大的大学试图通过大量增加教学科目来帮助学生选配伙伴,这种做法只是白费工夫罢了。由于受到课程、学科结构以及科层管理的制约,伙伴选配工作通常流于失败。在包括大学在内的学校中,大部分资源都被用来保证少数人能有时间和热情

---

[1] 复利,计算利息的一种方法。经过一定时间(如一年),将所生利息和本金加在一起算作新的本金,逐期滚动计算利息(区别于"单利"),俗称"利滚利"。——译者注

在一种仪式化的既定环境中去解决那些预先设定的问题。因此，取代学校的最根本的办法将是提供一种网络或者一种服务，这种网络或服务将为每个人提供能与他人探讨共同关心的问题的平等机会。

让我举一个如何在纽约市进行理智的伙伴选配的例子来说明我的上述观点。在进行这种选配时，每个人都可以在任何特定时间以最小的代价把自己的地址和电话号码输入计算机系统，用以表明自己的身份，并列出自己想寻找伙伴一起讨论的书、文章、影片或唱片的目录。几天之内，他便会收到邮寄来的列有近来有着同样需求的其他人的名单。这份名单将使他得以通过打电话与那些希望讨论相同主题的人约会见面，他们也正因为这个缘故而初次相识。

根据对某一具体标题的兴趣而进行伙伴选配是相当简单的，它只需根据双方就第三者的作品进行讨论的共同愿望来对双方身份加以确认，并把安排会面的主动权交给个人。这种简单的、清晰的选配方式通常会有三种反对意见。这些反对意见凸显着对于去学校化教育（deschooling education）以及对于摆脱社会控制的学习的抵抗。我在下面会对这些反对意见加以讨论，一方面想借此来澄清我所提出并阐明的理论，另一方面在于这一讨论或许有助于我们联想到那些尚未被用于学习的现存资源。

第一种反对意见是：为什么不能同时用某个观点或某个问题来表明自己的身份？此类主观性用语当然也可以在计算机系统中使用。各种政党、教会、工会、俱乐部、街道中心以及专业社团已经在用这种方式组织各自的教育活动，并且实际上扮演着学校的角色。它们都是为了探讨某些特定的"主题"而把人们选配在一起，然后采取讲习班、研讨会和科目研修等形式，把预先假定的"共同利益"套用于其中。顾名思义，这种按主题选配的方式，是以教师为中心的，也就是说，它需要有一个权威来为参与者们规定讨论的出发点。

与之相反，根据一本书、一部电影等作品的标题进行选配时，则完全依据作者对于一些特殊的语言、词汇以及用以叙述既定问题或事实的框架进行的界定。这种方式可以使接受这一出发点的人相互确认。比如，若围绕"文化革命"这一观念来选配，通常不是会造成思想混乱，就是会成为煽动性宣传。而如果把那些对于促进彼此对毛泽东、马尔库塞[1]、弗洛伊德[2]或古德曼的某篇具体文章的理解感兴趣的人选配到一起，那便是继承了从柏拉图[3]的《对话录》(*Dialogues*)——根据苏格拉底[4]的阐述整理而成——到阿奎那[5]对隆巴尔德[6]的评注所形成的自由学习（liberal learning）的伟大传统。这样，按标题选配的思想便和比如一些"名著"俱乐部所依托的理论有根本的不同，即是说，任何两个伙伴都可以挑选任何一本书进行深入分析，而不是依赖某些芝加哥的教授加以选择。

第二种反对意见是：为什么伙伴寻求者给出的身份确认信息中不包括年龄、背景、世界观、能力、经验或其他具有确定特征的内容？我再次强调，在把按标题选配作为其基本组织方式的一些大学中——不论是有围墙大学，还是无围墙大学[7]——都没有什么理由说在选配伙伴时不能且不应附加这些带有歧视的限制条件。可以想象，这些带有限制条件的伙伴选配或许是这样一些制度：这些制度或是鼓励对被预先选定的某本书感兴趣者相聚讨论，且该书作者或其代表也能出席；或是保证有一位专业的顾问出席讨论；或是仅

---

[1] 马尔库塞（Herbert Marcuse, 1898—1979），德国哲学家，法兰克福学派代表人物之一。著有《理性与革命》《爱欲与文明》《单向度的人》等。——译者注

[2] 弗洛伊德（Sigmund Freud, 1856—1939），奥地利心理学家、精神病医师，精神分析学派创始人。著有《梦的解析》《精神分析引论》等。——译者注

[3] 柏拉图（Plato，公元前427—前347），古希腊哲学家，柏拉图学派创始人，苏格拉底的弟子、亚里士多德的老师。著有《伊壁鸠鲁篇》《苏格拉底的申辩》《理想国》等。——译者注

[4] 苏格拉底（Socrates，公元前469—前399），古希腊哲学家。本人并无著作传世，其言行大抵见于其弟子柏拉图的一些对话体著作和色诺芬的《苏格拉底言行回忆录》。——译者注

[5] 阿奎那（Thomas Aquinas，约1225—1274），意大利神学家、哲学家，经院哲学集大成者。著有《神学大全》《反异教大全》等。——译者注

[6] 隆巴尔德（Peter Lombard，约1100—1160），意大利神学家，被誉为天主教"语录大师"。著有《四部语录》等。——译者注

[7] 无围墙大学，美国一些地方自20世纪60年代起进行的一种学校改革尝试，它将教育的空间拓展至整个社会，所有社会设施都可用来为教育服务，是比开放学校（Open School）更为激进的一种教育思潮与教育样式。——译者注

限于某个系或某个学院的注册学生参加讨论;或是仅限于彼此确认对方对于选定作品有着独特探讨方法的两个人进行讨论。所有这些限制条件对于达到特定学习目标都不无益处。但是我担心,人们之所以会提出这些限制条件,其真实原因多半在于由"人是无知的"这一假设而产生的一种轻蔑感,即是说,教育者们希望避免出现无知的会面,担心他们对于某个文本或许并不理解,只是凭兴趣读了读而已。

第三种反对意见是:为什么不顺便为伙伴寻求者的会面提供一些有益的帮助,如场所、时间表、放映屏幕以及保护措施?具备大型科层体制的所有低效能特征的学校倒是在提供此类帮助。但如果我们把安排会面的主动权交给伙伴寻求者自己,那么,现在尚未被人们归入教育类的那些组织或许能把这项工作做得更好。我想,餐馆老板、出版商、电话咨询服务机构、商场经理甚至通勤火车管理者们都可以通过为这种属于教育范畴的会面提供有吸引力的条件,来提升自身的经营服务。

比如,在咖啡馆初次会面时,会面者可以把要讨论的书放在自己的咖啡杯旁,以表明自己的身份。最初提议安排会面者很快就会知道用什么物品可引起自己在寻找的讨论伙伴的注意。与一个或数个陌生人讨论自行选择的话题或许会导致浪费时间、失望甚至不愉快,但这种风险肯定要小于申请升入大学所冒的风险。由计算机安排的在纽约第四大道岔路上的一家咖啡馆进行的、旨在讨论一家全国性杂志刊载的某篇论文的会面,将不会强求任何会面者同其初次相识者一起待上超过喝一杯咖啡的时间,会面者也不必非要同其他任何参与者再次见面。这种会面机会将有助于增加现代城市生活的透明度,有助于人们建立新的友谊,有助于人们自行选择工作,并可促进批判性阅读。(不可否认,联邦调查局可能会因此而获得个人的阅读书目与会面记录。这在1970年依然会让每个人都感到担忧,但这只会让自由人感到有趣,因为他的恶作剧使得一帮侦探们为搜集一些无关紧要的材料而疲于奔命。)

技能交换与伙伴选配都基于这样一个假设,即:为了所有人的教育(education for all)意味着由所有人来进行教育(education by all)。不是把人强制性地收容进专门的机构，而是让所有人都积极地活动起来，唯有如此才能催生大众文化（popular culture）。这种每个人均可发挥其学与教的能力的平等权利，现在已首先被持有执教许可证的教师独占，这反过来又使得教师的能力被局限于学校之中。而且，进一步来看，工作（work）与闲暇（leisure）相互异化，其结果是：工作者与观看者[1]都只能进入一个已为他们准备好的、合乎某种常规的工作场所。对于产品的设计、指导以及广告宣传的适应形塑着他们的角色，这一点和学校的正规教育没什么两样。要想让一个学校化了的社会发生根本转变，所需要的不只是为正规途径的技能学习及其具有教育意义的运用建立新的正规机制。一个去学校化社会意味着要创造一种新的方式，来进行随伴教育[2]或非正规教育（informal education）。

随伴教育不能再倒退到乡村或中世纪城市中的学习方式上去。传统社会更像是一套同心圆式的意义结构，而现代人则必须学会在和他只发生若即若离联系的诸多结构中发现意义。在乡村中，语言、建筑、劳动、宗教以及家庭习惯等都是和谐一致的，它们相互解释，相互强化，适应于其中之一也就意味着适应于其他所有。就连特定的学徒身份也是诸如制鞋、唱圣歌之类的专门化活动的副产品。如果一个学徒不可能成为师傅或学者，那么他也仍然会继续努力地做他的鞋子，或者继续在保持教堂礼拜的庄重气氛方面发挥作用。教育既不占用劳动时间，也不占用闲暇时间。几乎所有教育都是综合性的、终生性的且并非事先筹划的。

现代社会是有目的地设计的产物，教育机会的设计也必须包含其中。

---

[1] 工作者与观看者，从伊利奇在上文提到的工作场所本身也可成为技能中心（学习场所）的观点来看，这里意在指出，在如今已经学校化了的工作场所中，去学校化的技能学习不可能发生，因为"工作者"无法成为真正意义上的"技能教师"，而"观看者"也无法成为真正意义上的"技能学习者"，两者都已异化，且相互异化。——译者注

[2] 随伴教育（incidental education），也译为"偶发教育"。但"偶发"这个词在汉语里的准确含义是"偶然发生"，是小概率事件；而伊利奇所说的"incidental education"是指与工作、闲暇等所有社会活动、日常生活的过程如影随形、随时都有可能发生的教育，它远远超出"偶然发生"的概率，故译为"随伴教育"。——译者注

今后，我们对于学校的专门化的全日制教学的依赖将会减少。我们必须寻求学与教的更多途径，即是说，所有社会制度的教育品质都必须再次得到提升。不过，这一预测有多种含义。其中之一便意味着现代城市中的人一旦连本就贫乏的那么一点点批判的独立精神也被剥夺得荡然无存，那将愈发会成为广布于整个社会中的教学与操控的有效过程的牺牲品。而在如今的一些自由学校[1]中，倒是至少在为部分学生提供着批判的独立精神的存在空间。

这一预测还意味着，人们将很少再用其在学校获得的文凭来粉饰自己，如此便可获得"争辩"的勇气，并因此而对他们参与其中的那些制度加以控制与指导。为了确保这一点，我们必须学会根据劳动与闲暇所提供的教育交换（educational give-and-take）机会，对两者的社会价值进行评价。这样，人们在街道、工作场所、图书馆、新闻节目或医院的管理事务中的有效参与程度，便成为评价这些机构在多大程度上已成为具有教育意义的机构的最佳尺度。

我最近对一群发起抵制强迫升级运动的初中生发表了演讲。他们的口号是"要参与，不要模仿"。他们对于这一口号被误解成不是为了多受教育，而是为了少受教育这一点感到失望。这使我想起马克思（Karl Marx）在一百年前对《哥达纲领》[2]（*Gotha Program*）中关于宣布童工为不合法的主张所持的反对态度。马克思是从青少年的教育利益出发而反对这一主张的，因为当时青少年教育只存在于劳动之中。如果人进行劳动的最大成果应当是他从中所受的教育以及劳动赋予其主动教育他人的机会，那么，现

---

[1] 自由学校（liberal schools），起源于19世纪末欧美国家，泛指以自由为最高理念的学校。重视学生自发性学习理念，享受政府拨款，主要由慈善团体、商业机构、教育团体、教师和家长等创办，在经费、课程设置和教师薪酬等方面享受充分自由。起初主要有两种形态：一种是夏山式自由学校（summerhillian free schools），另一种是社区自由学校（community free schools），二者的侧重点有所不同。前者侧重于儿童中心和非强迫性学习，后者侧重于政治自由和社会公平。——译者注

[2] 哥达纲领，德国社会主义工人党的纲领。1875年5月，德国爱森纳赫派和拉萨尔派在哥达的合并代表大会上通过了该纲领。——译者注

代社会在教育学意义上的异化甚至比在经济学意义上的异化还要严重。

我的一位芝加哥黑人朋友对于朝向一个真正进行教育的社会迈进的过程中会遇到的主要障碍给出了非常清晰的界定。他对我说，我们的想象力已经"被彻底学校化了"。我们允许国家查明国民普遍存在的教育上的缺陷，并建立一种专门的机构去弥补这些缺陷。于是，如同前人制定了种种法律来界定何为神圣、何为亵渎一样，我们现在也幻想我们能区分对于他人而言，何为必要的教育、何为不必要的教育。

涂尔干[1]认为，正规宗教的本质就在于它能把社会现实分为两个领域。涂尔干论述道，虽然存在着自然宗教[2]与无神宗教[3]的不同，但两者都把世界中的事物、时间以及人区分为神圣的和世俗的（前一部分逻辑推论的结果）两个部分。涂尔干的这一见解可应用于教育社会学，因为从根本上来讲，学校也在以同样的方式对世界进行区分。

强制性学校的存在本身便把任何社会都划分为两个领域，即：有些时段、有些过程、有些安排、有些职业是"学术的"或"教育的"，其他的则不是。这样，学校便具有了划分社会现实的无穷力量：教育成了非世俗领域，而世俗世界则成了非教育领域。

自邦赫费尔[4]以来，一些现代神学家指出，将《圣经》启示与制度性的宗教混为一谈已成为如今的一种主流现象。他们基于经验事实指出，基督教中的自由与信仰通常得益于其世俗化过程。无疑，在许多教职人员看来，

---

[1] 涂尔干（Émile Durkheim, 1858—1917），另译迪尔凯姆，法国社会学家。著有《社会分工论》《宗教生活的基本形式》等。——译者注

[2] 自然宗教，将自然事物和自然力量作为崇拜对象的宗教。原始社会宗教的最初形式，如万物有灵论、拜物教等。——译者注

[3] 无神宗教，在涂尔干看来，宗教并非都具有神性的观念，"有些伟大的宗教并没有神和精灵的观念，或者至少可以说，在这些宗教里，这种观念仅仅能够扮演一种次要的、不起眼的角色。佛教即是如此。"（《宗教生活的基本形式》，上海人民出版社，2006年，第27页）这些并无神性观念的宗教便属于无神宗教的范畴。——译者注

[4] 邦赫费尔（Dietrich Bonhoeffer, 1906—1945），德国基督教神学家。因参加反希特勒活动，于1945年被绞死。著有《圣徒相通：教会社会学之教义性探讨》《行动与存在》《创世与堕落》等。——译者注

他们的这些论述似乎有渎神之嫌。毫无疑问,真正的教育过程将从社会的去学校化中获益,尽管这一要求在许多教师看来似乎有反启蒙之嫌。然而,如今在学校中正遭致扼杀的,恰恰是启蒙自身。

基督教信仰的世俗化仰仗于由教会熏陶出来的教徒为此而献身。同理,教育的去学校化则有赖于在学校中成长起来的人发挥引领作用。他们的学校教育背景不能成为他们逃避承担这一任务的借口,即是说,我们每个人都依然对导致我们成为如今这副模样的一切负有责任,哪怕我们所能做到的只是担负起这一责任并以此而告诫他人。

# 第二章　学校现象学

有些词因其变通性太强，以至失去使用价值，"学校"与"教"即属此类。这类词就像变形虫一样，可以钻进语言的任何缝隙之中。例如，反弹道导弹（ABM）"教"俄国人不要轻举妄动、IBM[1] 计算机"教"黑人儿童学习、军队可成为国民的"学校"，等等。

因此，要想探寻教育中的各种抉择，首先必须就我们所说的"学校"一词的含义取得共识。这或许可以采取几种方式。我们可以先列出现代学校教育制度的隐性功能，诸如监护、选拔、灌输以及促进学习等。我们也可以进行客户分析（client analysis），弄清这些隐性功能中哪些对教师、雇主、儿童、家长或专业人员起帮助作用，哪些起损害作用。我们还可以考察西方文化史以及人类学家搜集的资料，以便找出与今天的学校具有相似作用的那些制度。最后，我们可以重温自夸美纽斯[2]时代以来，甚至自昆体良[3]时代以来关于教育的诸多经典论述，看看现代学校教育制度与其中的哪些论述最为接近。然而，不论采取哪一种方式，都要求我们首先提出关于学校与教育之关系的某些假设。为了开发出一套用语，以便不必频频使用"教育"这个词也能谈论学校问题，我选择首先探讨以下或许可称之为

---

[1] IBM（International Business Machines Corporation），国际商业机器公司，是全球最大的信息技术和业务解决方案公司。前身为1896年成立的统计机制造公司，1924年改称现名。——译者注
[2] 夸美纽斯（Johann Comenius, 1592—1670），捷克教育家。著有《大教学论》《母育学校》等。——译者注
[3] 昆体良（Marcus Quintilianus, 约35—约100），古罗马演说家、教育家。著有《雄辩术原理》等。——译者注

公立学校现象学（phenomenology of public school）的一些问题。为此，我拟把"学校"界定为与教师有关的、要求特定年龄段的人全日制地学习必修课程的过程。

## 一、年龄

学校按年龄对儿童进行分类。这一分类基于三个尚未受到怀疑的前提，即：儿童隶属于学校、儿童在学校中学习、儿童只能在学校中接受教育。我认为有必要对这三个未经验证的前提提出严肃的质询。

我们对儿童的看法已经约定俗成。我们认定，儿童应该去上学，儿童应该按照成人吩咐的那样去做，儿童不应该有自己的收入和小圈子；我们希望儿童能知道自己的位置，言行举止要像个儿童；我们也会甜蜜地或伤楚地追忆起自己的孩童时光；我们被要求容忍儿童的幼稚行为。在我们看来，人类是既为照料儿童所苦，同时又会因之而乐的一个物种。然而，我们忘记了我们现在使用的"童年（childhood）"这个概念在西欧乃是近代之后、在美国则是更晚些时候才形成的。[1]

在人类历史的大部分时期，童年作为与幼年期、青年期或年轻时期相区别的一个阶段并不存在。在中世纪的几百年里，人们甚至不知道儿童身体各部分的比例。画家们把幼儿描绘成一个安坐于母亲怀抱中的小大人。在欧洲，儿童是与怀表以及文艺复兴时期的基督教债主一起出现的。在本世纪之前，无论是穷人还是富人，都不知道何为儿童服装、何为儿童游戏、何为儿童的法律豁免权。童年属于资产阶级。工人、农民以及贵族的子女都穿着与其父辈所穿款式一样的服装，玩着其父辈儿时玩过的游戏，并如其父辈一样被押上绞刑架。自从资产阶级发明了"童年"之后，这一切都

---

[1] 关于近代以来资本主义的产生与童年的出现齐头并进的历史，参见：Philippe Aries, *Centuries of Childhood*, Knopf, 1962。——作者注

发生了变化。只有某些教会在一段时期内，仍旧尊重青少年的尊严与成熟。在第二届梵蒂冈大公会议[1]之前，每一个儿童都被告知：一个基督教徒到7岁时应能进行道德判断与自由行动，其后若犯有罪行，将可能受到被永远打入地狱的惩罚。接近本世纪中叶，中产阶级家长们开始设法使其子女免受这一教规的影响，现在他们的儿童观对教会的实践具有广泛的影响。

直到20世纪，中产阶级家庭的"儿童"都是在家庭教师与私立学校的帮助下，在家庭中成长的。只是随着工业社会的出现，"童年"才得以成为普遍现象，并为大众享有。如同童年是近代社会的产物一样，学校教育制度也是进入近代社会后才出现的一种现象。

今天，大部分人都居住在工业城市以外的地方，他们经历不到童年。在安第斯山区，儿童一旦到了"有用"的年龄，就得去耕地；在此之前，则需照看羊群。如果身体发育良好，那么，到11岁时便应成为有用之人；如果身体发育不好，则到12岁时也应成为有用之人。最近，我和我的守夜人马科斯（Marcos）谈到他的在一家理发店工作的11岁的儿子。当我用西班牙语提醒他，说他的儿子还只是个"孩子"时，他十分惊奇，然后慈厚地微笑道："伊万先生，我想你是对的。"我这才知道，在我提醒他之前，这位父亲一直把小马科斯首先视为自己的"儿子"。我对于自己揭开了遮掩在两个有知有觉的人之间的童年的帷幕而深感不安。不用说，假如我对一个纽约贫民窟的居民说，他正在干活的儿子还只是个"孩子"，那么他是不会感到惊奇的，因为他十分清楚地知道，他11岁的儿子应当享有童年，并为其不能享有童年而感到愤恨。马科斯的儿子尚不知道渴望童年是何滋味，纽约贫民的儿子却感到被剥夺了童年。

这样，世界上大多数人不是不想就是无能为力让他们的子女拥有现代

---

[1] 第二届梵蒂冈大公会议（Second Vatican Council），简称"梵二会议"，罗马天主教会1962年10月11日—1965年12月8日在罗马梵蒂冈城举行的第二次世界性最高教务会议。会议主题为重新评估教会在现代世界中的地位和作用，会议成为罗马天主教会革新运动的开端。——译者注

意义上的童年。然而，对享有童年的少数人中的大多数人而言，童年却似乎是一种负担。他们中的许多人只是被迫度过童年，他们在扮演儿童角色时毫无快乐可言。对他们来说，经由童年的成长意味着被束缚于自我意识与角色之间的非人道的冲突过程之中，而这种角色是社会在其学龄时段强加给他们的。无论是代达罗斯[1]，还是波特诺伊[2]，他们都不喜欢自己的童年。我想，我们中的许多人在儿时也不喜欢被当作孩子。

假如没有以特定年龄段的人作为对象的强制性学习制度，自然也就不会出现什么"童年"，富裕国家的青少年便会免受童年的破坏性之害，贫穷国家也会终止其在赋予儿童以童年方面追赶富国的努力。倘若社会想要走出强制性赋予儿童以"童年时代"这样一个阶段，那就必须适合青少年生存。饰以人道主义伪装的成人社会与嘲弄现实的学校环境之间的不和谐状况不能再继续下去了。

废除学校还可以消除目前存在的有利于青少年，但不利于幼儿、成年人以及老年人的不公正现象。社会便可决定把教育资源优先用于那些错过了出生后最初四年的最佳学习期，其后也未能最大限度地实现自主学习愿望的国民身上，这在将来回首瞻顾时或许会使人感到奇妙无比。

制度性常识告诉我们，儿童需要学校，儿童在学校中学习。然而，这种制度性常识本身是学校的产物，因为正是这种"正统的常识"告诉我们，只有儿童才能在学校中接受教育；只有把一部分人归入"童年"这一范畴，我们才得以使他们服从于学校教师的权威。

---

[1] 代达罗斯（Stephen Daedalus），爱尔兰作家乔伊斯（James Joyce,1882—1941）的小说《尤利西斯》（*Ulysses*）中的主人翁。小说描写了卑微无能、逆来顺受的广告推销员布鲁姆（L. Bloom）寻找精神之子，而思想空虚、意志消沉的年轻教师代达罗斯寻找精神之父，两者同象征着现代人的孤独。——译者注

[2] 波特诺依（Alexander Portnoy），美国作家罗斯（Philip Roth,1933— ）的小说《波特诺伊的怨诉》（*Portnoy's Complaint*）中的主人翁。小说描写一位犹太年轻人因父亲望子成龙的期待与母亲的过度保护而变得无能，从而导致许多内心冲突、身心失调。——译者注

## 二、教师与学生

根据定义，儿童是学生。对于童年环境的需要，造就出一个无比庞大的有证教师（accredited teachers）市场。学校是基于学是教的结果这一信条而建立起来的一种制度。尽管否定这一信条的证据比比皆是，但制度性常识却一直认同这一信条。

我们所知道的大部分东西都是在学校之外学到的。学生的大部分学习都是教师不在场时自己进行的；即使教师在场，学生也经常是自己进行学习的。但最可悲的是，大多数人尽管从未进过学校，却也受到学校的影响。

每个人都在学校之外学习如何生存。我们在没有教师干预的情况下学习说话、学习思考、学习爱、学习感知、学习玩耍、学习诅咒、学习搞政治以及学习干活。这一点就连处于教师日夜照料之中的孩童也不例外。孤儿也罢、低能儿也罢、教师自己的孩子也罢，都是在为他们设计的"教育"过程之外学到他们所知道的大部分东西的。教师在试图促进穷人子女的学习方面显然并不成功。穷人家长之所以想让孩子上学，所关心的与其说是孩子将学到的东西，莫如说是通过学习将获得的文凭以及将挣到的钱。中产阶级家长之所以将孩子置于教师的照管之下，是为了防止他们去学习穷人子女在街头所学的那些东西。越来越多的教育研究表明，儿童是从同辈群体、连环画杂志以及偶然观察中，且尤其是从参加学校的例行活动中，学习着教师自诩要教给他们的大部分东西的。而教师则往往对发生于学校中的这些学习起着阻碍作用。

当今世界上半数的人从未跨进过学校大门，他们和教师没有任何接触，甚至连成为辍学者的资格也被剥夺了。然而，他们却十分有效地接受着学校传递的一个信息，即：他们应当去上学，应当不断接受更多的学校教育。学校通过那些向他们征缴学校教育税的税务官，或者通过那些煽动他们求学欲望的蛊惑民心的政客，或者通过他们自己的痴迷着想要上学的孩子，而使他们感到自卑。于是，穷人们便接受了唯有学校教育才能拯救自己这一信条，结果却丧失了自尊。教会至少还会在他们临终之际给他们一个忏悔的机会，而学校则留给他们一个期待（一个虚幻的希望），即期待其孙辈将会获得成功。不用说，这仍然是指望其孙辈能有更多的学习机会，这些学习机会来自学校，而不是来自教师。

学生们从未相信教师对自己的大部分学习能有多少帮助，聪明的学生也好，愚钝的学生也罢，其学习都是或因鞭棍所逼，或为理想职业所诱，他们总是靠死记硬背、阅读以及临场机智来应付各种考试。

成年人容易把自己所受的学校教育浪漫化。他们在回顾既往时会把自己的学习归功于教师，会赞赏教师的忍耐，并且他们也学会了这种忍耐。但同样是这些成年人，当放学后匆忙回家的孩子告诉他们从每位教师那里学到了些什么时，则又为其精神健康而担忧不已。

不论学生们能从教师那里学到什么，学校总是在为教师们提供着就业机会。

## 三、全日制就学

每个月我都能看到美国的一些企业向国际开发总署（Agency for International Development）提出各种建议的清单，这些企业建议用训练有素的系统管理者或者就用电视机来取代拉丁美洲国家的"班级教师"。在美国，由教育研究人员、设计人员以及技术操作人员实施的团队教学正逐渐为人们所接受。然而，不论教师是一个女学究，还是一组身着白上衣的男士团队，不论他们执教的学校课表中所列课目的教学成功与否，专业教师都在制造着一种神圣的环境。

专业化教学的未来难以预料，这使课堂教学陷入困境。假如教育专业人员想在促进学生的学习方面进行专业性探索，那就不得不摒弃目前这种一年里需将学生聚集750～1000次的教育制度。当然，除此之外，教师所做之事还有很多。关于学校的制度性常识告诉家长、学生以及教育者们：教师要想进行教学，就必须在一种神圣空间里行使其权威。即使对于其学生的大部分时间都在开放式教室（classroom without walls）中度过的那些教师来说，这一点也同样毋庸置疑。

根据其自身属性，学校往往会对其成员提出时间和精力上的全面要求。结果，教师便成了监护人（custodian）、说教者（preacher）和治疗专家（therapist）。

在充当这三种角色时，教师分别基于不同的要求而行使其权威。作为监护人的教师扮演的是仪式引导者的角色，他引导学生通过那漫长的、迷宫般的一系列程序。他对学生遵守规章的情况加以评判，并根据那些纷繁复杂的陈规引导学生的人生。其最好的结果是使学生进入获取某些技能的准备阶段，就像教师自己一直在做的那样。他并不奢望激发学生进行任何深入的学习，他只是对学生进行一些基本常规的训练。

作为说教者的教师扮演着家长、上帝或国家的代理人的角色。他对学生进行灌输，告诉他们在学校乃至整个社会中，哪些是对的，哪些是错的。他以家长的姿态出现在每一个学生面前，以确保所有学生都感到他们是同一个国家的未来一代。

作为治疗专家的教师则觉得自己有权深究学生的个人生活，以便帮助学生成长为一个人。当这一功能是由集监护人与说教者这两种角色于一身的教师来执行时，则意味着教师通常会说服学生在洞察真理以及正确感知方面听从教师的训导。

关于自由社会可以建立在现代学校基础之上的主张自相矛盾。教师在处理与学生有关的事宜时，把对于个人自由的保护抛弃得一干二净。当教师集法官、思想宣传家和医生的功能于一身时，社会的基本样态也就被原本应为生活做准备的过程本身扭曲了。法律规定儿童在法定身份或经济上属于未成年人，并且限制儿童的自由集会或自由居住的权利，而将上述三种权利集于一身的教师对于儿童自由的限制比这些法律更甚。

教师绝非唯一的提供治疗服务的专业人员。精神病医生、学业咨询人员、职业咨询人员甚至律师等，都可以帮助其服务对象做出决定、发展个性、进行学习。不过，常识告诉这些服务对象：这些专业人员应当避免把自己的是非评价强加给服务对象，应当避免强迫任何服务对象听从他们的劝告。与此不同，学校教师与神父则是在对受其控制的服务对象进行说教的同时，还自认为自己有资格窥探其隐私的仅有的两种专业人员。

当儿童站在作为世俗神父的教师面前时，无论是美国宪法第一修正案还是美国宪法第五修正案[1]，都保护不了他们。儿童不得不面对一个戴着如同罗马教皇所戴的却又看不见的三重冕[2]的人，这顶三重冕是集上述三种权威于一身的标志。对儿童来说，教师如同牧师、先知以及神父一般自以为是地说教，即是说，教师同时充当着神圣仪式的引领者、传授者以及管理人。在一个承诺绝不让某一种既存的强制性制度——不论是教会还是国家——同时行使上述几种权利的法治社会中，教师却把中世纪教皇所拥有的这些权利集于一身。

强迫儿童成为全日制学生，使得教师能对他们行使很少受宪法与习俗限制的权力，这比其他一些封闭的社会场所里的监护者所行使的权力要大得多。因为儿童尚未达到一定年龄，所以他们得不到被送进现代收容机构——精神病院、修道院或监狱——中的成年人可得到的那些日常保护。

在教师的权威主义眼光中，不同层面的价值观的秩序叠加于一体，道德、法律以及个体价值这三者之间的区别被混淆乃至最终被抹消。对其中任何一种价值的侵犯均被教师视为对这三种价值的同时侵犯。他们希望违

---

[1] 美国宪法第五修正案（Fifth Amendment to the U.S. Constitution），美国权利法案的一部分，1791年12月15日获得通过。该修正案规定，除军事案件外，任何非经大陪审团的起诉或指控，不受判处死罪或其他不名誉罪之审判；任何人不得因同一罪行而两次受审；不得在任何刑事案件中被迫自证其罪；不经正当法律程序，不得被剥夺生命、自由或财产；不给予公平赔偿，私有财产不得充作公用。——译者注

[2] 三重冕（triple crown），罗马教皇所戴的礼冠，象征着掌管现世、阴间以及炼狱的权力。——译者注

规者意识到自己破坏了规章、行为不端,并使自己蒙羞。一个在考试中投机取巧的学生会被告知,这种行为是违反纪律的,是道德败坏的表现,在人品上是可耻的。

进入课堂使得儿童与西方文化的日常世界相分离,使他们陷入一种极不开化、匪夷所思且极为痛苦的环境之中。假如学校不把儿童长期禁锢于这种神圣空间中,那么就不会形成这样一种不受日常生活规则约束的封闭环境。全日制就学的规定使得课堂就像一个神奇的子宫,一到每天放学时和学年结束时,便将学生分娩而出,直至最终将他们逐入社会。假如没有学校,就不会出现大众化的、漫长的童年,也不会产生令人窒息的课堂气氛。不过,即便这两种现象都不出现,学校作为一种强制性学习的通道也依然会存在,依然比我们迄今已知的其他任何东西都更具有压制和破坏作用。为了弄懂究竟何为去学校化社会,而不只是弄清何谓改革既存教育,现在我们必须聚焦于学校教育中的隐性课程。我们在这里并不直接述及穷人聚居的贫民窟街道的隐性课程,或者富人享用的火车特等卧铺车厢的隐性课程。我们所关心的是吁请人们注意一个事实,即:学校教育的各种仪式或例行活动本身便构成了此类隐性课程。就连最优秀的教师,也无法使其学生完全不受隐性课程的影响。学校教育的这种隐性课程不可避免地会使社会愈发对其部分成员怀有偏见、抱有歧视,并赋予其他已经享有特权者一种新的权力,即对没有特权的大多数人示以关怀的权力。同样不可避免的是,无论对于富人还是穷人来说,这种隐性课程都具有一种仪式的作用,这种仪式把他们诱入一个以增长为取向的消费社会之中。

# 第三章　仪式化了的进步

大学毕业生所受的教育使他们选择跻身于富人世界。不论美国大学毕业生们的主张同第三世界有何关联，其人均所耗费的教育费用比全世界处于中等收入水平的半数人一生平均收入的5倍还要多。一个拉丁美洲学生要想进入这一高傲人群，则其所耗费的公共教育资金至少等于本国中等收入水平的同胞所耗费的350倍。穷国大学毕业生们几乎毫无例外地感到，同来自北美与欧洲的大学毕业生在一起，要比同未受学校教育的本国同胞在一起轻松自在。所有被学校"科学地"加工过的学生，都只有和同为教育机器（educational machine）之产品的消费者伙伴们在一起时才会感到愉悦。

现代大学把话语权赋予那些经过考试被归为未来有望成为能挣钱或能掌权的人。除非能同时以文凭来证明自己获得的学业成绩，否则任何人都不会获得税收资金对其业余自学的支持，也不会获得教育他人的权利。在拾级而上的每一个教育层次，学校都把在初始阶段便证明对现存秩序没有风险的那些人挑选出来。由于大学既垄断着学习资源的分配，又垄断着社会角色的赋予，因此，大学也就把未来的发明家与潜在的反对者尽收囊中。学位为其消费者的履历打上了永久性的身价标签。持有文凭的大学毕业生能适应的只是这样一个社会——这个社会给大学毕业生标以身价，并因此而决定着社会的期望水平。在任何一个国家，大学毕业生的消费总量决定着其他所有人的消费标准。不论是有职业者，还是无职业者，要想成为文明人，都会向大学毕业生的生活方式看齐。

于是，大学便在工作与家庭生活两方面都制约着人们的消费标准，这在任何国家中、任何政治制度下都是如此。一个国家的大学毕业生越少，其文明需求就越会被本国其他社会成员仿效。在俄国、中国和阿尔及利亚，大学毕业生与普通国民之间的消费差距比美国更大。在社会主义国家，拥有磁带录音机、小汽车以及乘飞机旅行会让一个人同其他人的区别更为明显。在这些国家中，获取这些东西所需要的是学位，而不只是金钱。

大学拥有影响人们确定自己的消费目标的能力是新近的事情。在许多国家中，只是在20世纪60年代，随着人们普遍开始抱有公共教育机会平等的幻想后，大学才获得了这种能力。在此之前，大学虽然保护着个人言论自由，但并未使个人知识自然而然地转变为物质财富。在中世纪，成为学者便意味着成为穷人乃至乞丐。出于职业需要，中世纪的学者们学习拉丁文，这既受到农民、贵族、市民和神职人员的尊敬，同时也为他们所鄙视，他们成了社会的局外人。为了出人头地，这些学者首先不得不参加公共服务活动，尤其是教会的公共服务活动。过去的大学是进行科学探索、讨论新旧观念的一块自由领地。导师与学生聚集在一起，阅读早已谢世的其他导师的著作，并从他们的那些仍为今人所使用的鲜活语汇中，寻求审视现今种种谬误的新视角。因此，大学曾经是一种追求学术、思想活跃的共同体。

在现代巨型大学中，这种共同体已逃离到边缘地带，人们只能在某条小路旁、某个教授的办公室中或某个学校牧师[1]的宿舍里寻觅到它的踪影。从结构上看，现代大学的意图与传统意义上的探究已几无关联。自谷登堡[2]以来，严谨的批判性探索方面的交流大多已从大学的"讲座"转移到印刷品之中。现代大学不可能再为人们的相遇、相识提供一种纯粹的交流环境——这种环境鼓励人们进行自主决定而又无拘无束的、有所聚焦而又随兴所至的、热情奔放的交流。现代大学所选择的，是对所谓的研究与教学

---

[1] 学校牧师(chaplain)，即学校中的牧师。在西方国家，特定组织中往往设有自己的牧师，如院(医院)牧、军(军队)牧、监(监狱)牧等。——译者注
[2] 谷登堡(Johannes Gutenberg, 1400—1468)，德国人，铅活字印刷的发明者。——译者注

赖以产生的过程加以管理。

自苏联人造卫星上天以来，美国一直试图使其大学毕业生的数量赶上苏联。现在，德国人也在抛弃其学术传统，为赶上美国而建造"大学校园"。他们打算在10年内把初中与高中的教育经费从140亿马克增加到590亿马克，并把高等教育经费增加到现在的3倍。法国也计划到1980年将学校教育经费占国民生产总值的比例提高到10%。福特基金会（Ford Foundation）则一直在推动拉丁美洲的穷国将其"应受尊敬的"大学生人均教育经费提高到北美国家的水准。学生把他们的学习视为可获得最高回报的经济投资，国家则把他们视为促进发展的一个关键因素。

对于将谋取大学学位作为主要目标的大多数人来说，大学并未失去其声誉。但是，自1968年以来，大学在其信徒心目中的地位已明显下降。学生们拒绝为战争做准备、反对污染环境、批评顽固不变的偏见。教师们则支持学生向政府的合法性、政府的外交政策、教育制度以及美国人的生活方式发起挑战。不少人拒绝接受学位，并为在超越于文凭社会的反主流文化中生活做准备。他们似乎选择了中世纪的法兰提塞里派[1]与宗教改革运动[2]中的阿隆白郎陶斯派[3]所走过的道路，这些人可以说是那个时代的嬉皮士[4]与离经叛道者。其他的人则意识到，为建立一个反主流社会所需要的各种资源已经被学校垄断。因此，他们一方面遵守例行学术规范，另一方面

---

[1] 法兰提塞里派（Fraticelli），一译"方济会属灵派"，欧洲中世纪被视为异端的一个教派。坚持过清贫的生活，对抗教廷的指示，否认教会拥有财产的权利。15世纪遭到宗教法庭的惩罚。——译者注

[2] 宗教改革运动，16世纪欧洲新兴资产阶级以宗教改革为旗号发动的一次大规模反封建的社会政治运动。主要反对教皇通过教会对各国进行控制以及大主教会内的骄奢腐化。——译者注

[3] 阿隆白郎陶斯派（Alumbrados），也称"光照派"，中世纪基督教的一个神秘派别，出现于1575年左右。与其他光照派相同，该派强调个体对《圣经》的自我体验，从中直接获得上帝的特别光照启示，不必依赖教会。该派成员过着退隐的生活，强调祈祷和沉思。17世纪初遭到宗教裁判所的严厉迫害，许多人被烧死。——译者注

[4] 嬉皮士（hippies），20世纪60年代出现于美国的对社会采取消极反抗态度的"亚文化群体"。其特点是蓄长发、穿奇装异服、吸毒、反对主体文化、主张非暴力行动。——译者注

则为了正直地生活而寻求相互支持。可以说，他们是在等级制度内部制造着异端的温床。

然而，大部分普通国民对这些现代神秘主义者以及现代异教创始者投以警惕的目光，认为他们威胁消费经济、民主权利以及美国人的自身形象。然而，他们不会如人所愿地退出历史舞台。而且，他们当中通过耐心说服而能使其改变信仰者或借助巧妙方法——比如，让他们讲授他们所倡导的异端——而能使其受缚于校园者越来越少。于是，人们便寻求一些可能的手段，或者将异端者逐出校门，或者削弱作为其反抗主流社会之基地的大学的重要地位。

花费了高昂个人成本才对大学的合法性产生怀疑的学生与教职员们，当然不会意识到他们决定着社会成员的消费标准或者刺激着社会的生产系统。在从根本上改变数百万年轻人对外国现实的认识方面，那些诸如关心亚洲问题学者委员会（Committee of Concerned Asian Scholars）与拉丁美洲问题北美代表大会（North American Congress on Latin America）之类的团体的创建者们发挥了极为重要的作用。还有一些人则试图用马克思主义来解释美国社会，或者竭力使嬉皮士盛行起来。他们的成果进一步强化着这样的观点：大学的存在是保证社会批判得以持续的必要条件。

毋庸置疑，现在的大学提供着一种独特的环境，这种环境允许其部分成员对整个社会进行批判。大学向他们提供其他社会成员无法同样享有的优越条件——时间、社会流动、结交伙伴与获取信息的机会以及一定的免受惩罚权。不过，大学并非向谁都提供这种自由，它只向那些已被引入且深陷于消费社会之中，并且强烈期盼某种类型的强制性学校教育的人提供这种自由。

今天的学校行使着有史以来那些权力巨大的教会所共有的三重功能。它既是社会神话的收藏者，又是将社会神话所含的种种矛盾加以制度化的专业机构，同时还是日常仪式的实施场所，这些日常仪式再生产出并掩饰着社会神话与社会现实之间的矛盾。今天的学校教育制度，尤其是大学，为批判这些神话并抵制这些神话对社会现实的制度性歪曲提供了大量机会，然而，要求人们对神话与制度之间的种种根本矛盾予以宽容的学校日常仪式却依然未受多少挑战，原因就在于意识形态批判也罢，社会行动也罢，都不可能造就一个新社会。只有从对社会生活中处于核心地位的日常仪式的沉湎中清醒过来，与之决裂并对其加以改革，才能带来社会的根本变化。

美国大学的"人生导引仪式（initiation rite）"是迄今为止世界各国大学的人生导引仪式中最为包罗万象的，现在它已走到了尽头。有史以来，没有任何一个社会无须日常仪式或神话便可存续，但像美国这样需要把如此沉闷、漫长、具有破坏性且代价高昂的日常仪式变成神话的社会，则尚无先例。当代世界文明也有史以来第一次发现，借教育之名将具有根本意义的人生导引仪式加以合理化的必要性。因此，除非我们首先明白学校教育的日常仪式既不可能推动个人学习，也不可能促进社会平等，否则，我们就无法开始教育改革。除非我们首先明白不论强制性的公立学校教育在教些什么，都必然会再生产出消费社会，否则，我们就不可能超越这样的社会。

我提出的打破神话的计划不能仅限于大学范围。大学是整个学校教育制度中的一个有机组成部分，任何不关注整个学校教育制度的大学改革，就好像企图从十二层楼以上的高度对纽约市进行城区改造一样。目前正在进行的大部分高等学校的改革，看上去就像是在建造高层贫民窟。唯有非经义务教育而培养的新一代才有望重建大学。

# 一、制度化价值观的神话

除了上文所述特征之外，学校还制造出无限消费的神话。这个现代神话基于这样一种信念：过程必定会产生出某些有价值的东西，因此，生产活动也就必然会制造出相应的需要。学校告诉我们：学是教的产物。学校的存在本身便导致了对学校教育的需要。而一旦我们学会对学校提出需要，那么我们的所有活动往往都会求助于各种专门机构。一旦自学的价值得不到认可，那么所有非专业性活动的价值均会遭到质疑。在学校里，我们被告知：有价值的学习是上学的结果；学习的价值随着所受教育的量的增多而提升；而且，这一价值最终可通过成绩和文凭来衡量与证明。

其实，学习是他人操控越少越好的一种活动。大部分的学并不是教的产物，而是不受束缚地参与到富有意义的情境之中的结果。大多数人都是在身心"投入"时学得最好，但学校则要人们把自己的人格与认知的发展看成学校精心计划与操控的结果。

人们一旦承认学校的必要性，那么也就容易成为其他制度的俘虏。青少年一旦听任课程教学形塑自己的想象，那么也就会习惯于接受任何一种制度性计划。"教学"窒息了他们的想象。他们不会被出卖，但总是被欺骗，因为他们已经被告诫用期待（expectations）来代替希望（hope）。他们将不再为他人的善行或恶行而感到惊奇，因为他们已经被学校教会对于每个与自己受到同样教育的人应当抱有何种期待。期待对象为人时是这样，期待对象为机器时也同样如此。

这样，责任便从个体自身转嫁到了制度身上，其结果必然导致社会倒退，尤其是当这种责任被视为一种义务时更是如此。于是，那些反抗母校的教师们并不是鼓起勇气，通过自己的个别教学[1]去影响别人，并对其后果承担责任，而是常常与母校的教职员们同流合污。这一现象预示着提出一种新俄狄浦斯[2]说的可能，即：俄狄浦斯式教师为得其子而娶其母[3]（学校）。如今，在学生时代曾沉湎于受教过程而不能自拔的男教师们，想从对学生的强制性教学中寻求安全感，而将自己的知识视为学生时代所经历的教学

---

[1] 个别教学（personal teaching），指以学生为中心的、面对面的教学。——译者注
[2] 俄狄浦斯（Oedipus），希腊神话中底比斯王拉伊俄斯（Laius）之子。因神预言他将杀父娶母，出生后被其父弃在山崖，后为牧人所救。长大后，想逃避杀父娶母的命运，却在无意中杀死亲父。因除去怪物斯芬克斯，被底比斯人拥为新王，并娶前王之妻，即其生母伊俄卡斯达（Jocasta）为妻。发觉后在悲愤中自刺双目，流浪而死。——译者注
[3] 为得其子而娶其母，伊利奇这里的意思是说教师在学校工作只是为了自己的个人目的，而并非为了学生的发展。——译者注

过程之产物的女教师们，则希望她的学生也能产生同样的体验。

## 二、价值观测量的神话

学校所灌输的制度化价值观都是些量化的价值观。学校把青少年引入一个一切均可加以测量的世界，包括对他们的想象力——事实上也是对他们整个人本身——的测量。

然而，个人的成长并不是一个可测量的实体，它是个人饱经磨炼、与众不同的发展结果，既无法依据任何尺度或任何课程来加以测量，也无法将之同他人的成就相比较。在这种"成长"的学习中，人只是在富有想象力的努力方面同他人竞争，是走自己的路，而不是仿效他人。我所赞赏的学习乃是无以测量的再创造行为。

学校自诩可将学习内容细分为各种学科"材料"，然后把这些如同积木般的现成材料组合成课程教给学生，并用一种国际通用的尺度评估学生的学习结果。个人一旦甘于接受别人用他们制定的标准来测量自己的个人成长，那么也就很快会用同样的标准来自行测量。此时，个人已无须任何外在强制，便可自行进入他人指定的位置，不敢越雷池一步。而就在这一过程中，他们也使其同伴同样安就其位，直至所有人、所有事项最终都适应这一过程。

已经被学校化了的人无法获得那些测量不到的体验。对他们来说，不可测量的东西是次要的、不安全的。他们未必是被剥夺了创造性，而是经过学校的教学而忘记了去"做"自己的事情或"成为"他自己，并且认为只有已经做成的事情或可以做成的事情才是有价值的。

人们一旦在学校的训导下形成了价值观可以被生产出来且可以被加以测量这一观念，往往便会认可所有类型的等级划分，包括国家发展水平的衡量尺度、婴儿智力的测量标准，甚至连和平的进步都可根据战争中的死亡人数来计算。在一个学校化了的世界中，人们认为幸福之路乃由消费指数铺就。

## 三、套装价值观的神话

学校出售课程。同其他商品一样,课程也是按照同样的过程生产出来并有着同样结构的一捆商品。对大多数学校而言,课程生产(curriculum production)起始于所谓的科学研究,教育技术人员根据研究结果,在经费预算以及有关规定允许的范围内,对未来所需设置的课程以及用于课程生产流水线的各种工具进行预测。作为销售者的教师(distributor-teacher)则把已完成之产品的课程交付给作为消费者的学生(consumer-pupil),学生的反应则被加以仔细研究并制成图表,以便为建立新的教学模式提供研究资料。这些新的教学模式包括"不分年级的教学""学生设计的教学""团队教学""直观教学"或"问题中心的教学"等。

课程生产过程的产品看上去与现代社会中其他任何主要商品都很相似。它是一组预先规定的意义,是一套预先设定的价值观,是一种因对数量足够多的消费者具有相对平衡的市场吸引力,从而能确保收回生产成本的商品。作为消费者的学生们被告诫:必须使自身的愿望适应市场价值观的需要。这样,在学校的训导下,学生们便形成了相应的就业期待。如果没有按照消费者研究所示明的那样去学习,没有获得就业所需要的成绩与文凭,那么他们就会感到问心有愧。

教育者们会根据自己的观察结果而把设置收费更贵的课程的做法加以合理化,即:课程收费高低同课程学习难度成正比。这是对帕金森定律[1]的一种运用,该定律认为,工作本身会随着可用于工作的资源的增多而增加。这一定律在学校的各教育阶段都可得到证明。例如,在美国,阅读困

---

[1] 帕金森定律(Parkinson's Law),由英国历史学家诺斯古德·帕金森(Northcote Parkinson,1909—1993)在其《帕金森定律》(*Parkinson's Law*)一书中提出,认为行政官员为完成某项任务往往会制定一套烦琐的实施办法,并在任务已不需要的情况下仍然采用。根据该定律,即便任务减少,官僚机构仍会扩大。——译者注

难自1950年开始成为学校教育中的一个重要问题；而在法国，则是在其人均教育经费达到美国1950年的水平时，阅读困难才开始成为学校教育中的重要问题。

事实上，当精力充沛的学生们发现自己受到比预想的要更为广泛的操控时，他们常常会对学校教学加倍反抗。这种反抗并不是某所公立学校以权威主义方式压制的产物，也不是某些自由学校以富有魅力的方式诱惑的结果，而是可归因于一切学校所共有的根本观念，即：一个人可以判定另一个人必须学什么以及什么时候学。

## 四、永恒进步的神话

具有讽刺意味的是，即使在学习的经济收益递减时，人均教育成本的增加也会抬高学生对自己的估价及其在劳动市场上的身价。学校几乎不惜一切代价地要让学生达到可以加入课程消费竞争的水平，并使他们不断向更高层次迈进。为激励学生继续留在学校所消耗的费用随着学生的升级而猛涨。在学校教育的高级阶段，增加费用的借口是建造新的足球运动场、学校附属教堂以及实施所谓的国际教育计划。即使学校不教其他任何东西，它也会向学生灌输不断进取的价值，即美国人的行为方式的价值。

眼下正在进行的越南战争便符合这一逻辑。评价其成功与否的尺度是被价格低廉而又耗资极巨的枪弹所击毙的敌方人员的数量。这种非人性的计算方法被恬不知耻地称作"尸体计算法"。恰如做买卖就是做买卖，就是永无休止地赚钱一样；战争就是杀戮，就是永无休止地增加尸体的数量；同理，教育就是学校教育，对其漫无尽头的过程的计算指标就是学生的课时。各种过程均不可逆转且自我佐证。按照经济标准，美国将越来越富有；按照尸体数量标准，美国永远会赢得战争；而按照学校标准，则会有越来越多的美国国民成为有教养的人。

学校有计划地激发学生对于教学的持续渴求。然而，即使这种渴求能引导学生不断汲取教学内容，学生也绝不会因满足求知欲望而感到快乐。各门学科都是源源不断地"提供"教学套装让学生持续消费。而且，过时包装年年依旧。生产教科书这一行当就建立在对这种教学套装的需要的基础之上。教育改革者们许诺要为下一代提供最新最好的东西，而公众则在他们的诱导下产生了对于他们所提供的东西的需求。那些永远不会忘记自己失去了什么的辍学者，以及那些在新毕业生面前感到自卑的老毕业生，都清楚自己在越来越具欺骗性的日常仪式中处于何种位置，并且都持续不懈地支持这样一个社会——这个社会把由日趋普遍的挫败感所导致的社会分裂委婉地称作"日益强烈的革命期待"。

然而，被视为无限消费——永恒进步——之过程的增长永远也不可能走向成熟。热衷于无节制的数量增加，只会泯灭有机发展的可能性。

## 五、仪式游戏与新的世界宗教

在发达国家，义务教育年限延长的速度快于人均预期寿命增加的速度。若以图示，这两条增长曲线将在10年内交会。这就向米特福德[1]以及研究"终结性教育[2]"的专家们提出了一个问题。我想起了中世纪末，当人们希望教会提供的服务也能扩展至死后的安排时，便创造出了"炼狱"，以便在进入永久安宁之前能在教父的监督下净化自己的灵魂。从逻辑上讲，这首先催生了以恕罪为营生的行当，其次导致了宗教改革的尝试。而现在，无限消费的神话取代了对于永生的笃信。

汤因比[3]指出，伴随着一种伟大文化的衰落，通常会产生一种新的

---

[1] 米特福德（Jessica Mitford, 1917—1996），美国新闻记者、作家。著有《美国人的死亡方式》（*The American Way of Death*）等。——译者注
[2] 终结性教育(terminal education)，指在学校教育阶段，受教育者所接受的最后一个阶段的教育。亦为实施终结性科目 (terminal program) 的一种教育。——译者注
[3] 汤因比（Arnold Toynbee, 1889—1975），英国历史学家，历史形态学派的主要代表人物。著有《历史研究》（*A Study of History*）等。——译者注

世界宗教（World Church）。这种世界宗教在满足新的武士阶层（warrior class）的需要的同时，也为国内底层阶级带来了更多希望。在我们这种日渐衰败的文化中，学校似乎特别适合扮演世界宗教的角色。在当今世界，没有任何一种制度能像学校一样，更为巧妙地对其成员掩饰社会原则与社会现实之间的深刻矛盾。由于学校是世俗的、科学的，且否认自己会消亡，因此它是弥漫着现代氛围的一块领地。学校所饰以的经典性与批判性的伪装，使它看上去即便不是反宗教的，也是多元论的。学校的课程界定着科学，其自身也由所谓的科学研究来界定。任何人都不能说已不再需要学校。对于任何已从学校毕业的人，学校都会向其敞开大门，提供再次教育的机会，即矫正教育、成人教育以及继续教育。

由于学校的结构同学校中逐步升级的仪式性游戏相吻合，因此它是社会神话的有效编造者与维护者。对学校而言，引导学生进入这种冒险的日常仪式比教给学生什么以及怎样教给他们更重要。学校教给学生的、融入其血液的且形成其习性的东西，正是这种游戏本身。整个社会都被诱导相信可以无限消费各种各样的服务这一神话，以至不论在何处，对于无休止的日常仪式的象征性参与都成了义务性的、强制性的。学校把这种仪式竞争发展成为一种国际游戏——这种国际游戏强迫竞争参与者们把那些不能或不想参与者指责为世界的祸害。学校所进行的是一种诱导仪式，它把新加入者诱入不断消费的神圣竞赛之中；学校所进行的也是一种安抚仪式，学术神父（academic priests）在其信徒与拥有特权及权势的诸神之间起着沟通协调的作用；学校所进行的还是一种赎罪仪式，它把辍学者作为牺牲品，使他们成为教育落后的替罪羊。

甚至那些最多只受过两三年学校教育的人——这部分人在拉丁美洲、亚洲和非洲占绝大多数——也会因其未能受到充分的学校教育而感到羞愧。在墨西哥，法律规定实行六年义务教育，但在占总数三分之一的低收入家庭的儿童中，只有三分之二的人能念完小学一年级；且他们当中也只有4%的人能完成六年义务教育。而在占总数三分之一的中层收入家庭的儿童中，这一比例便会增至12%。以此来看，在提供公共教育方面，拉丁美洲其他25个共和国还不如墨西哥。

不论在哪个国家，所有儿童都知道，在强制性教育这种博彩活动中，他们被赋予了一次抽奖机会，尽管这是一种不平等的机会。这样，预先设定的关于机会平等的国际标准，如今把辍学者的原有贫困与他们自我强加并承受的歧视混为一体。在学校的训导下，他们已经相信应不断提高自己的期望值，现在，他们还会把自己在学校之外遇到的日渐增多的挫折归因于未曾受到学校的恩惠。他们被拒于天国门外，因为他们虽曾受过洗礼，但并未去过教堂。由于生而负有的原罪，他们接受了洗礼，进了小学一年级；但因其个人的缺陷，他们又掉进了"地狱"（Gehenna，希伯来语中意为贫民窟）。如同韦伯[1]曾对拯救灵魂乃是对财富积累者的恩宠这一信念的社会效应进行的探究一样，我们现在则可发现，神的恩宠如今已成为受过长期学校教育者的专利。

## 六、未来王国：普遍抱有的期待

学校把消费者的期待与生产者的信念结合在一起，消费者的期待反映在学校的各种权利主张中，生产者的信念则体现在学校的日常仪式中。学校教育是一种带有礼拜仪式[2]色彩的遍及全球的"货物崇拜[3]"的表现方式。说到货物崇拜，使人想起20世纪40年代流行于美拉尼西亚群岛[4]的一种膜拜仪式。这种仪式让狂热的信徒们深信，只要他们把一条黑色领带系在自

---

[1] 韦伯（Max Weber, 1864—1920），德国社会学家、历史学家、经济学家。著有《新教伦理与资本主义精神》《宗教社会学》《经济与社会》等。——译者注

[2] 礼拜仪式，基督教新教的主要宗教活动。多在礼拜堂举行，由牧师主礼。内容包括祈祷、唱诗、读经、讲道等。认为耶稣基督"受难"后，在星期日"复活"，故以该日为礼拜日。——译者注

[3] 货物崇拜，19世纪末至20世纪初主要在美拉尼西亚群岛流行的宗教运动的统称。相信来自超自然资源的特殊商品——"货物"即将到达，幸福的新时代即将开始。——译者注

[4] 美拉尼西亚群岛（Melanesia），位于西南太平洋。——译者注

已裸露的身体上，那么，耶稣便会乘一艘汽船而来，带给每人一台冰箱、一条裤子和一台缝纫机。

学校使得学生愈发丢人现眼地依赖教师，使其愈发不切实际地自感无所不能。这两者融为一体，并且后一种状况在那些想要走出校门、向全世界宣扬要自我拯救的学生中尤为典型。学校的日常仪式是专为培养学生严格的劳动习惯而制定的，其目的在于颂扬无限消费的人间乐园之神话，而建立这种乐园被说成不幸者与无产者的唯一希望。

对于现世生活得寸进尺的期待，是人类历史进程中普遍存在的现象，这在殖民地以及所有文化的边缘群体中尤为明显。罗马帝国时期的犹太人中有艾赛尼派信徒[1]与弥赛亚[2]；宗教改革时期的奴隶中有闵采尔[3]；从巴拉圭（Paraguay）迁至达科他[4]的一贫如洗的印第安人中也有富于感染力的舞蹈家。这些宗教团体总是受某个先知的引领，将希望寄托在挑选出来的少数人身上。而学校引导人们对于未来王国的期盼，与其说是预言性的，莫如说是缺乏人情味的；与其说只是针对特定地方的，莫如说是涉及整个世界的。人已经成了创造其自身救世主的工程师，并承诺对那些日益增多的顺从于这位救世主操控的人，投以无尽的科学回报。

---

[1] 艾赛尼派信徒（Essenes），意为"圣者"或"虔诚者"。公元前2世纪—公元1世纪盛行于巴勒斯坦的一个犹太教派别。该派严守律法、教规，过着严格的禁欲生活，但也容许婚姻以繁衍种族；避免和外界接触，寻求理想中的和平；任何对神不敬的言语和行为都会被处以极刑；相信命运，相信灵魂不朽，但不相信身体会永恒。异教徒需经过长时间考察并宣誓遵守教规后才会被接纳加入。——译者注

[2] 弥赛亚（Jewish messiahs），原意为"受膏者"。古代犹太人封立土君、祭司等职位时，常举行在受封者头上敷膏油的仪式，故君王等人有"受膏者"之称。在犹太王国灭亡后，犹太人中流行一种说法，称上帝终将重新派遣一位"受膏者"来复兴犹太王国，弥赛亚遂成为犹太人期盼的"复国救主"的专称。基督教产生后沿用此说法，宣传耶稣就是弥赛亚，但不是"复国救主"，而是"救世主"，凡信基督耶稣的人，灵魂便可得到拯救。——译者注

[3] 闵采尔（Thomas Münzer, 1489—1525），德国农民战争领袖，宗教改革家。1525年在米尔豪森城（Muhlhausen）建立并领导革命政权"永久议会"，组织军队，号召全德起义。——译者注

[4] 达科他（Dakota），美国过去一地区名，现分为南、北达科他州。——译者注

## 七、新的异化

学校不仅是一种新的世界宗教,而且也是全世界发展最快的劳动市场。消费者工程学现在已成为经济学的一个主要发展领域。在富有国家中,随着生产成本的降低,资本与劳动力越来越集中到那些将人们的消费引导至特定方向的大型企业里。在过去10年中,与学校系统直接相关的投资的增长速度甚至超过国防费用的增长速度。裁军只会加速学习产业成为国民经济中心产业的进程。只要学校的破坏性尚未被人们认识到,只要为缓解其破坏性所耗费用在持续增加,那么,学校便会为合法化浪费提供无限的机会。

假如我们把参与全日制教和学的人数加在一起,那么便会发现学校这个所谓的上层建筑已成为社会中的主要雇主。在美国,有6200万人生存于学校之中,8000万人在其他场所工作。这一点常常被新马克思主义分析家们忘记,他们声称,必须推迟或暂不考虑去学校化进程,因为在此之前,必须首先通过经济与政治的革命来解决其他的社会失序问题,即传统意义上的更为基本的问题。然而,只要学校被理解为一种产业,那么就可以制定具有现实意义的革命策略。在马克思看来,为使人们产生对于商品的需要而投入费用几乎毫无意义。但在今天,大多数人都从事着各种需要的生产,能够满足这些需要的是集约使用资本的产业。而在这当中,学校扮演着最主要的角色。

传统意义上的异化是雇佣劳动所带来的一个直接后果。这种雇佣劳动剥夺了人进行创造并得以被再创造的机会。如今,在年轻人进入社会之前,学校就已经通过把他们与社会相隔离而将他们预先异化了。他们自认为既是自己所掌握的知识的消费者,同时也是这种知识的生产者,但实际上这些知识不过是学校这一市场中所出售的一种商品。学校使这种异化成为年轻人为适应生活所做的准备,这就剥夺了教育的现实性与工作的创造性。学校通过训练学生产生被教育的需要,而让学生做好适应未来生活中这种异化的制度化的准备。学生一旦学会这种准备,便会失去自主发展的欲望,便不会再发现同自主发展相关联的诸多事物的魅力,便会把自己关在制度并未预先设定,但人生慨然给予的诸多惊奇的大门之外。学校直接或间接地雇用着大部分社会成员。学校不是使人们终生自我封闭,就是确保人们将适应某些制度。

学校这一新的世界宗教是一种知识产业,它既生产精神鸦片,又供应精神鸦片,其纠缠于人一生中的岁月越来越长。因此,去学校化乃是任何一种人的解放运动之根基。

## 八、去学校化的革命潜力

当然,学校绝不是以形塑人的现实观为主旨的唯一的现代制度。在对人的世界——视觉、语言、需要等——的制度性操控过程中,家庭生活、征兵制度、卫生保健、所谓的职业精神或者传播媒介等所蕴含的隐性课程也起着重要作用。但学校的操控更为深刻且更为系统,因为人们相信,唯有学校才具有形成人的批判性判断能力这一主要功能。但荒谬的是,学校是通过让学生依靠套装过程(prepackaged process)去学习关于自身、关于他人以及关于自然的知识而试图实现这一功能的。学校与我们之间的联系如此密切,以致任何人都无法指望借助其他什么办法把自身从学校中解放出来。

许多自封的革命家其实是学校的牺牲品。他们甚至把"解放"也视为制度性过程的产物。只有把自身从学校中解放出来,才能抛弃这种幻想。"大部分的学都不需要教"这样一种发现,就既不可能是他人操控的产物,也不可能是事先筹划的结果。我们每个人都负有对自身进行去学校化的责任,且只有我们才拥有这种力量。任何人都不能为自己未从学校教育中解放出来而寻找借口。当初若不是有一部分人将自身从英国国教中解放出来，那么人们便无法摆脱英国国王的统治。[1] 同样，如果今天的人们不将自身从强制性的学校中解放出来，那么也就无法从不断升级的消费中解放出来。

我们在生产与消费这两个层面都卷入了学校教育。我们盲目地相信，我们能够且应当进行有效学习；与此同时，我们也能使他人进行有效学习。在试图摈弃学校这一概念时，我们将会感受到来自自身的阻力。这同我们在试图拒绝无限消费、拒绝所谓为了他人好而可操控他人这一广为认同的推断时，感受到的来自我们自身的阻力如出一辙。在学校教育的过程中，任何人都无法完全避免对他人的剥夺。

学校既是最大的雇主，同时也是最不为人所注意的雇主。事实上，学校是继行会、工厂以及公司之后出现的最典型的新型企业。跨国公司曾在经济活动中占支配地位，如今则是一种补充的角色，也许有一天它会被多国共同筹划的超国家服务机构取而代之。这些机构的服务方式让所有人都感到不得不消费其服务，它们采用国际标准，在世界各地按照大致相同的节奏定期重新确定其服务的价值。

以新型汽车和高速公路为依托的"交通运输"，不论其各个组成部件是否由国家生产，都同样制度性地服务于人们对舒适、声望、速度以及精巧配置等一整套的需要。不论医疗费用是由国家支付还是由个人支付，"医疗保健"的器材都界定着某一种特定类型的健康的含义。同理，无论学校的经营者是谁，以获取文凭为目的的升级决定着学生在合格人才的金字塔中将占据的位置，世界各国皆然。

在所有这些例子中，雇用都是一种潜在的受益，即，我们现在必须把私人汽车的司机、不得不住院治疗的病人或教室中的学生都看成新的"雇

---

[1] 伊利奇这里指的是1620年11月11日，不堪忍受英国国内宗教迫害的120名清教徒乘坐"五月花"（May Flower）号大帆船，经过66天的海上漂泊到达美洲大陆。在上岸之前，船上的41名男乘客经过反复讨论协商，签订了一份公约，即后人所说的"五月花号公约"。由此结成了一个世俗的公民政治体，成为美国政体发展的第一块基石。——译者注

工"阶级的组成部分。发端于学校、以教师与学生——同时也是剥削者与被剥削者——的觉醒为基础的解放运动,应能预见其未来的革命策略。一项彻底的去学校化计划,应能在一种崭新的革命中对年轻人加以训练,而这种崭新的革命对于向一个以强制性的"健康""富有""安全"为特征的社会系统进行挑战来说是必不可少的。

反抗学校的危险无以预见,不过它并不像发端于其他任何主要制度的革命那么可怕。学校尚未像一个民族国家那样,或者甚至尚未像一个大公司那样在自我保护方面组织得卓有成效。从学校的支配下解放出来可以是不流血的。劝学员及其在法庭与雇佣机构中的同行们在对付违规者,尤其是对付贫穷的违规者时使用的武器,或许是采取无情的处罚措施。但面对群众运动的浪潮,他们会变得无能为力。

学校已成为一个社会问题,它正陷于四面楚歌之中。在世界所有国家中,国民及其政府都在支持各种打破常规的实验。这些实验诉诸各种独特的统计手段,以使人们继续信任学校,保全学校的面子。一些教育者的心态与梵蒂冈大公会议后天主教主教们的心态十分相似。一些所谓的"自由学校"的课程则同由民谣与摇滚乐构成的一些礼拜仪式颇为相像。中学生们要求拥有自己选择教师的话语权,被认为同教区居民们要求拥有自己选择神父的话语权一样尖锐刺耳。然而,假如学校教育失去这一十分重要的少数人群的信任,那么社会风险将会更高。它不仅会危及建立在商品生产及对商品需要的生产合二为一的基础上的经济秩序的存续,而且同样会危及建立在单一民族国家基础上的政治秩序的存续,而学生们正是由学校配置到这一秩序之中的。

我们的选择十分清楚。要么继续相信制度化了的学习是无限投资过程的一种结果,这一结果反过来又证明这种无限投资是值得的;要么重新认识到,假如立法、计划以及投资对于正规教育有什么作用,那就应当主要用来清除目前阻碍人们获得学习机会的那些障碍,而这种学习只能是一种个体活动。

如果我们不向有价值的知识是在特定环境中强迫知识消费者接受的一种商品这一臆断发起挑战，那么，社会将愈发会被险诈而虚伪的学校与极权主义的信息管理者们支配；教育诊疗专家们将会更加起劲地"毒害"学生，以便把学生教得更好；而学生们则会更加起劲地"吸毒"，以便从教师的压力下及文凭竞赛中挣脱出来；越来越多的官僚将会摆出一副教师的面孔。教师的语言早已被选用于广告，而如今，将军与警察也试图通过假扮教育者的姿态，来为其职业增光添彩。在一个学校化社会中，发动战争与压制民众均可找到教育方面的缘由。越南战争式的教育战争将愈发被正当化为向人们灌输不断进步乃是最高价值这一观念的唯一途径。

压制民众将被看成为加速机器操控的救世主（mechanical Messiah）的到来而进行的一种传教式努力。越来越多的国家将会诉诸巴西和希腊业已施行的对于教育的拷问。这种拷问并非为了获悉情报或满足施虐狂的心理需要，而是出于对整个国民的统合性遭致破坏，以及对技术专家们发明的各种教学成为轻而易举之事而不时产生的恐慌。除非我们现在就把自己从教育傲慢中解放出来，从人能够为上帝所不能为这一信念中解放出来，也即从人可以为了拯救他人而操控他人这一信念中解放出来，否则，具有全面破坏作用而又持续加剧的强制性教育便会实现它的最终逻辑。

许多人刚开始意识到，当今的生产活动具有无情破坏环境的趋势，但个人改变这种趋势的力量微乎其微。发端于学校中的对于人的操控，如今也已达到无法回头的地步，而大多数人对此仍毫无察觉。如同福特三世[1]建议发展公害较少的小汽车一样，这些人仍在鼓动学校改革。

贝尔[2]指出，我们这个时代的特征是文化与社会结构之间严重断裂。前

---

[1] 福特三世（Henry Ford Ⅲ, 1917—1987），美国实业家，汽车大王亨利·福特的孙子。生前曾担任福特汽车公司总经理达34年之久。——译者注

[2] 贝尔（Daniel Bell, 1919—2011），美国社会学家。著有《意识形态的终结》《资本主义文化矛盾》《后工业社会的来临》等。——译者注

者忠实于启示录[1]的精神,后者则专注于技术决策。对许多教育改革者来说,情况确实如此,他们觉得不得不对现代学校的几乎所有特征都加以谴责,但与此同时又提出要建设新型学校。

库恩[2]在《科学革命的结构》(*The Structure of Scientific Revolutions*)一书中认为,这种失调现象在新的认知范式出现之前是不可避免的。例如,自由落体观察者、从地球另一边归来者以及新式望远镜使用者们所报告的诸多事实,就与托勒密[3]对地球的见解不同。于是,牛顿[4]范式一下子被人们接受。现今许多年轻人身上出现的失调特征与其说是认知方面的问题,不如说是态度方面的问题,即对于社会可以容忍到什么程度方面的感受问题。而令人惊讶的是,相当多的人对于这种失调现象都具有承受能力。

这里需要对人们追求相互矛盾的各种目标的能力加以说明。根据格拉克曼[5]的观点,任何社会都有对其成员掩饰这种失调现象的手段。他提出,掩饰失调正是日常仪式的目的。日常仪式甚至能对其参与者掩饰社会原则与社会组织之间的矛盾与冲突。只要一个人没有清醒地意识到形塑其自身世界的各种力量对他的诱导过程所具有的仪式性特征,那么,他就不可能打破这种过程的魔咒,形成自己的新世界。同样,只要我们没有觉察到学校对于欲望日增的消费者——经济的主要资源——进行形塑的仪式性特征,那么,我们也就无法打破这种经济的魔咒而建立一种新的经济。

---

1 启示录,基督教《圣经·新约全书》的卷末。作者自称为约翰。运用当时犹太人中流行的"启示文学"体裁,以"见异象""说预言"的方式描绘了一幅"世界末日"和"基督再来"的景象。——译者注

2 库恩(Tomas Kuhn,1922—1996),美国科学史家、科学哲学家,科学哲学中历史学派的创始人。著有《科学革命的结构》《哥白尼革命》等。——译者注

3 托勒密(Claudius Ptolemaeus,约90—168),古希腊天文学家、数学家、地理学家和地图学家。著有《天文学大成》《地理学》等。——译者注

4 牛顿(Isaac Newton,1643—1727),英国物理学家、数学家和天文学家,被誉为"近代物理学之父"。著有《自然哲学的数学原理》《光学》等。——译者注

5 格拉克曼(Max Gluckman,1911—1975),出生于南非的英国社会人类学家。人类学中曼彻斯特学派的创始人。著有《非洲部落中的秩序与反抗》(*Order and Rebellion in Tribal Africa*)、《部落社会中的政治、法律和宗教仪式》(*Politics, Law and Ritual in Tribal Society*)等。——译者注

# 第四章　制度光谱

空想主义的蓝图与未来学的构想大都需要耗资昂贵的新技术，富国与穷国都只能以同样的价格购买这些技术。在委内瑞拉、阿根廷以及哥伦比亚，卡恩[1]都可找到其门徒。贝纳德斯[2]曾为他的巴西同胞描绘过一个绚丽的美梦，他许诺到2000年，巴西将比现今的美国拥有更多的新机器，而届时美国将因其陈旧不堪的导弹发射场、飞机场以及20世纪60年代与70年代水准的城市而背上沉重的包袱。受富勒[3]鼓舞的未来学家们想来会求助于耗费更少且更为新奇的技术手段。他们期望采用具有可行性的新技术，这些新技术显然可以使我们更多地制造出轻型单轨铁路，而不是超音速飞机；可以使我们的居住空间往高延伸，而不是在平面上铺摊。现在，所有未来学规划者都试图使技术上可行的东西，同时也具有经济上的可行性，但却拒绝面对必然会产生的社会后果，即：所有人对商品与服务的渴求都日趋强烈，而享用这些商品与服务则仍是少数人的特权。

我相信，一个值得憧憬的未来有赖于我们刻意选择一种行动的生活

---

[1] 卡恩（Herman Kahn, 1922—1983），美国物理学家、军事战略家。坚决主张热核战争与常规战争只有程度上的区别，应当用同样的方法去分析和计划。著有《论热核战争》（*On Thermonuclear War*）。——译者注

[2] 贝纳德斯（Sergio Bernardes, 1919—2002），巴西建筑师。在20世纪70年代末提出"研究实验室概念"，设计解决社会问题的独特方案，诸如建造30000千米长的输水管道抗旱工程、建筑1000米高的住房等。——译者注

[3] 富勒（Buckminster Fuller, 1895—1983），美国建筑师、工程师、发明家、哲学家、诗人。主张发展全面的、长期的技术发展计划，"使人类成为宇宙间的一项奇迹"。——译者注

（life of action），而不是消费的生活（life of consumption）；有赖于形成一种能使我们具有自发性、自主性而又相互联系的生活方式，而不是维持一种只会让我们去制造与毁灭、生产与消费的生活方式——这种生活方式只会让我们走向耗竭资源与污染环境的末路。未来更多地有赖于我们选择支持行动的生活的各种制度，而不是去发展各种新思想与新技术。我们需要有一套标准，这套标准将会让我们辨识那些助人成长、而非纵人"吸毒"的制度；我们还需要有一种意志，这种意志可让我们将技术资源优先用于发展这些助人成长的制度。

我们是在两种根本对立的制度类型中进行选择的。这两种类型都可以在某些现存制度中找到范例，尽管其中的一种类型赋予了现代社会以特征，以至几乎界定了什么是现代社会。我把这种占支配地位的类型称为"操控型（manipulative）"制度。另一种类型也存在于现实社会中，但还不稳定。这一类型的制度比较低调，不太引人注目，但我还是将它们视为更理想的未来模式。我把这些制度称为"友好型（convivial）"制度，并将它们置于制度光谱（institutional spectrum）的左端。这既是为了表明在光谱的左右两端之间存在着各种制度，也是为了说明在历史进程中形成的各种制度，随着其功能从促进活动转变为促进组织生产，其在制度光谱中的位置会发生相应的变化。

这种从左到右渐次变化的光谱，迄今通常被用来区分人及其观念的特征，而不是用来区分我们的各种社会制度及其不同样式的特征。用这种光谱对人——不论是个体还是群体——进行分类，常常并未带来新的认识，而是招致激愤的情绪。以一种非常规方式来使用常规手段，可能会引起重大异议，但我希望通过这种方式使那些用于讨论的术语由枯燥无味变得丰富多彩。这种讨论将可清楚地表明，位于制度光谱左端的人们对于那些位于制度光谱右端的操控型制度未必总是持对立的态度。

在制度光谱的右端，聚集着各种最有影响的现代制度。例如，随着司法执行的职能从县治安官转由联邦调查局（FBI）与五角大楼（Pentagon）

承担，其在制度光谱中的位置也就移到了右端。再如，现代战争如今已成了一种高度专业化的、专司杀戮的行当，它已到了以尸体数量来衡量其效果的地步。其维护和平的潜在作用能否得到发挥，有赖于参战一方能否令友方与敌方都相信本方具有无限的杀伤力量。今天的弹药与化学武器如此有效，以至一旦准确击中目标，便能以极低的成本让对方非死即伤。不过，其费用也在飞快上涨，每杀死一个越南人的成本已从1967年的36万美元增加到1969年的45万美元。只有经济规模达到近乎种族自杀（race suicide[1]）地步的国家，才会让现代战争具有经济效益。而战争的回飞镖效应[2]正变得愈加明显。例如，越南人死得越多，则美国在国际上树敌也越多；同样，其在为消除战争的副作用的无效努力中，为建立另一个操控型制度——被人们讥讽为"安抚制度"——所付出的代价也就越大。

同样在制度光谱右端，我们还可以发现一些专司操控其服务对象的社会机构。这些社会机构与军队相似，随着操控范围的扩大，往往会产生同其目标相悖的效果。这些社会机构的操控同样是适得其反的，只是不如军队那样明显。为了掩饰这种自相矛盾的结果，许多社会机构都装扮成一副关怀同情、治病救人的面孔。例如，直到两个世纪之前，监狱一直被用来作为对那些等候判刑、等候受残刑、等候受极刑或等候被流放的人实行拘禁的场所。而且，关进监狱有时还会被蓄意作为折磨人的一种方式。只是到了不久之前，我们才开始提出，把人关进牢房有助于矫正其性格与行为。现在，相当多的人开始认识到，监狱的存在既导致了犯罪种类的增加，又导致了罪犯数量的增长；事实上，它经常将一些单纯的违规者也作为罪犯关押进来。然而，只有极少数人似乎认识到，精神病院、疗养院以及孤儿院的作用与监狱完全相同。这些机构为其服务对象提供着对他们的人格

---

[1] "race suicide"这个词所说的种族自杀，原本是指由于限制生育或不愿生育的原因，使得出生率低于死亡率而导致种族渐次灭绝。——译者注

[2] 回飞镖效应（boomerang effect），回飞镖是澳大利亚等地土著人用作武器或狩猎工具的一种飞镖，如未击中目标能飞回原处。此处意指自食其果。——译者注

具有损毁作用的自我形象，即精神病患者、老朽无用者或流浪儿；同时也为所有在这些机构服务的专家们提供了存在的理由，就好像监狱的存在为看守带来了收入一样。位于制度光谱右端的这些制度都具有强制性，表现为以下两种方式，即或者是强行看管，或者是提供有选择的服务。

位于制度光谱左端的各种制度，即"友好型"制度，以服务对象自主使用为特征。电话交换台、地铁运输网、邮政网、公共市场以及交易所等无须软磨硬泡地诱使顾客去使用其服务，人们也无须接受关于使用污水处理系统、饮用水系统、公园以及人行道等的好处的制度性宣传，就会使用这些设施。无疑，任何制度的运行都需要某些规章。但是，那些并非为了生产什么东西，而只是为了供人们使用的友好型制度所需要的运行规章，与那些以安排为特征的操控型制度所需要的运行规章，在性质上完全不同。前一种规章主要用来防止制度的滥用，这种滥用会妨碍对于制度的广泛而方便的利用。例如：必须保持人行道畅通无阻，必须限制工矿企业对饮用水的使用，在公园中打球必须限于特定区域等。现在，我们需要制定法律来限制计算机系统对电话线路的滥用，限制广告业对邮政服务的滥用，并防止工业用水对我们的下水道系统造成污染。友好型制度的规章对制度的使用加以某些限制。随着一种制度从位于制度光谱左端的友好型转向位于制度光谱右端的操控型，其运行规章也就越来越要求人们违己所愿地进行消费或参与。而在为争取到更多服务对象所花成本方面的差异，只是友好型制度与操控型制度相区别的诸多特征之一。

在制度光谱的左右两端，我们都可以发现一些服务性的制度。但是，在制度光谱右端，服务是强制的、操控性的，其服务对象成了广告、攻击、灌输、关押或电击的牺牲品。而在制度光谱左端，服务则是在正式规定的范围内向人们提供更多机会，服务对象依然是自由的主体。位于制度光谱右半侧的各种制度往往都有十分复杂且成本昂贵的生产过程，在这一过程中，这些制度会耗费大量财力精心设计，千方百计地说服消费者们相信：若无该制度提供的产品或安排，他们将无法生存。而位于制度光谱左半侧的各种制度则往往是一些网络，这些网络为由服务对象发起的沟通或合作提供便利。

位于制度光谱右端的操控型制度导致人们不是社会性地，就是心理性地"成瘾"。社会性成瘾（social addiction）或曰逐步加码（escalation），说的是倘若数量较少的安排未能得到期盼的结果，那么人们往往会要求提供更多的安排。心理性成瘾（psychological addiction）或曰成为习惯（habituation），则出现在消费者陷入对过程或产品产生越来越多的需求而难以自拔时。而位于制度光谱左端的自我激励型制度（self-activated institutions）则倾向于自我约束。与那些旨在满足纯粹消费行为的生产过程不同，这些自我激励型制度的网络是为超越于反复使用之外的目的而服务的。一个人对他人有话要说时便拿起话筒，想要进行的交谈一结束便会挂上话筒。除了十多岁的年轻人，谁也不会纯粹因为对着电话机讲话有十足的乐趣才打电话。假如打电话并非最佳的联系方式，则人们便会写信或登门造访。而位于制度光谱右端的各种制度，如同我们在学校的例子中可以清楚地看到的那样，既强制性地要求人们反复使用其服务，又阻挠人们通过其他途径取得类似的结果。

对于那些在自身领域同其他企业竞争，但尚未开始进行引人注目的广告宣传的企业，我们可将它们置于制度光谱的偏左部分，但不是左端。手工洗衣店、小面包店、理发师以及某些律师和音乐教师等值得一提的专业人员都属于此类。接下来，具有代表性的位于制度光谱的中心之左侧的是一些个体经营者。他们的服务已经制度化了，但并未进行制度化的广告宣传，他们通过个人交往与服务质量去赢得顾客。

饭店与咖啡馆更靠近制度光谱的中心。像希尔顿（Hilton）这种在美化自身形象方面耗资极巨的大型连锁酒店，其所作所为常常让人觉得它所经营的机构似乎位于制度光谱的右端。不过，希尔顿与喜来登（Sheraton）之类的企业所提供的服务通常并不比那些以同等价格独立经营的公寓更多，事实上，它们所提供的服务常常更少。酒店广告牌中招揽旅客的方式与路标基本相同，广告牌上写的并非"到公园一歇不如到本店一眠"，而是"请君留步,此处可供君安卧"。

生产主要食品以及大多数易损生活消费品的厂家位于制度光谱的中心位置。这些产品满足着人们的一般需要,其价格中除了含有生产与流通的成本之外,还包括由购买者承担的广告宣传成本与特殊包装成本。越是满足基本需要的产品——商品也好,服务也罢——竞争也越为激烈,其结果往往会导致对其销售价格的限制。

大部分消费品生产商在制度光谱中的位置已向右移动了许多。它们或直接或间接地引发着人们对于一些附属品的需要,这些附属品使得产品的实际销售价格远远高于生产成本。通用汽车公司与福特汽车公司生产交通工具,但更重要的是,它们也左右着公众对于交通工具的口味——这种口味让公众产生的是对私人小汽车的需要,而不是对公共汽车的需要。它们在让人们幻想能驱车前往任何地方的同时,还让人们产生操控机器的欲望以及驾驶豪华舒适的汽车飞速驰骋的欲望。然而,它们出售的并不只是一些毫无价值的大型马达、多此一举的精巧装置,或者迫于纳德[1]以及那些要求保护新鲜空气的院外说客[2]的压力而不得不生产的新的附加设备。产品定价中不仅含有大功率发动机、空调设备、安全带以及控制尾气排放装置的费用,而且含有并未告明司机的其他成本费用,这些成本费用除了在我们的城市中因交通拥堵而造成的时间浪费、心情焦躁以及呼吸不到新鲜空气之类的无形成本之外,还包括汽车公司的广告费、销售费、燃料费、保养费、备品费、保险费以及贷款利息等。

我们对具有社会功用的各种制度的讨论必然引申出一项格外令人关注的制度,即"公用"高速公路系统。它在汽车的全部成本中占主要部分,我们有必要对它加以更详尽的探讨,因为这可以使我们的讨论直接指向制

---

[1] 纳德(Ralph Nader, 1934— ),美国律师。常为维护消费者利益而呼吁、辩论。著有《任何速度都是不安全的》(*Unsafe at Any Speed*) 等。——译者注
[2] 院外说客(lobbyists),受雇对议员和政府官员等进行游说、疏通的说客,多为院外活动集团的成员。——译者注

度光谱的最右端。而我最关注的制度——学校——便位于这一区段。

## 一、虚假的公用事业

高速公路系统是用于较长距离移动的一种道路网络。作为一种网络，它似乎应位于制度光谱的左半侧。但在这里，我们必须对高速公路与真正的公用事业的性质加以明确区分。真正适用于各种用途的道路是名副其实的公用事业，而高速公路则由私营公司经营维护，这些私营公司采用欺骗手段，将其部分经营维护成本强摊给了公众。

电话、邮政以及高速公路系统都是网络，它们所提供的都不是无偿服务。对电话网络的使用是通过计时收费的方式加以限制的。通话费用相对比较便宜，且无须改变电话系统的性质便可降低话费。打电话丝毫不受通话内容的限制，尽管最善于使用电话者是那些能用对方理解的语言清楚表达的人，而希望使用电话网络者一般都具有这种能力。邮费通常也很便宜，使用邮政网络极少会受到笔与纸的价格以及书写能力方面的限制。不会写信者通过口述，让其亲戚或朋友代笔，仍可使用邮政服务；假如他想邮寄一盘录音磁带，则也同样如此。

高速公路系统则与之不同，它不会仅仅因为某人学会了开车便可供其使用。电话网与邮政网是为了想要使用电话与邮政服务的人而建立的，而高速公路系统则主要充当着私人小汽车的附庸。前者是真正的公用事业，后者则是面向小汽车、卡车以及公共汽车所有者的一种公共服务（public service）。公用事业的存在目的在于为人们之间的交往提供便利，而高速公路系统，则和位于制度光谱右端的其他制度一样，其存在目的在于为某种产品服务。如前所述，汽车制造厂商在制造汽车的同时，也制造着人们对于汽车的需要，以及对于多车道高速公路、桥梁以及油田的需要。在位于制度光谱右半侧的一堆制度中，私人小汽车处于核心位置。基本产品的精细生产使得所有部件的成本上涨，而销售基本产品也就等于诱引社会产生对于同基本产品相关的全套产品的需要。

为了将高速公路系统规划为一种真正的公用事业,应当贬抑把高速以及个性化舒适度视为交通之主要价值的那些人的需要,更多地关注把机动性以及到达目的地视为交通之主要价值的那些人的需要。这就是两种不同公路网的区别:一种是尽可能地让更多人得以利用的四面延伸的公路网,一种是仅供特权者在有限范围内享用的公路网。

如果把视线转向发展中国家,那么我们便可对现代制度的特性进行严格检视。在十分贫穷的国家中,道路的质量通常只能允许一些车轴位置较高的、用来装载杂货、牲畜和人员的特殊货车通行。这类国家当然需要将其有限的资源用于建设能通往所有地区的蜘蛛网般的公路网,并用于进口仅限于两三种极为经久耐用且可在所有道路上低速行驶的不同类型的车辆。这将使车辆维修与备件贮存简单方便,可以昼夜不停地提供运输服务,并可让所有国民都能获得最大限度的机动性,使他们能选择自己的目的地。这将需要对多用途车辆进行工程设计,这种多用途车辆装有结构简单的T型发动机[1],使用最先进的合金材料以确保车辆经久耐用,内置有可将车速控制在每小时24公里以内的限速装置,而且足够结实,以便能在任何崎岖不平的地面上行驶。如今这种车辆不在市场上出售,因为它们没有市场需求。事实上,这种需求按理说是有必要形成的,在严格的法律保护下也是极有可能形成的。但在今天,这种需求一旦稍有显露,很快就会被旨在向全球推销小汽车的反向广告宣传淹没。目前在美国,这种广告宣传要从纳税人的腰包里掏出建造高速公路所需的资金。

为了"改善"交通运输,所有国家——甚至连最穷的国家——都在为客车与高速房车[2]规划高速公路系统。这些车辆适合于精英阶层中追求交通快捷的少数生产者与消费者。这种做法常常被加以合理化,被说成是为

---

[1] T型发动机,一种结构简单、经久耐用的老式发动机。——译者注
[2] 房车,一种可移动、装有居家必备基本设施的车辆类型,兼具"房"与"车"两大功能。——译者注

了节约穷国最宝贵的资源,即医生、学校督察员[1]或政府官员的时间。不用说,这些人几乎只是为那些和自己一样已经拥有或希望有一天能够拥有小汽车的人服务的。地方税收和宝贵的外汇就这样被浪费在虚假的公用事业上了。

移植到穷国的"现代"技术分属三大范畴,即:商品、商品生产厂家以及服务机构。这些服务机构——主要是学校——使人成为现代生产者与消费者。大多数国家都将最大比例的预算支出用于学校;学校培养出来的毕业生则产生了对于那些引人注目的公用事业的需要,诸如工业用电系统、铺设优良的高速公路、现代化医院以及飞机场等;而这些公用事业转而又催生出一个原本为富国而生产的商品市场。于是,用不了多久,往往就会产生从富国引进生产这些商品的过时工厂的需要。

在所有"虚假的公用事业"中,学校最为阴险。高速公路系统仅仅使人产生对于小汽车的需要,而学校则使人产生对聚集于制度光谱右端的全套现代制度的需要。一个对高速公路系统的必要性持怀疑态度的人或许会被斥责为空想主义者,而他若是对学校的必要性提出质疑,则立刻就会被攻击为冷酷无情者或帝国主义者。

## 二、作为虚假公用事业的学校

如同高速公路一样,乍看起来,学校给人的印象似乎是对所有人平等开放。但实际上,学校只对那些想要不断获得更高层次的文凭的人开放。恰如高速公路给人的印象是,若要利用高速公路出行,就必须按年支付目前水准的费用一样,接受学校教育也被认为是在使用现代技术的社会中获得所需能力的必要前提。上文已经通过指出高速公路对于私人汽车的依

---

[1] 学校督察员,对学校教育和教学工作进行指导、提出建议、实施监督的教育行政官员。——译者注

赖，揭露了它是一种骗人的公用事业。学校也同样建立在具有欺骗性的假设基础之上，这个假设便是：学习是课程讲授的产物。

高速公路是人们对机动性的期望和需求被扭曲为对私人小汽车的需要所导致的结果，而学校自身便把人所具有的成长和学习的自然倾向扭曲为对于教学的需要。这种对于制造出来的成熟的需要远比对于制造出来的商品的需要，更容易使人放弃自发性活动的欲望。在制度光谱中，学校不但位于高速公路与小汽车之右，而且与位于最右端的全面监护的精神病院相毗邻。即便是战争制造者，所杀害的也只是人的躯体；而学校则通过使人放弃对于自己成长的责任，而导致许多人走向一种精神自杀。

高速公路的部分费用是由使用者支付的，因为过路费与汽油费税只向司机收取。而学校则是一个完全靠累退税制来维持的系统，那些享有特权的毕业生是依靠全体国民纳税才得以完成学业的。当然，学校要向升级的学生收取人头税[1]，但学校教育没有得到充分利用所造成的损失，要远远大于高速公路没有得到充分利用所造成的损失。一个洛杉矶居民若无小汽车可能寸步难行，但倘若他能设法到达工作场所，那么他仍可获得并持有一份工作，而辍学者则没有代替学校的其他教育途径可以选择。对于一个住在郊外并拥有林肯牌新车的人和他住在乡间、驾驶着一辆破旧老爷车的表哥来说，高速公路的用途基本上没什么两样，尽管前一辆车的价格要高出后一辆车30倍以上。一个人所受学校教育的价值被认为是他完成就学的年数与学校收费水平的函数。法律不强求任何人开车，却强迫每一个人上学。

根据在制度光谱中所处的位置而对一些制度进行的分析，使我得以阐明我的一个信念，即：要进行根本的社会变革，首先必须改变人们的制度意识；并使我得以说明为什么一个有希望的未来取决于制度样式（institutional style）的返老还童。

---

[1] 人头税（head tax），以人口为课税对象所征收的税。随着所得税、消费税的普遍实行，此税逐渐废止。伊利奇此处使用这一概念，指的是学费。——译者注

# 第四章　制度光谱

在20世纪60年代，诞生于法国大革命[1]不同时期的种种制度全都成为过时之物。杰斐逊[2]时代或阿塔蒂尔克[3]时代建立起来的公立学校教育制度，连同第二次世界大战后建立起来的其他学校教育制度，全都成了科层性的、自我合理化的以及操控性的制度。同样的变化也发生在社会保障制度、劳动工会、主要教会组织、外交事务、老年人看护以及死后安置等方面。

例如，在今天，哥伦比亚、英国、苏联以及美国的学校教育制度之间的相似之处，要更甚于19世纪90年代后期的美国学校教育制度与今天的美国学校教育制度之间的相似之处。现在，所有学校都是强制性的、开放性的、竞争性的。制度样式的趋同现象也影响着医疗保健、商业、人事管理以及政治生活等领域。所有这些制度的变化过程都呈现出向制度光谱中具有操控性质的右端聚集的趋向。

科层体制的全球趋同便是上述制度趋同的结果。现在，连哥斯达黎加或阿富汗的规划委员会都效仿西欧国家的模式来确定学校的样式、等级系统以及各种配套用品（从教科书到计算机）的标准。

在任何国家，这些科层体制似乎都只聚焦于同一个任务，即：促进位于制度光谱右半侧的那些制度的发展。它们所关心的是制造物品、制定例行规则、规定与修正"行政真理（executive truth）"。所谓行政真理，指的是一些观念或法令，这些观念或法令决定着产品物当所值的现价。技术的使用赋予这些位于制度光谱右半侧的科层体制以日益强大的权力，而位于制度光谱左半侧的那些制度则似乎日趋衰败，这并非因为它很难通过技术来扩展人的行动范围，并使个人获得发挥想象力与创造力的时间，而是因

---

[1] 法国大革命（French Revolution），1789—1794年法国推翻封建专制统治、确立资本主义制度的革命。——译者注

[2] 杰斐逊（Thomas Jefferson，1743—1826），美国第三任总统（1801—1809），资产阶级民主派代表人物，民主共和党创始人。曾参与起草《独立宣言》。——译者注

[3] 阿塔蒂尔克（Mustafa Kemal Atatürk，1881—1938），土耳其军人，改革家、作家。曾任土耳其共和国第一任总统（1923—1938）。著有《走向自由》《国民革命》等。——译者注

为技术的使用并不会增加管理它的精英阶层的权力。邮政局局长无权控制人们大量使用邮件，电话交换台话务员或贝尔电话公司总经理也无权阻止人们利用电话网来策划通奸、谋杀或颠覆活动。

人类生活的本质便在于身处困境时，必须在制度光谱的右半侧与左半侧这两者之间做出选择。人不得不选择是要拥有丰富的物品，还是要享有使用物品的自由；不得不选择是尝试与现今生活样式截然不同的新的生活样式，还是延续同现今生活样式密切联系的各种生产计划。

亚里士多德[1]早已发现"制作与行动（making and acting）"并不相同。事实上，由于两者差异极大，所以其中一者不能包含另一者。"因为，行动不是一种制作方式，制作也不是一种真正的行动方式……建筑术是一种制作方式……它是做出某种东西。这种东西的原型存在于制作者的头脑中，而不是物品中。而制作总是有着制作之外的目的，而行动则并非如此；善的行动自身便是这一行动的目的。完美的制作是一种艺术，完美的行动则是一种美德。"[2]亚里士多德用来表达"制作"一词的是"poesis"，用来表达"行动"一词的则是"praxis"。若一种制度在制度光谱中的位置向右移动，则意味着该制度在为增强其"制作"能力而进行着重构；若向左移动，则意味着该制度在为增强其"行动"能力而进行着重构。现代技术增强了人把物品"制作"交由机器去完成的能力，从而增加了人可用于"行动"的时间。今天，人在"制作"生活必需品方面已无须耗费多少时间。失业便是这种现代化的结果，即是说，失业成了懒人的标志，对失业者来说，已没有什么东西可去"制作（make）"，他也不知道应该"做（do）"些什么——即应该如何"行动（act）"。与亚里士多德的观点相反，对于一个认为制作物品或从事劳动乃美德、游手好闲乃恶行的人来说，失业是可悲的懒惰之

---

[1] 亚里士多德（Aristotle，公元前384—前322），古希腊哲学家。著有《形而上学》《工具论》《物理学》《伦理学》《政治学》等。——译者注

[2] 《尼格马科伦理学》（*Nichomachean Ethics*），第1140页。——作者注

表现。失业是接受了新教伦理[1]的人所产生的一种体验。根据韦伯的观点，闲暇是人得以工作的必要条件。而在亚里士多德看来，工作是获得闲暇的必要条件。

技术为人们提供了可用于"制作"或"行动"的自由支配的时间。在痛苦的失业与愉快的闲暇之间进行选择的机会，现在已向所有文化开放，这取决于文化所选择的制度样式。这种选择在以农耕制或奴隶制为基础的古代文化中无法想象，而对于后工业化时代的人来说，则已不可避免。

打发可自由支配时间的一种途径，是既刺激人们对商品消费的需求不断增长，同时又刺激人们对提供服务的需求不断增长。前者意味着建立这样一种经济，这种经济向人们提供更多更新的物品，它使人们处于制造、消费以及浪费物品的周而复始的过程之中。后者意味着进行一种无效尝试，即尝试"使"人的善行成为那些"服务性"制度的产物。这导致人们把学校教育视同于真的教育，把医疗服务视同于增进健康，把观看节目视同于欢愉快乐，把高速行驶视同于有效移动。如今，这些"视同"中的前者在促进发展的名义下畅行无阻。

打发可自由支配时间的根本替代途径，是生产种类有限的且更为耐用的商品，并为人们享用能够增进人际互动的机会与愿望的各种制度提供方便。

同以有意废弃商品[2]为基础的经济截然相反，以生产耐用品为基础的经济意味着要限制商品生产的种类与数量。在这种经济中，商品必须成为这样一种东西，即：它为人们提供了可最大限度地用它来"做"些什么的机会，诸如自行组装、自助、重新使用以及修理等。

---

[1] 新教伦理（protestant ethic），指基督教新教发展起来的"职业""天职"观念。认为上帝允许的唯一生存方式，不是要人们以苦修的禁欲主义超越世俗道德，而是要完成个人在现实生活中所处的角色赋予他的责任和义务；要珍惜时光、辛勤劳作、增加资本、节制、不图悠闲享乐，才能为上帝效劳。——译者注
[2] 有意废弃商品，指为增加销量而故意制造不耐用的商品。——译者注

对于经久耐用、可修理且可重新使用的商品的种类和数量的补充,不在于增加那些按制度提供的服务,而在于构建能不断引导人们去行动、参与以及自助的制度框架。在我们现在的社会中,所有制度都在向后工业化的科层体制行进;在未来的后工业化的友好型社会中,行动的力量将会战胜产品的力量。而要从现在走向未来,就必须从重建各种服务性制度开始,而且首先必须重建教育制度。 一个理想且又可行的未来社会是否能够诞生,取决于我们是否乐意把我们的技术知识用于促进友好型制度的成长。在教育研究领域,这意味着需要进行与目前趋势截然相反的变革。

# 第五章　荒谬的一致性[1]

我相信，解决当代教育的危机，与其说需要对非个人自主的规定性学习的种种强制性方法加以检视，不如说需要对这种学习的观念本身进行反思。辍学者与离职者比例之高，尤其是初中辍学者与小学教师离职者比例之高，反映了人们希望对教育进行彻底的全新审视的普遍要求。那些将自己视为自由教师（liberal teacher）的"课堂实践者"越来越陷于四面楚歌之中。自由学校运动[2]把纪律与灌输混为一谈，把教师描绘成一种具有破坏性的专制者角色；教育技术专家们不断地论证教师在测量与矫正学生行为方面拙劣无能；而学校管理则让教师感到强制性学习显然不可能成为一种自由的活动，从而逼得教师不得不认可夏山学校[3]与斯金纳[4]的教学方法。这样，教师离职者的比例高于学生辍学者的比例也就绝非不可思议。

---

[1] 本章原为作者1971年2月6日在纽约召开的一次会议中向美国教育研究协会（The American Educational Research Association）提交的论文。——作者注

[2] 自由学校运动（free-school movement），亦称新学校运动或另类学校运动，一般指20世纪60年代至70年代初的美国教育改革运动。旨在通过另类、独立的社区学校改变正规学校教育。关于该运动持续的时间至少有两种观点：一种最保守的估计是自由学校运动兴起于1965年，结束于1973年，持续了8年；另有一种说法认为自由学校运动兴起于1963年，至少存在到1998年。——译者注

[3] 夏山学校（Summerhill），英国教育家尼尔（A. S. Neil, 1883—1973）于1921年在英格兰东萨弗克郡里斯顿镇（Leiston, Suffolk）创办的学校。重视个人需要与兴趣，被誉为"最富人性化的快乐学校""因材施教的典范"。——译者注

[4] 斯金纳（Burrhus F. Skinner, 1904—1990），美国心理学家、教育家，新行为主义教育代表人物之一。著有《有机体的行为》（*The Behavior of Organisms*）、《教学技术》（*The Technology of Teaching*）等。——译者注

现已清楚无疑的是，美国在青少年义务教育方面所做的努力同其在越南强制推行民主所做的虚假努力一样徒劳无功。传统学校在这方面显然无能为力。虽然自由学校运动对不因循守旧的教育者们具有诱惑力，但它最终还是支持学校教育的传统观念。教育技术专家们许诺，只要经费充足，他们就能研究并开发出对付青少年反抗强制性学习的一些根本解决办法。这一许诺听起来让人信心十足，但其实同军事技术专家们的类似许诺一样愚不可及。

行为主义者与新一代激进主义教育者对于美国学校教育制度的批评似乎截然相反。行为主义者们旨在运用教育研究成果，"开发出一种借助个体化学习包（individualized learning packages）引导自订学习目标的教学"。虽然他们所采取的方式与通过非指令性地将青少年纳入成人监督下建立起来的开放式共同体（liberated communes）的方式大相径庭，但从历史的角度来看，两者不过是公立学校教育制度的那些看似矛盾、实则互补的目标在当代的表现形式。自20世纪初以来，学校一方面充当着社会控制的主角，另一方面则扮演着自由合作的主角。这两种角色都是为"好社会"服务的，这个"好社会"被认为是高度组织起来的、具有和谐运行结构的社会。受急剧城市化的影响，儿童成了经学校形塑后提供给工业社会的一种自然资源。进步主义政治与效率崇拜合为一体，共同促进了美国公立学校的发展[1]，就业指导与初级中学便是此类思考的两个重要产物。

因此，对学校教育而言，试图使学生行为出现可测量且测量数据可处理的特定变化似乎只是问题的一个方面，问题的另一个方面则是使年轻一代参与到专为他们设计的封闭的环境之中，这种封闭的环境将诱导他们进入年长一代的理想世界。对于社会中的这些安静祥和的小环境，杜威[2]曾有

---

[1] 见斯普林：《教育与公司式国家的诞生》，跨文化文献中心编：《纪要》第50期，1971年。（Joel Spring, *Education and the Rise of the Corporate State*, Cuaderno NO.50, Centro Intercultural de Documentación, Cuernavaca, Mexico, 1971.）——作者注

[2] 杜威（John Dewey，1859—1952），美国哲学家、教育家，实用主义芝加哥学派创始人。著有《学校与社会》《民主主义与教育》《哲学的改造》等。——译者注

过很好的描述，他希望我们"使每个学校都成为一种雏形的社会生活，以反映大社会中各种类型的职业活动，并充满着艺术、历史与科学的精神"。[1] 基于这一历史视角，把目前在现行学校体制维护者、教育技术专家以及自由学校这三者之间出现的争论解释为教育革命的前兆，乃是极大的错误。这一争论莫如说反映着一个阶段，在这一阶段中，人们试图将古老的梦想逐步变为现实，并最终使一切有价值的学习都成为专业化教学的结果。大多数教育改革方案都聚焦在培养具有合作精神的人的过程中所蕴含的那些目标上，而在美国的制度中，这种具有合作精神的人的个人需要乃是通过自己的专业化才得以满足的。这些改革方案的取向是对我所说的学校化社会——尚未找到更合适的词——加以改良。甚至连那些对学校教育制度似乎持激进批判态度的人也不情愿抛弃这样一种观念，即：不论是奉以爱心，还是施以威胁，他们对青少年尤其是对贫困青少年都有一种义务——一种对他们进行加工并把他们输送给社会的义务。这个社会不仅要求消费者与生产者都成为训练有素的行家，而且要求他们完全信奉经济发展优先的观念。

上述争论掩盖了"学校"这一观念本身固有的矛盾。现有的教师工会、技术行家以及教育解放运动[2]都在竭力使整个社会都信奉一种学校化世界（schooled world）的基本原理。这在某种程度上有点像许多和平运动与抗议运动的做法，这些运动竭力使其成员——不论是黑人、妇女、青少年，

---

[1] 此处所引杜威原话参考赵祥麟的译文（杜威. 学校与社会·明日之学校 [M]. 赵祥麟，等，译. 北京：人民教育出版社，1994：41）。可顺便提及的是，杜威的《学校与社会》（The School and Society）撰写于1899年，而他在1897年撰写的《我的教育信条》（My Pedagogic Creed）中则说："我认为学校作为一种制度应简化现实的社会生活；不应当像过去那样把它缩小为一种社会雏形。"详见：杜威. 学校与社会·明日之学校 [M]. 赵祥麟，等，译. 北京：人民教育出版社，1994：6。——译者注

[2] 教育解放运动，未见有确切的界定，可视为对美国20世纪60—70年代兴起的教育改革运动的总称。旨在批判隐藏于各种不平等现象背后的、受权力支配的、异化的社会关系，重构教育制度，建立更加平等、更加民主、促进而不是阻碍个人发展的学校教育制度，创造更加自由的学校环境。——译者注

还是穷人——相信可以通过增加国民总收入来寻求社会正义。

　　这里不难列举出目前尚未受到挑战的一些信条。首先一个为人们普遍持有的信条是，学生在教师指导下习得的行为对学生具有特殊的价值，并且特别有益于社会。这个信条与人只有在青年期且只有在学校这种特殊环境中逐步成熟，才能真正成长为社会人这一假设有关。然而，人们对学校的期待不尽相同：有些人希望学校宽容温和，另一些人希望学校物品繁多，还有些人则希望学校闪烁着自由主义传统的光辉。此外，还有一个为人们普遍持有的关于年轻人的信条，这个信条带有心理上的浪漫情调与政治上的保守色彩。按照这个信条，要想使社会发生变化，就必须让年轻人担负起改革的责任——但这只能是在他们最终从学校毕业之后。基于这一信条所建立的社会，很容易确立起一种对年轻一代进行教育的责任感，而这就不可避免地意味着某些人可以制订、区分并评价他人的个体目标。博尔赫斯[1]在其"想象的中国大百科全书节选"一文中力图表明，这样的分类尝试定会让人晕头转向。他告诉我们，在这种大百科全书中，动物被分成以下类别："(a) 属于皇帝所有的动物，(b) 已变成木乃伊的动物，(c) 饲养的动物，(d) 乳猪，(e) 海妖，(f) 传说中的动物，(g) 来回游荡的狗，(h) 包括在上述类别中的动物[2]，(i) 疯疯癫癫的动物，(j) 数量多得数不清的动物，(k) 用极为高级的驼绒毛笔画成的动物，(l) 零零星星的动物，(m) 毁坏水壶的动物，(n) 远道飞来形同苍蝇的动物。"[3]如今，谁也不会使用这种分类，除非有人觉得这种分类对他有用。我想，这里"有人"所说的"人"便是指收税官。如同教育目标分类对教育科学论著的作者来说是有意义的一样，至少对收税官来说，这种动物分类一定是有意义的。

---

[1] 博尔赫斯（Jorge Borges, 1899—1986），阿根廷作家。著有《小径分叉的花园》《沙之书》等。——译者注

[2] 包括在上述类别中的动物，原文为"those included in the present classification"。——译者注

[3] 此段关于动物分类的文字完全照译。毕竟只是博尔赫斯基于想象的分类，想来没有哪本中国大百科全书会如此进行分类。——译者注

当农民看到别人有权使用这种难以理解的逻辑对其家畜进行评价时,一定会感到无能为力、沮丧失望。与此相似,学生在正经八百地按照课程要求去学习时,通常也会疑窦丛生。他们甚至难免比我所想象的中国农民还要担惊受怕,因为被打上令其费解的标记的,并不是他们的家畜,而是他们的人生目标。

上面引自博尔赫斯的一段文字颇为有趣,因为它使人联想到荒谬的一致性逻辑,这种逻辑导致卡夫卡[1]与凯斯特勒[2]所描述的科层制既是危及日常生活的严重灾祸,又是日常生活的真实再现。荒谬的一致性使得那些从事联手共谋、训练有素的敲诈活动的犯罪同伙们如痴如醉。这是科层制行为(bureaucratic behavior)所导致的一种逻辑。它也成为这样一个社会所奉行的逻辑,这个社会要求其教育制度的管理者们担负起改变学生行为的公共责任。那些经过激发而能对教师强迫自己去学习的那些套装式教育内容(educational packages)之价值予以认同的学生,同那些在博尔赫斯展示的纳税申报表中能填入有关自家牲畜内容的中国农民相比,可谓半斤对八两。

在过去两代人的某些时段里,信奉精神治疗在美国文化中占支配地位,教师也开始被视为精神治疗专家。人们认为,任何人只要希望享受美国宪法规定的、与生俱来的平等与自由的权利,那就需要教师的精神帮助。现在,作为精神治疗专家的教师们提出接下来应进一步提供终身教育治疗(life-long educational treatment)。关于这一治疗的方式,目前正在讨论之中:是应当采取成人补习班的形式?还是应当利用电子技术使学习者痴迷于其中?抑或应当定期进行敏感性训练?所有教育者都乐于联手推

---

[1] 卡夫卡(Franz Kafka, 1883—1924),奥地利作家,现代主义、表现主义文学的重要代表人物。著有《审判》《变形记》《城堡》等。——译者注
[2] 凯斯特勒(Arthur Koestler, 1905—1983),匈牙利裔英国作家。著有《正午的黑暗》(*Darkness at Noon*)、《创造行动》(*The Act of Creation*)、《机器幽灵》(*The Ghost in the Machine*)等。——译者注

倒阻隔课堂与外部世界联系的围墙，以使学校成为整个社会文化的缩影。

虽然美国人关于教育未来的争论辞藻华丽、喧嚣震耳，但实际上比其他公共政策领域中的一些话语要更加保守。在外交政策方面，起码还有一个有组织的少数派在不断提醒我们：美国必须停止扮演世界警察的角色；在经济政策方面，激进的经济学家们，甚至连不怎么激进的经济学教师们，现在都对把经济总量增长作为理想目标持怀疑态度；在医疗政策方面，一些院外游说集团提出预防应重于治疗；在交通运输政策方面，另外一些院外游说集团强调交通运输应优先考虑机动性而不是速度。而唯独在教育领域，要求社会彻底去学校化的呼声却依然稀弱无力。现在缺少的是有力的论证与成熟的领导集团——这种领导集团旨在废除为强制性学习服务的一切制度。眼下，社会彻底去学校化这一事业尚未得到某个政党的支持。在12—17岁的青少年对所有形式的制度性的有计划教学都进行着日趋强烈——尽管有点无序——的抵抗的今天，这种现象让人尤为惊奇。

教育革新者们依然将教育制度的功能设想为可用来灌输他们所提供的各种套装式教育内容的漏斗。在我看来，问题并不在于这些漏斗的形式是课堂，还是电视台，或是"自由学习区"[1]；同样也不在于所提供的套装式教育内容丰富还是贫乏、新鲜刺激还是平淡无味、难度大且可测定（如数学Ⅲ）还是无法定量评价（如感受性），而在于教育被设想成由教育者所管控的制度性过程的结果。只要教育者与受教育者的关系依然是供给者与消费者的关系，那么，教育研究仍将是一个循环论证的过程。这种研究将不断借助科学证据，来证明人们需要更多的套装式教育内容，而且需要将这些套装式教育内容更精准地分配给每一个受教育者，这同某些社会科学去论证解决争端需要更多地诉诸军事手段别无二致。

教育革命能否成功，取决于能否实现以下双重转变：一是确立教育研

---

[1] 自由学习区，在西方国家，教室乃至学校的空间往往会按照学科分成不同的区域，如科学活动区、语音活动区、创造活动区以及此处所说的自由学习区等。——译者注

究的新取向，二是对正在兴起的反主流文化的教育样式获得新的理解。

现在，操作性研究（operational research）正致力于让沿用至今的研究框架发挥最大效能，而对这一框架本身人们从无半点怀疑。这一研究框架具有用来灌输套装式教育内容的漏斗所特有的一种句法[1]结构（syntactic structure）。取代这一框架的办法是建立一种教育网络，这种教育网络可使每一个学习者都能自主而又自律地组合各种学习资源。这种教育制度的新结构正是迄今我们进行操作性研究的思维盲点。假如能聚焦于这种新结构，那么我们的教育研究将会发生真正的科学革命。

教育研究的这一盲点反映出把技术专家的控制与技术的发展混为一谈的社会所持有的文化偏见。在技术专家看来，环境的价值随着个人与环境之间有计划联系的增多而提升。在这个社会中，监管者或计划者可操控的选择，同时也就成了被监管的所谓受益人能够进行的选择。自由已被降格为只能在套装商品中加以选择的自由。

正在兴起的反主流文化重申，语义[2]内容（semantic content）的价值大于日臻繁多且愈发精细的句法的功效；内涵比形式更重要；人们自己选择的与他人相识所产生的意外收获，比凭借专业化教学获得的文凭来证明的素质更重要。寻求个人惊奇，而非看重制度性设定的价值，这样一种重新定位将可瓦解现存社会秩序，直到我们把日益增多的对有助于个人相识的那些技术手段的有效利用，同技术专家对这种相识的日益增多的控制区分开来。

现存的种种教育制度是为教师的目标服务的。我们需要的是这样一些关系结构，这些关系结构将使每一个人都能通过学习与帮助他人学习来界定他自己。

---

[1] 句法，语法学的组成部分之一。包括词组的构成、句子的构成、句类和句型等内容。——译者注

[2] 语义，语言所表达的意思，即语言所包含的意义内容。——译者注

# 第六章　学习网络

　　上一章讨论了人们开始出现的对学校的普遍抱怨，例如，卡内基委员会[1]最近的一份报告就反映了这种抱怨：在学校中，注册学生为了获取文凭而顺从于持有执教许可证的教师；教师与学生都感到失望，且都抱怨经费、时间或建筑设施等资源短缺——这是导致他们彼此失望的原因。

　　这种批评促使许多人提出是否有可能采取与现今不同的学习方式。但具有讽刺意味的是，同样是这些人，一旦被要求具体说明他们是如何获得知识与价值的，他们马上便会承认自己在校外学到的东西常常多于在校内所学。他们所拥有的关于事实的知识以及对人生与劳动的理解，一方面来自观看电视或阅读书籍，来自伙伴的示范或在街头遭遇的挑战，另一方面则来自友情或爱情。或者，他们可能是通过加入某一街头团伙所须经过的入伙仪式，通过进入医院、报纸的本地新闻编辑室、管道工场或保险公司办公室，而学到知识的。改变对于学校的依赖，不是要利用公共资源来建造"使"人们进行学习的某些新设施，而是要创造出人与环境之间的新型教育关系。为了促使这种关系的形成，必须同时改变我们现在对于人的成长的态度，改变可用于学习的种种手段以及日常生活的品质与结构。

---

[1] 卡内基委员会（Carnegie Commission），原文如此，应为"卡内基促进教学基金会（Carnegie Foundation for the Advancement of Teaching）"或"卡内基基金会（Carnegie Corporation）"之误。前者由安德鲁（Andrew Carnegie, 1835—1919）于1905年创设，后者由安德鲁于1911年创设。
　　——译者注

对于人的成长的态度已在发生变化。以依赖学校为荣的观点已经过时。消费者们对知识产业的反抗也在增多。许多教师和学生、纳税人和雇主、经济学家和警察恐怕也不愿再依赖学校。他们之所以既对学校感到失望，又不去构建新的制度，是因为他们不仅缺乏想象力，而且常常缺少合适的语言表达以及与文明精神相符的对自身利益的思考。他们要么无法预见去学校化社会的未来，要么无法设想废除学校后社会中的教育制度的前景。

本章旨在表明，与学校截然不同的教育制度是可能的：我们可以诉诸自我激励的学习（self-motived learning），而不必雇用教师来诱感或强迫学生挤时间、靠毅力去学习；我们可以为学习者提供他与世界之间的新的连接，而不必继续由教师按照预定的教育计划进行灌输。我将讨论学校教育与学习的一般区别，并将概述四种主要类型的教育制度，这些教育制度不仅对许多个人，而且对许多现存利益群体，都会具有吸引力。

## 一、一种异议：当下无处可通的桥梁对谁有用

我们已习惯认为学校是依附于政治与经济结构的一个变量，认为若能改变政治领导方式，或者增加这个或那个阶级的利益，或者将生产资料所有制的形式从私有转变为公用，那么学校教育制度也会发生变化。然而，尽管人们现在对于学校的失望本身是推动社会安排（social arrangement）产生新的变化的一种主要的潜在力量，但我要倡导建立的教育制度所服务的并不是现存社会。对此，人们已经提出了明确的异议：为什么不首先去改变政治与经济制度，而是首先去改变学校？为什么要耗费精力去建造一些当下无处可通的桥梁？

然而，这种异议既低估了对学校教育制度的有效挑战中所蕴含的政治潜能，也低估了学校教育制度自身所具有的基本的政治属性与经济属性。

学校现在已基本上不再被任何政府或市场组织声称的意识形态左右。

社会中的其他一些基本制度，如家庭、政党、教会或出版社等的情况或许会因国家而异。但不论在哪个国家，学校教育制度都具有相同的结构。而且，不论在哪个国家，学校教育制度的隐性课程也都具有相同的影响。学校塑造出来的消费者必然会认为制度性商品的价值要大于邻里所提供的非专业化服务的价值。

不论在哪个国家，学校教育的隐性课程都诱引国民相信这样一个神话，即：在科学知识指导下的科层制是高效率的、乐善好施的；不论在哪个国家，同样是这种隐性课程，都向学生灌输着这样一个神话，即：生产的发展将带来生活的改善。而且，不论在哪个国家，这种隐性课程都助长着人们形成放弃自身努力、一味依赖他人服务的习惯，都助长着异化的生产活动，都助长着人们对制度依赖（institutional dependence）的迁就以及对制度性分等（institutional rankings）的认可。无论教师做出怎样的反向努力，无论何种意识形态在学校中占优势地位，学校教育的隐性课程都具有上述全部影响。

换言之，不论是法西斯国家，还是民主国家或社会主义国家，不论大国还是小国，不论富国还是穷国，学校的作用都基本相同。学校教育制度的这种同一性迫使我们认识到，尽管关于学校的神话极为多样，但学校神话的存在、编造神话的方式以及通过神话进行社会控制的方法等都具有深刻的世界同一性。

从这种同一性的观点出发，无论在何种深刻的意义上，将学校视为社会变革的因变量的主张都是不切实际的幻想。这意味着，人们通常抱有的社会与经济变革将带来学校教育制度产生根本变革的期盼，也是一种不切实际的幻想。而且，这一幻想使得作为消费社会之再生产机构的学校获得了近乎毋庸置疑的免责权。

正是在这一点上，中国的例子很能说明问题。在3000年的历史中，中国不是根据人们的学习过程，而是通过官方考试来录用官员、授予特权，从而对较高层次的学习起到了保护作用。[1]为了成为世界强国与现代民族国家,中国不得不采用世界各国普遍采取的方式来实施学校教育。

在任何国家中,即便一点一点地逐步创建与现在的学校迥然相异的新型教育机构,也将是对在国家的组织下形成的这一普遍现象中最敏感的连接部位的一种冲击。一个没有明确认识到去学校化之必要性的政治纲领不是革命性纲领,而是蛊惑人们产生更多的相同索求的纲领。对于20世纪70年代中任何一项重要的政治改革纲领,都应进行如下评估:它在多大程度上清楚地阐明了去学校化的必要性?并且,它在多大程度上提供了实现它所提出的改善社会的教育品质这一目标的指导方针?

反抗国际市场与大国政治的支配,或许会超出一些贫困地区或贫困国家的能力范围,然而,这更加有力地表明,应当强调通过彻底改变教育结构来解放所有社会的重要意义,而这种改变是任何一个社会的财力都能承受的。

## 二、新的正规教育制度的一般特征

一个好的教育制度应当具有三个目标:第一,向所有希望学习的人提供其一生中任何时候均可使用的学习资源;第二,让所有希望与他人分享自己的知识的人都能找到想从他们那里学到这些知识的人;第三,向所有希望公开提出争议的人提供表达的机会。这样一种制度需要宪法对教育的保护。不应强迫学习者去学习某门必修课程,或忍受因没有某种证书或文凭而导致的歧视,也不应利用累退税强迫公众去供养由教育者和建筑物构成的庞大的专业教育机构,实际上,这些专业教育机构只把公众的学习机会限定在专业人员愿意向市场提供的服务范围之内。应当利用现代技术使

---

[1] 伊利奇对我国官员产生制度的了解有误。严格来讲,我国通过官方考试选拔官员的历史应从隋炀帝实行科举制(公元605年)算起,至今也只有1400多年。即便宽泛一点,从汉文帝于公元前165年在察举制中设立考试("对策")并区分等第算起,迄今也不到2200年。——译者注

言论自由、集会自由以及出版自由真正成为所有人均可享受的权利，并因此而使这些自由具有充分的教育意义。

学校是基于以下假设来设计的：人生万事皆存秘密；人的生活质量高低取决于是否知晓人生秘密；唯有经过按部就班的连续过程，才能掌握人生秘密；唯有教师才能正确揭示人生秘密。一个在心态上已经被学校化了的人，会把社会设想为一座由业已分门别类的各种套装品（packages）所组成的金字塔，唯有贴着合适标签者才可进入其中。新的教育制度将会砸碎这座金字塔，其目的必须是帮助学习者获得进入社会的机会，即是说，即使学习者不能进入控制室或议会大厦的大门，也应允许他们从窗外往里面观看。而且，这种新的教育制度应当为学习者提供不受文凭或血统所限而获得学习机会的途径，亦即为学习者提供能同那些并非近邻的同伴与长者接触的公共空间。

我相信只需四种——也许只需三种——不同性质的学习通道或学习交换（learning exchanges），便可涵盖真正的学习所必需的全部资源。儿童是在充满各种物品的世界中成长起来的，作为其技能与价值观学习之榜样的人们围绕在他的周围。儿童会寻找那些能激己争论、同己竞争、与己合作并促己理解的伙伴，并且，倘若幸运，儿童还会得到真正关心他的有经验的长者的挑刺或批评。物品、榜样、伙伴和长者是学习活动的四种资源。为确保所有人都能充分利用这些资源，需要对每一种资源都加以不同形式的安排。

为了阐述上述每一种资源的特殊获取方式，我想用"机会互联网（opportunity web）"这一概念来取代"网络（network）"的概念。不幸的是，"网络"这个概念常常被用来指称专门传递由他人选择的用于灌输、教学以及娱乐的那些材料的通道。不过，它也可以用来指称电话服务或邮政服务，这些服务主要是为那些希望相互传递信息的个人提供的。我希望我们能找到其他词语来指称这种可共同使用的网状结构。这个词应很少会招致误解，很少会因其属于通常用法而显得品位不高，且应更能使我们联想到这样一个事实，即：对于上述资源的任何安排都包括法律的、组织的以及技术的层面。因为尚未找到这样的词，所以，我将用"网络"作为"教育互联网（educational web）"的同义词，并对表达不尽之处加以补充说明。

我们现在需要的是易为公众所用且旨在扩大学与教之平等机会的新型网络。

这里可举一例说明。现在用于电视机与磁带录音机的技术已处于同一水准。电视机已进入拉丁美洲所有国家。在玻利维亚（Bolivia），政府已于6年前投资建设了电视台，400万国民中现在有不到7000台电视机。而目前整个拉丁美洲专门用于发展电视的资金本来可用来为五分之一的成年人每人提供一台磁带录音机。除此之外，这笔钱原本还可用来提供大量空白录音带，并足以建造一座几乎没有收藏数量限制的，甚至偏僻乡村也能拥有其分馆的录音带图书馆。

无疑，这种磁带录音机网络与现在的电视机网络根本不同。它将向人们提供自由表达的机会，即有文化的人与文盲都能录制、保存、传播及重申自己的观点。与此相反，现在用于电视的投资则为官僚们——政治家也好，教育者也罢——提供了一种权力，即在全国播放他们或其赞助者认为对国民有益或为国民所需的那些制度性地制作出来的电视节目的权力。

因此，技术既可用来促进人们的自主性与学习，也可用来强化官僚政治以及为之服务的教学。

## 三、四种网络

建立新的教育制度的计划不应起始于确定校长的管理目标、专业教育者的教学目标或设想中的任何特定阶级的人群的学习目标。这一计划一定不能起始于"某些人应当学习什么"的问题，而应起始于"学习者为了学习想要接触什么样的人和事"的问题。

想要学习的人都知道，他既需要信息，也需要他人对于自己使用信息的批评意见。信息可被储存于物品和人脑之中。在一个好的教育制度中，学习者应可随意使用各种物品，尽管若想得到信息提供者的帮助，则需其本人同意。对学习者的批评意见会来自伙伴或年长者两方面，即是说，或来自同自己有着直接的相似学习兴趣的学友，或来自愿意同自己分享已有经验的先学者。伙伴可以是和自己一起提出问题的同事，可以是和自己一起愉快地（或刻苦地）阅读或散步的伴侣，也可以是任何竞赛中的挑战者。年长者则可以成为顾问，他们告诉学习者在特定时间段应学习何种技能、应采用何种方法以及寻找什么样的同伴。他们可以引导学习者在伙伴中提出恰当的问题，并发现自己解答问题的不足之处。上述这些资源大部分都十分丰富，但它们通常并未被视为教育资源，也不易被学习者——尤其是穷人——获取并用于学习。我们必须细致地构想，建立新的关系结构，以便帮助任何想要寻求这些教育资源的人都能容易地获取。为了建立这些形如网状的结构，我们有必要进行管理、技术，尤其是法律方面的准备。

教育资源常常被根据教育者确定的课程目标加以分类。与之相反，我建议把可使学生获得教育资源的途径分为以下四种，这些途径有助于学生明确并实现自己的目标。

### 1. 教育物品查询服务

这种查询服务可以为了解正规学习（formal learning）所需的那些物品或过程提供方便。其中，有些物品是专为查询服务而存放的，它们收藏于图书馆、租借公司、实验室以及诸如博物馆、剧院之类的陈列室中。其他物品则可存放在工厂、机场或农场中，服务于日常用途，但也允许学生在见习或课外活动时使用。

### 2. 技能交换

个人可以列出自己所掌握的技能、愿为那些想要学习这些技能的人进行演示的各项条件以及自己的联系地址。

### 3. 伙伴选配

这是一种沟通网络，个人可以描述他们为能找到一起探究的同伴而希望参加的学习活动。

### 4. 广义教育者[1] 查询服务

人们可以在名簿上留下联系地址和自我简介，包括本人是专业人员、准专业人员还是自由职业者，以及获得他们所提供的服务需要的各项条件。如同下面将要述及的那样，可通过民意调查或向曾接受过他们服务的人咨询而对这些教育者进行选择。

## 四、教育物品查询服务

物品是学习的基本资源。环境的品质及人与环境的关系决定着人在环境中能自然而然地学到多少东西。正规学习一方面需要有使用普通物品的特殊机会，另一方面需要有便利且可靠地使用教育专用物品的机会。作为前者的一个例子，是向学习者提供可在车库里操作或拆解汽车的特殊权利；作为后者的一个例子，是向学生提供使用算盘、计算机、书籍、植物园或生产中已不再使用的机器并可任意处置的一般权利。

现在，人们的注意力集中在富人子女与穷人子女在使用物品的机会，以及在使用这些物品进行学习的方式方面所存在的差异。鉴于此，美国经济机会局（OEO）与其他一些机构试图通过向穷人提供更多的教育设备，全力以赴地解决教育机会平等的问题。而在一种更为激进的观点看来，则应当人为地使城市中的富人与穷人都远离其周围的大部分物品。

---

[1] 广义教育者，根据伊利奇的观点，在去学校化社会中，任何有某种知识或一技之长的人只要有同他人分享的意愿，都可以成为教育者，他们不受雇于特定机构或部门。此处的"广义教育者"便是在这个意义上说的。——译者注

生于塑料制品泛滥成灾及效率专家[1]横行霸道的时代的儿童，不得不冲破阻挡他们理解世界的两道障碍：一道是内在于各种物品之中的障碍，另一道是环绕在各种制度周围的障碍。工业设计的结果，创造出一个本质属性藏而不露的物品世界，而学校却将学习者关在具有丰富意涵的物品世界的门外。

一位来自墨西哥乡村的妇女在对纽约进行短暂访问之后对我说，她对纽约的商店里尽出售些"乔装打扮"的商品印象深刻。我理解，她的言下之意是说工业产品具有吸引顾客的诱人外表，但顾客对其真实面目则不得而知。工业发展的结果，使得人们已经被人工产品包围，而这些人工产品的内部装置只有专家才会知晓。外行们已经失去了弄懂诸如钟表何以滴答滴答响、电话铃何以会响或者电动打字机何以会动等问题的勇气，因为他们被警告如果试图去触碰，那么会把这些物品弄坏。他可以从别人那里得知收音机的工作原理，但自己无法去发现它。这种设计方式往往能巩固一个非创造性社会，在这个社会中，专家们发现越来越容易让自己的专业知识不为公众所知，并让公众无从评价。

如同大自然对于原始人来说不可思议一样，人工环境对于现代人来说也变得不可思议。与此同时，教育材料（educational materials）已经被学校垄断。简单的教育物品已经被知识产业加以费用昂贵的包装，成了专业教育者们的专用工具，其价格随着为刺激教师周围的人或教师本人的购买欲望所进行的加工而成倍上涨。

教师倍加小心地保护其教科书，他把教科书视为自己的专业用具。学生会变得讨厌实验室，因为他把实验室同作业联系在一起。学校行政人员则为自己所持的保护图书馆的态度进行辩护，指出这是对那些不是利用耗资昂贵的公共设施去学习，而是来玩耍的人进行防范。在这种氛围中，学生们只是迫于课程学习的需要，才会在很少的时间里去频频使用地图、实验室、

---

[1] 效率专家，指专门从事帮助企业减少浪费、降低成本、最大限度地提高生产与管理效率的专业人员。——译者注

大百科全书或显微镜。就连那些伟大的经典作品也未能给学生的人生带来新的转折，而只是成为"大学二年级学生"教学内容的一部分。学校将这些物品贴上了教育用具的标签，从而使这些物品失去了日常用途。

倘若我们打算进行去学校化，那么，上述两种倾向都必须彻底得到扭转。必须让任何人都可利用普通物质环境，必须让任何自主学习者都可使用那些已被降格为教学用具的有形学习资源。只把物品作为课程内容的一部分来使用的做法，要比仅仅把物品与普通环境相分离的做法对学生产生的影响更糟糕，因为它会腐蚀学生的态度。

游戏便是一个很好的例子。我这里所说的"游戏"并不是指学校中的体育系用以增加收入、提高声望且耗资甚巨的那些"比赛"（如足球、篮球等）。运动员自身也十分清楚，这些活动采取军事比武的方式，其目的是为了增强学校的竞争性，它们破坏了体育的乐趣。我心中所企盼的是教育游戏（educational games），它可提供一种洞察正规制度的独特方式。对于进行游戏的某些人来说，可以在游戏中毫不费力地弄懂集合论、语言学、命题逻辑、几何学、物理学乃至化学的知识。我的一个朋友曾带了一套叫作"Wff'n证明（Wff'n Proof）"的游戏器具到墨西哥人的一个市场去。这套游戏器具由一些印有十二个逻辑符号的骰子组成。他向孩子们示范用哪两个或哪三个骰子配对，便可组成一个合乎规范的命题。结果，有些围观的孩子在开始后不到一小时便通过归纳掌握了组合规则。在接下来两三个小时里进行的形式逻辑证明的愉快过程中，有些孩子已能够向其他孩子演示命题逻辑的基本证明。其余的孩子则信步走开了。

事实上，对有些儿童来说，这些游戏是解放的教育（liberating education）的一种特殊形式，因为这些游戏可使儿童更加清晰地认识到这样一个事实，即：合乎规范的系统是根据一些可变换的原理建构而成的，概念操作具有与游戏相类似的性质。而且，这些游戏结构简单、费用低廉，并在很大程度上可以由游戏参与者自行组织。这种在课程之外进行的游戏，为人们提供了发现与发展儿童独特才能的机会，而学校心理学家[1]却常常认为这样的儿童存在反社会倾向、精神病态或心理失衡的危险。在学校中以竞赛方式进行游戏时，游戏已不仅被排斥在娱乐领域之外，而且常常成为一种工具。人们借助这种工具而把玩耍变为竞争，把缺乏抽象推理能力的儿童标定为差生。一种训练对有些类型的学生来说具有解放的价值，而对其他类型的学生来说则成为束缚的枷锁。

学校对教育设备的控制还会产生其他影响，它会使本来十分便宜的物品的费用大幅增长。一旦这些物品被限定在特定时间内使用，那么就得向那些对领取、保管以及使用设备进行监督的专职人员支付薪水。而且，倘若学生因宣泄对学校的不满而毁坏这些设备，那么学校还得重新购买。

学生不但不能自由触碰教学用具，而且无法知晓现代器具的奥秘。在20世纪30年代，任何一个有自尊心的少年都知道如何修理汽车，但如今汽车制造商则把汽车内部的线路复杂化了，而且，不向除了专业技工之外的任何人提供修理手册。过去，一台老式收音机中含有许多线圈、电容器等器件，它们足够用来组装一台可向街坊中所有收音机发送信号的无线电发射机。而现在的半导体收音机虽然较为轻便，但谁也不敢把它拆开。在高度发达的工业化国家，改变这一状况将会极为困难。然而，至少对第三世界国家来说，我们必须强调改变这一状况所蕴含的教育意义。

我将提出一种模式来说明我的观点。假如能提供1000万美元，那么便可在秘鲁这样的国家修建一个由1.8米宽的小道组成，从而把4万个小村庄连接起来的交通网，并可对之进行维修保养。除此之外，还能添置20万辆三轮小机动车——平均每个小村庄5辆。但几乎所有与秘鲁差不多大的穷国每年花在小汽车与公路上的费用都不低于1000万美元，而现在这些小汽车与公路主要限于富人及其雇员们使用，穷人则依然困守在自己的村庄里。简单而又耐用的三轮小机动车每辆价值125美元——其中一半是传动装

---

[1] 学校心理学家，这里指受过专业心理学训练、在学校里从事心理教育工作的人。——译者注

置与一台六马力发动机的费用。这种车的时速可达24千米,并可装载385千克重的货物(即是说,除了大树干与钢梁之外,一般的物品均可运载)。

显然,建设这样一种交通运输系统对于农民来说具有政治上的号召力。同样显而易见的是,那些当权者——当然也就拥有小汽车——为何对花钱修筑乡间小道不感兴趣,为何对小机动车无法在封闭的公路上行驶漠不关心。只有当国家的统治者们愿意对全国所有车辆的时速加以限制,比如限制在40千米之内,并使公共制度与之相适应,那么小机动车才有可能普遍发挥作用。但假如这一举措仅被视为权宜之计,则这种模式也不会奏效。

这里我不打算详尽探讨这一模式在政治、社会、经济、财政以及技术方面的可行性。我只想指出,在用低廉实用的小机动车交通运输来取代耗资昂贵的交通运输时,其中的教育考量至关重要。如果我们把每台小机动车的价格提高大约20%,那么就有可能实施这样一个计划,即尽可能让每一个将会拥有小机动车者花一两个月的时间去制造小机动车所需的部件、理解其工作原理,并学会修理。用这20%的追加费用,还有可能把小机动车生产分散至各地的工厂。其额外的好处不仅在于可把教育成本涵盖于生产过程之中,而且更重要的是,生产小机动车中经久耐用的马达要比生产先进国家的小汽车中复杂的发动机具有更大的教育价值,因为实际上任何人都能学会修理这种马达,而且,理解了它的工作原理,便可运用这一原理去修理犁具和水泵。

现在,不光是现代器具,甚至连现代城市中的一些据称是公共场所的地方也已变得难知其详。在美国社会中,儿童被拒于大多数物品与场所之外,理由是这些物品与场所乃私有财产。然而,即便在一些已宣称废除私有制的国家中,儿童也还是被拒于同样的物品与场所之外,因为这些物品与场所被视为只有专业人员才准许进入的特殊领域,对未成年人则具有危险。从上一代人开始,铁路调车场就和消防署一样,已成为闲人免进的地方。其实,只要稍加设计,保障此类场所的安全并不困难。为了从教育角度出发对这些人工物品进行去学校化,就需要让任何人都能接触这些人工物品及其生产过程，并认识到其中所蕴含的教育价值。当然，有些工作人员或许会感到让学习者接触这些物品将带来不便，但这些不便一定会换来教育收益。

此外，可以禁止私人小汽车进入曼哈顿（Manhattan）。这在五年前还无法想象。现在，纽约的某些街道已规定在每个奇数钟点禁止私人小汽车通行，这一趋势或许将持续下去。其实，在大多数十字路口都应禁止汽车通行，且应禁止在任何地方停车。在一个对公民开放的城市中，可以把眼下被锁在储藏室和实验室中的教学用具拿出来，分别放在临街的一些自营商店的仓库间里。这样，儿童与成年人便可去查询、使用，而无须担心有被汽车碰撞的危险。

假如学习目标不再由学校和教师决定，那么，学习者市场将更为多样，对"可用于教育的人工物品（educational artifacts）"这一概念的界定也会更加宽泛，工具店、图书馆、实验室以及游戏室等都将会出现；摄影实验室和胶印机将可让邻近读者印刷许多报纸；有些临街的学习中心可设有闭路电视收看室，另一些学习中心则因有可供使用与修理用的办公设备而具特色；自动点唱机或录音机将成为寻常之物，其中有些专门播放古典音乐，有些专门播放各国民歌，还有些则播放爵士乐；电影俱乐部之间将会相互竞争，同时也会和商业电视竞争；各博物馆门前的广场可成为多半由各种各样的都市博物馆组织的艺术品巡回展出的网络，这些艺术品中既有旧品，也有新品，既有原物，也有复制品。

这种网络所需的专业人员将更多地带有看管人、博物馆导游或图书馆馆员的性质，而不是教师。他们可以带领学习者从博物馆中位于某个角落的生物陈列室开始，然后参观贝壳展示处，或者接下来引导学习者到某个放映室观看生物学录像片。这些博物馆可以提供关于控制虫害、日常饮食以及其他预防性医学方面的指导，也可将那些希望得到一些忠告的人引见给可担此任的"年长者"。

为建立"学习物品"网络而筹措经费可有两种不同的方式。社区可以确定所需经费的最大限度的预算，以及这一网络的所有部分均可向所有来访者开放的合适时间。或者，社区可以决定按年龄向市民发放有限额的许可证。一方面，任何人均可使用比较简单的物品；另一方面，许可证持有者可享有使用某些价格昂贵且数量稀少的物品的特殊机会。

  为购置教育专用物品而筹集财源只是建设一个教育世界（educational world）的全部工作中的一个方面——或许是花费最少的一个方面。目前在为学校日常仪式服务的那些神圣物品方面所花的钱，可以用来为所有国民提供更多贴近城市现实生活的机会。假如雇用条件符合人道主义标准的话，那么，我们便可对那些每天以两三小时雇用8～14岁儿童的雇主在征税方面予以特别优惠。我们应当恢复受戒礼[1]或坚振礼[2]的传统。我的意思是说，我们应当首先限制，继而消除剥夺青少年的公民权的现象，并允许一个12岁的少年完全担负起参与社区生活的责任。许多学龄儿童比社会工作者或议员们更熟悉自己所在的街区。当然，他们也会提出一些令人尴尬的问题，并且会提出威胁科层体制存在的解决办法。他们应被视同于成年人，以便他们能运用自己的知识以及调查事实的能力而为民主政治服务。

  与警察局、消防署或娱乐业中的学徒制相比，学校的危险性迄今仍为人们所低估。人们很容易替学校辩护，认为它起码还是保护青少年的一种手段。但这种观点常常站不住脚。我最近访问了哈莱姆黑人居住区的一个卫理公会[3]的教堂，该教堂被一群因罗丹（Julio Rodan）之死而发起抗议

---

[1] 受戒礼（bar mitzvah），犹太男孩在13岁时举行的成人仪式。——译者注
[2] 坚振礼（confirmation），天主教和东正教圣事的一种，也称"坚信礼"，是入教者在接受洗礼后，为使圣灵降于其身，从圣灵获得恩典、勇气和力量，以坚定信仰振奋心灵而举行的一种礼仪，象征着一个人通过洗礼同上帝建立的关系得到巩固。通常由主教施行，包括按手礼、敷圣油，特殊情况下也可由主教委派的神父施行。在东正教，儿童同时接受洗礼、坚振礼和第一次圣餐。信教部分教派也有此礼，但不称为圣事，仅为公开声明信仰的一种行为。——译者注
[3] 卫理工会，英文全文为"Methodist Church"。基督教新教卫斯理宗教会之一。英国的约翰·卫斯理（John Wesley，1703—1791）于1738年独立传道，1784年脱离圣公宗，将"牛津圣社"发展为独立的卫斯理宗（Wesleyans）。该教派主张圣洁生活与改善社会，注重在群众中进行传教活动。美国独立后，美国卫斯理宗教徒脱离圣公会而组成独立的教会，后陆续分为美以美会、监理公会、美普会、循道会等。1939年，前三派又合并为现今的卫斯理宗教会。——译者注

的身带武装的"青年贵族"占领。罗丹是被发现在牢房中自杀的一名波多黎各青年。我认识这个抗议团体的首领们，他们曾在库埃纳瓦卡跨文化文献中心参加过一个学期的研讨班。当我惊奇地问起曾经是他们中一员的胡安（Juan）为何不在时，他们告诉我说："他又犯了毒瘾，回州立大学去了。"

我们的社会为建造各种工厂和设备投入了巨额资金，我们可以通过制订计划、推出激励措施以及立法等来发掘蕴含于工厂与设备之中的教育潜能。只要企业可以利用保护个人隐私的《人权法案》（*Bill of Rights*）来强化其经济力量，那么，教育物品就难以得到充分利用。而支撑企业经济力量的则是其数百万消费者、数千名雇员、股东以及产品供应厂家。这个世界的很多技术及其大部分生产过程与设备都被封闭在企业的高墙之内，不仅一般公众被拒于门外，而且其消费者、雇员以及股东们也无法涉足。法律规定与保护设施使得企业能够有效实行这种封闭措施。在资本主义国家，目前花费在制作广告上的钱倒是可转用于通过诸如通用电气公司（General Electric）、美国全国广播电视公司（NBC-TV）或百威啤酒公司（Budweiser）等大企业来实施教育，即是说，应当将各种工厂与事务所重新加以组织，以便其日常运行更方便公众涉足，使得公众的学习成为可能。而且，事实上，这样做可能会使那些从企业学有所获者找到对企业予以回报的途径。

一些更有价值的科技物品与资料可能会以国家安全为由而对公众保密，甚至也对一些真正的科学家保密。在过去很长一段时间里，科学的功能一直都像是无政府主义者梦想中的一个公开论坛，任何有研究能力者都享有使用研究工具，以及向同行们为自己的研究辩护的大致同等的机会。而现在，科层体制化（bureaucratization）与组织管理却把许多科学置于公众可涉足的范围之外。事实上，过去的那种科学信息国际网如今已支离破碎，变成了研究群体之间的竞争场域。科学共同体的研究成果和研究人员都已被捆绑在国家与公司的以实绩主义为取向的研究项目之中。其结果是，支撑着这些国家与公司的人们处于极度的精神贫困之中。

在一个被国家与公司控制并为其所有的社会中,教育物品的使用机会永远都会受到限制。但随着那些可供人们分享的物品日渐增多地用于教育目的,或许能带给我们充分的启迪,帮助我们冲破这些最终的政治障碍。公立学校的出现使物品的教育用途控制权从私人转移到专家手中,而学校制度的彻底颠覆将可让这一权利重新回到个人手中。倘若最终能彻底祛除私人或团体对于"物品"在教育层面的控制,那么,真正的公共所有权或许就会诞生。

## 五、技能交换

吉他教师不同于吉他,他既不能被归入博物馆一类,也不可能为公众所有,并且也不可能从教育物品仓库中租借。因此,技能教师是与技能学习所需要的教育物品不同的一种资源。这并不是说在任何情况下技能教师都必不可少。比如,我不仅可以借到一把吉他,而且可以借到吉他教学磁带以及附有文字说明的指弦图。借助这些东西,我便可以自学弹奏吉他。事实上,这种自学方式具有一些优点。比如,倘若能借到的磁带中吉他教学的质量优于能物色到的技能教师的教学质量;倘若可用于学习吉他的时间只能是深夜;倘若想弹奏的曲子国人尚未听过;倘若因为害羞而宁愿独自悄悄摸索着弹奏,那么,这种自学方式就更为合适。

技能教师的姓名和地址必须登记在册,与技能教师联系的渠道也应不同于获取物品的渠道。一件物品由使用者——或者说可以由使用者——随意取用,而一个人只有当其本人首肯时,才会正式成为一种技能资源。而且,他还可以根据自己的选择来确定指导的时间、地点和方法。

此外,还必须把技能教师同学习伙伴区分开来。希望进行某项共同探究的伙伴首先必须具有相同的兴趣和能力;他们聚集在一起练习或提高他们共同学习的某项技能,如篮球技能、舞蹈技能、搭建宿营地的技能,或者商讨下次选举事宜。而技能的首次传授则不同,聚集在一起的参与者中有些已经掌握了技能,有些则尚未掌握而又希望掌握技能。

"技能演示者(skill model)"是指具有某项技能并愿意进行实际演示的人。这种演示对于有潜力的学习者来说,常常成为一种必要的学习资源。现代技术使我们得以把这种演示录制成磁带、拍成视频或绘成动作图,尽管如此,但还是有许多人希望能看到当面演示,尤其是沟通技能的当面演示。已经有大约一万人在我们位于库埃纳瓦卡的跨文化文献中心学习过西班牙语,其中大部分人都强烈希望自己的第二语言能讲得几乎同母语为西班牙语的人一样流利。当他们被要求在两种学习方式——一种方式是在语言实验室里按照周密的教学计划进行学习,另一种方式是两个学生在母语为西班牙语的人的指导下,接受严格的日常会话训练——中加以选择时,大部分人都选择了后者。

对于已被许多人掌握的那些技能的学习来说,技能演示者是我们所需要且能够获取的唯一的人力资源。不论是在说话还是在驾驶,不论是在烹调还是在使用通信设备,我们往往都很少意识到自己在进行正式的教与学,尤其是在我们已经接触过那些和技能有关的物品之后,更是如此。我不认为用同样的方式就不能学习其他复杂的技能,诸如使用外科医疗器械、演奏小提琴、阅读或使用各种说明书与目录等。

学习欲望强烈且无特殊障碍的学生除了接受技能演示者的帮助之外,通常不再需要其他人的帮助。有人认为,有技能的人在演示其技能之前应当首先取得执教资格。这一观点基于以下两种执着主张中的任意一种:一种主张是人们总得学习一些自己并不想学的东西,另一种主张是所有人——甚至是那些有特殊身体障碍的人——总得在人生的特定阶段,最好是在特定环境中去学习某些特定的东西。

如今,教育市场中之所以出现技能教师短缺的情况,是因为存在制度上的限制,即:除非持有表明正式认可的某种证书,否则那些能够进行技能演示的人不能传授技能。我们强调,帮助别人习得某种技能的人同时也应知道如何诊断学习中的困难,并能激发人们学习某种技能的欲望。简言之，我们要求他们能成为教育者。只要我们学会在教师职业之外去发现能进行技能演示的人，那么，技能演示者的来源便会充足起来。

当年那些公子王孙接受教育时，他们的父母强烈主张任教者应当集教师与技能拥有者于一身。尽管这种主张在今天已不再具有合理性，但在当时是可以理解的。然而，如果今天的家长全都期望自己的子女能像亚历山大[1]那样受教于亚里士多德，则显然无法实现。如今既能激发学生的学习欲望，又能向学生演示一项技能者少之又少，且如此难以发现，以至即便公子王孙的父母们为其孩子请到了教师，教师往往也只是诡辩者，而不是真正的哲学家。

对于一些稀有技能的需要倒是能很快得到满足，尽管能演示这些技能的人数量很少。然而，这些演示者必须能够容易找到。在20世纪40年代，电子管收音机进入拉丁美洲后不到两年，就出现了能修理这种收音机的人。他们中的大多数人没有接受过同修理工作有关的学校教育，直到价格便宜但无法修理的晶体管收音机问世，进而导致他们失业之前，他们都一直从事着这种修理工作。现在的技术学校毕业生修不好过去的修理工匠所当然能修好的电子管收音机，这些电子管收音机的用途与晶体管收音机相同，但更为经久耐用。

如今，日渐趋同的利己主义倾向鬼使神差地阻止个人与他人分享自己所掌握的技能。掌握技能者通过维持其技能的稀缺性，而不是通过向他人传授技能来获益。掌握技能的师傅们不愿助推自己的徒弟在技能领域崭露头角，这便让学校中的专职技能教师从中受益。而公众则被灌输了这样一个信条：唯有经由正规学校教育而习得的技能才是有价值的、可靠的。劳动市场的存在靠的是使技能成为稀缺之物，并保持其稀有价值，其途径或者是禁止未经正式许可就使用与传授技能，或者是规定只有那些有机会获

---

[1] 亚历山大（Alexander，公元前356—前323），即亚历山大大帝，马其顿帝国国王（公元前336—前323）。亚里士多德的弟子。——译者注

得稀缺工具或稀缺信息的人才可以对物品进行操作与修理。

这样，学校的存在便导致有技能者的数量短缺。一个很好的例子是：在美国，四年制本科护理专业迅速增加的结果，反而导致护士数量的减少，因为那些原本打算学习两年制或三年制专业的穷人家的女孩子，现在完全被关在了护士职业的大门之外。

强调将许可证作为教师的必要条件，是维持技能稀缺状态的另一条途径。如果鼓励在职护士自己训练护士，如果雇用护士的标准是看其是否确已掌握注射、填写图表以及配药等技能，那么，训练有素的护士的短缺问题很快就会得到解决。现在，许可证制度常常会剥夺人们的教育自由，因为它把同他人分享知识的公民权转变成了只有学校教师才享有的学术自由特权。为了保证任何人都有机会进行有效的技能交换，我们需要制定法律来保障所有人的学术自由。传授技能的权利应当属于保护言论自由的范畴。一旦取消对于传授技能的种种限制，那么，对于学习技能的种种限制也将很快得以解除。

我们需要采取一些措施来吸引技能教师为学生服务。在初始阶段，至少可以通过两种简单的方式将公共资金分配给无许可证的教师。一种方式是通过建立向公众开放的免费技能中心而使技能交换制度化。这些中心可以且应当设在工业化地区，它们起码可用于交换进入某些师徒制职业所必需的基本技能，诸如阅读、打字、记账、使用外语、计算机编程、数字操作、阅读电子线路之类的特殊符号文本以及操作某类机器等技能。另一种方式则是向某类群体提供教育券，持券者可免费进入那些对其他光顾者按市场价格实行有偿服务的技能中心。

更为激进的办法是建立一种为技能交换服务的"银行"。每个国民均可得到一笔用于习得一些基本技能的基本贷款。除此之外，技能传授者还将获得更多贷款，不论其演示技能的场所是在有组织的技能中心，还是在自己家中，或者是在学校操场上。只有对他人进行了一定时间的技能传授，才有权提出让更高层次的技能教师对自己进行同等时间的技能传授。

这将有助于产生一个完全新型的精英人群，这个精英人群通过分享的方式为别人提供教育，从而换取自己所需的教育。

那么，父母是否享有通过自己的技能传授而为其子女挣得技能贷款的权利呢？因为这将使特权阶级获益更多，所以，采取这种方式时应当向处境不利人群提供更多的技能贷款，以资补偿。技能交换的实施将仰仗于这样一些机构，这些机构应当便于收集与扩充技能交换参与者的信息，并保证这些信息可自由获取，费用低廉。这样一种机构还可以提供考试及授予证书等辅助性服务，并有助于实施必要的法律来打破并防止技能垄断。

从根本上来说，必须通过法律来保证所有人均享有技能交换的自由。法律所允许做出的区分，并不是基于人们所拥有的教育背景，而只能是基于人们经考核而被证实的技能状况。劳动市场可通过这种技能考核对求职者进行甄别，这就必然需要公众对技能考核进行监督。若非如此，为社会选拔而服务的一整套复杂的考试就有可能在工作场所卷土重来。为了使技能考核具有客观性，尚有许多工作要做，比如，可以只对某些特殊的机器或系统的操作进行技能考核。容易进行客观性考核的技能包括：打字（根据速度、错字率以及能否根据口授打字等加以测定）、会计系统操作、水压起重机操作、车辆驾驶以及COBOL[1]数据录入等。

实际上，许多真正具有重要实践价值的技能都可以进行这样的考核。而且，从人力资源管理的目的来看，考核一个人某项技能的现有水平，比了解其20年前学习打字、速记以及会计等课程时是否让教师满意要有用得多。当然，对于是否需要进行正式的技能考核这个问题本身，也可以进行探讨。就我个人的观点而言，为了避免给人贴上标签而对其名声造成不应有的伤害，则与其禁止技能考核，不如对之加以限制。

---

[1] COBOL，全称"Common Business Oriented Language"，商业通用语言。第一个被广泛使用的商业应用高级编程语言。在相当长的时间里，许多薪水册、会计账目和其他商业应用程序都使用COBOL来编写。随着编程语言的发展，COBOL已逐渐过时，通常被视为旧的应用程序。
——译者注

## 六、伙伴选配

对学校而言,最糟糕的状况是它仅仅把全班学生聚集到同一间教室,并以同样的流程对所有学生进行数学、公民以及拼写等科目的教学;最良好的状况则是允许每个学生在限定的若干种科目中选择一种。但不论哪一种状况,学生都是根据教师的目标而被组成同伴群体。与之相反,一个理想的教育制度将会让每个人都有适合于自己的活动,并为之而选择学习伙伴。

学校确实向学生提供了摆脱家庭束缚与结识新朋友的机会。但与此同时,这一过程也向儿童灌输了一种观念,即:他们应当从与自己一起被分在同一个学习群体中的那些人中选择朋友。与之不同,如果从年轻人的人生最初阶段开始便为其提供机会,引导他们结识、评价并寻找伙伴,那么将为其在整个一生中都持有为从事新活动而寻觅新伙伴的兴趣打下基础。

一个国际象棋高手总是喜欢找到与自己旗鼓相当的对手,同样,初学者也喜欢与初学者对弈。在这方面,俱乐部能满足他们的需要。希望对特定的著作或论文进行讨论的人,多半会努力寻觅讨论伙伴。想玩游戏者、想去短途旅行者、想建造养鱼池者或者想给自行车安装马达者,也会很有耐心地寻觅伙伴。找到伙伴,便是对他们的这种努力的回报。而如今的一些所谓的好学校则力图使学习相同课程的注册学生都形成共同的学习兴趣。与学校截然相反的将是这样一种制度:无论这种制度是否与学校有相同之处,它都可以为那些在某段时间里有相同的特殊兴趣的个人提供更多相识的机会。

与伙伴选配不同,技能传授(skill-teaching)给教学双方带来的益处不尽相等。如前已述,在技能传授中,除了给予技能教师教学酬金外,还需对其予以其他激励。技能传授是一种来来回回进行的反复操练,事实上,越是对那些最有必要学习技能的学生进行传授,则越是枯燥无味。因此,为了使技能交换得以正常开展,就需要向技能教师发放技能教学酬金、技能教学贷款或其他有形的物质奖励，哪怕技能教师进行技能交换的目的就是为了挣得酬金。与此不同，伙伴选配系统（peer-matching system）所需要的则并非此类激励，而只是一种联系网络。

录音带、检索系统、程序教学以及声像复制等技术的出现，使许多技能领域对于教师的需要逐渐减少。这些技术的运用提高了教师的工作效率，并使个人能在一生中学会更多技能。与这一趋势齐头并进的是，人们同有兴趣享用新近所获技能的他人结识的需要也增加了。一个在学校放假前已学会希腊语的学生，可能想在其开学返校后用希腊语讨论希腊克里特人[1]的政治事务问题；居住在纽约的墨西哥人可能想找到能和他一起阅读《永久》（*Siempre*）周刊[2]或最流行的连环画杂志《罗斯·阿加查多斯》（*Los Agachados*）的伙伴；还有一些人则可能想结识同自己一样对鲍德温[3]或玻利瓦尔[4]的著作产生更大兴趣的伙伴。

伙伴选配网（peer-matching network）的操作将会比较简单。使用者可在计算机中输入自己的姓名、地址，并对想寻求伙伴一起参加的活动加以说明。计算机则会向他反馈所有活动兴趣相同的人的姓名和地址。令人惊讶的是，如此简单实用的方法迄今从未被广泛运用于具有公共价值的活动之中。

在最初阶段，伙伴选配网会把伙伴选配申请者的填报信息处理结果以邮寄方式反馈给申请者。而在大城市中，带有打字机的计算机终端则可立即显示反馈信息。通过计算机检索有关人员的姓名和地址所需做的，只是

---

[1] 希腊克里特人（Greek Cretan），曾被认为好说谎。他们生活在希腊最大的岛屿克里特岛上。——译者注

[2] 《永久》周刊，墨西哥一家有影响的刊物，创刊于1953年。——译者注

[3] 鲍德温（James Baldwin, 1924—1987），美国黑人作家。被认为在第二次世界大战后的美国黑人文学发展进程中具有承上启下的作用。著有《无人知道我的名字》（*Nobody Knows My Name*）、《另一个国家》（*Another Country*）等。——译者注

[4] 玻利瓦尔（Simon Bolívar, 1783—1830），委内瑞拉军事家、政治家。在南美地区领导了摆脱西班牙殖民统治的独立战争。1819年创建大哥伦比亚共和国并担任总统，其后陆续解放委内瑞拉、厄瓜多尔、秘鲁、玻利维亚等国家，并担任秘鲁和玻利维亚总统。——译者注

往计算机里输入自己想要寻找伙伴一起参加的活动的名称与说明。只有潜在的伙伴，才会获知伙伴选配申请者的相关信息。

作为对计算机系统的一种补充，可以建立一个由告示栏和报纸的分类广告栏组成的网络。当通过计算机系统未能找到可匹配的伙伴时，申请者可以把对自己想要寻找伙伴一起参加的活动的说明，刊登于告示栏和报纸的分类广告栏。这时可不必注明姓名，感兴趣者看到后将会把自己的姓名输入计算机系统。提供一个由公共资金支持的伙伴选配网，或许是保障人们自由集会的权利并训练人们参与这种最基本的公民活动的唯一途径。

自由集会的权利在政治上已获得认可，在文化上也已被接受。但我们现在应当看到，由于法律把参加某种形式的集会规定为义务，所以这一权利反而受到侵害。尤其是在按照年龄、阶级或性别等条件而强迫人们聚集在一起且极为浪费人们的时光的那些制度中，这种现象尤为明显。军队即为一例，学校则更是令人难以容忍。

去学校化意味着禁止一个人握有强迫他人参加某个集会的权利，同时也意味着承认任何年龄或任何性别的人均享有召集聚会的权利。如今，这种召集聚会的权利已经因为集会的制度化而被极大地减损。"聚会"原本是指个人间的聚集行为的一种结果，而如今却被认为是某些机构的制度性产品。

在赢得顾客的能力方面，服务性制度要远远强于那些不依赖制度性传媒[1]来发声的个人。这些制度性传媒只对那些具有新闻价值的人感兴趣。用于伙伴选配的各种设施应当像乡村中用于召集村民开会的大钟那样，便于召集聚会的人使用。学校建筑可经常服务于这一目的，尽管这些建筑是否会被转用于其他目的值得怀疑。

事实上，学校教育制度可能很快便会遇到教会此前已经遇到的一个问题，即：如何处置因信徒的离去而出现的多余的、空空如也的场所。同寺院一样，学校也难以出售。使这些场所得以继续利用的一个途径，是将其

---

[1] 制度性传媒，也即大众传媒。伊利奇这里意在强调"大众传媒"也已带有"制度性"特征。为保持原味，此处按照伊利奇的原文直译。——译者注

委托给学校附近的居民。这些居民可以说明打算利用空闲教室开展活动的内容与时间，并可在告示栏中注明来访者可以参加的活动项目。来访者可以免费或者凭教育票单（educational vouchers）进入"教室"，"教师"的报酬甚至可根据其在两节课的时间里所吸引的学生人数来支付。可以想象，在这种制度下，最杰出的两种人物将会是相当年轻的领导者与优秀的教育家。同样的方式也可以在高等教育领域中采用。可以向大学生们发放教育票单，他们借此每年可以向他自己挑选的教师进行10小时的单独请教，并可借助图书馆、伙伴选配网以及学徒制等进行其他学习。

当然，我们必须承认，这种面向公众的选配方式也有可能像电话与邮政网那样，为了达到榨取性的和不道德的目的而被滥用。因此，如同电话与邮政网一样，伙伴选配网也必须有一些防范措施。我在别处曾提出可设置一种选配系统（matching system），该系统除了列有伙伴寻求者的姓名与地址外，只受理有关的打印材料。这样一种系统完全可以从实质上防止不当滥用。此外，通过其他一些安排，还可以添加书籍、电影、电视节目或选自某个特殊类别的其他事项。我们不能因担心这种系统有被不当滥用的危险而忽视其所具有的极为重要的价值。

与我同样关心言论与集会自由的一些人可能会认为，伙伴选配是把人们聚集到一起的一种人为的手段，而最需要选配伙伴的穷人可能并不会利用它。另外一些人一旦得知有人提出要安排社区生活传统中所没有的特别见面会，便真的会变得焦躁不安。还有一些人则对利用计算机对伙伴选配申请者的兴趣进行分类与选配的建议表示反对。他们认为，不能用这种非人工的方法把人们拉拽到一起；共同探究必须扎根于多种不同层次的共有体验之中，且必须在这些共有体验——比如发展邻里组织的体验——的基础上向前推进。

我对这些反对意见表示理解，但我觉得，持反对意见者既偏离了他们自己的出发点，也未真正领会我的观点。首先，把邻里生活重新作为展示创造性表达能力的主要中心的做法，实际上对于将邻里重建为一种政治单元可能会产生阻碍作用。事实上，把各种需要都寄希望于邻里生活，会忽视城市生活对于人的解放的一个重要方面，即一个人具有同时参加几个不同伙伴群体的能力。而且，一个重要的常识是，从未在同一个社区里一起生活过的人们之间，有时可能会比自儿时起就相互熟悉的人们之间有着多得多的共同体验。那些伟大的宗教总是能清楚地认识到与远道来访者相会的重要性，其信徒们也总是能通过这些远道来访者而发现自由。朝圣、修道院的生活以及对寺院与圣殿的共同维护便反映了这种意识。伙伴选配对于清晰地知晓城市中存在的许多潜在的受压抑人群会很有帮助。

社区共同体是有价值的。但随着人们日趋增多地听任各种服务性制度限定自己的社会关系圈，社区共同体也在逐渐消亡。科特勒[1]在其近著中指出，"城市商业区"帝国主义剥夺了邻里生活的重要政治价值。而将邻里生活重建为一种文化单元的保护主义尝试，则只会对这种科层制帝国主义起支持作用。与人为地使人脱离当地环境（local context）而加入抽象群体（abstract groupings）的做法大相径庭，伙伴选配应能促进城市中正趋消亡的当地生活的恢复。一个重新获得召集伙伴进行有意义对话之主动性的人，便不会再甘于因受办公室中的礼节或郊外别墅中的规矩的限制而同伙伴分离。人们一旦懂得能否同他人一起做事取决于自己是否决心这样去做，他们甚至会主张社区共同体应更加开放，以有利于进行创造性政治交流。

我们必须清楚地认识到，城市生活费用将会变得十分昂贵，因为居民们一定会被告诫：应当依靠各种复杂的制度性服务来满足自己的每一种需求。在城市中，哪怕是维持最低水准的生活也花费极高。城市中的伙伴选配将可成为市民们迈向摆脱对科层性市民服务的依赖的第一步。

---

[1] 科特勒（Milton Kotler, 1935— ），美国科特勒咨询集团（KMG）创始人，"现代营销学之父"菲利普·科特勒（Philip Kotler）的弟弟，有"世界营销实战大师"之称。著有《邻里政府：政治生活的地方基础》（Neighborhood Government: The Local Foundations of Political Life）等。——译者注

伙伴选配也将成为提供新手段以建立公众信任的必要一步。在一个学校化社会中，我们已变得越来越依赖教育者对他们的教育结果做出的专业判断，来决定应该对哪些人予以信赖。我们之所以向医生、律师或心理学家求助，是因为我们相信，任何经由我们的专业同行进行了必要的专业化教育的人都是值得信任的。

而在一个去学校化了的社会中，专业人员将无法凭借经由课程学习而获取的学位来寻求其服务对象的信任，也无法只通过让其服务对象向能证明其所受学校教育之价值的其他专业人员咨询的办法来保住自己的地位。可能的情况应该是，对于任何一个需要服务的人来说，不是盲目相信专业人员，而是随时利用计算机或其他手段建立起来的其他伙伴选配网，向那些已有体验的服务对象了解他们对于专业人员的满意程度。这样的网络可被视为公用事业，它允许学生选择教师，允许患者选择医生。

## 七、专业教育者

随着国民能对学习进行新的选择并获得新的机会，其寻求指导的愿望也会变得更加强烈。可以预料，他们对于保持自身独立性与寻求指导的必要性都将有更深刻的体验。随着从他人操控下解放出来，他们应当学会如何从别人的毕生训练所得中受益。去学校化教育应当促进——而不是阻碍——我们去发现这样一些人：他们既有实践智慧，又乐意帮助进入教育探索领域的新人。由于这些技能导师并不主张把自己视为信息提供优势者或技能演示者，因此，他们把自己看成实践智慧优势者的观点将使人感到真实可信。

随着对导师需求的增加，导师的供给也应增加。随着学校教师这个职业逐渐消亡，有助于产生独立教育者这个职业的相应条件将会形成。这看起来似乎明显存在概念上的矛盾，因为迄今为止学校与教师完全是相互依存的。不过，这恰恰是前面所述三种教育交换通常会产生的结果，而且也将是这三种教育交换得以充分利用的必要条件。这是因为,家长及其他"未经专门训练的教育者"需要他人指导,学习者个人需要他人帮助,网络需要有人管理。

家长在引导其子女担负起自主学习的责任方面需要得到指点,学习者在遇到困难时需要得到有经验的指导者的指点。这两种需要有着显著的区别:前者是对于教育方法指导的需要,后者是对于其他所有知识领域中的智性指导(intellectual leadership)的需要;前者需要的是关于人的学习与教育资源方面的知识,后者需要的是基于探究经验的智慧。对于教育工作的有效性来说,这两者不可或缺。而学校如今将这些功能集于一身,并对任何撇开学校去发挥这些功能者,即便不去辱其名声,起码也会投以怀疑的目光。

其实,我们应当明确区分三种特殊的教育能力。第一种是这里已经略述的创建与操作教育交换或交换网络的能力;第二种是指导学生与家长使用这些网络的能力;第三种是在困难的智性探求旅程中充当首领的能力。只有前两种能力可被视为自主职业所需能力的组成部分,也即作为教育管理者的能力与作为教育顾问的能力。设计与操作我所描述的网络并不需要很多人,但它需要对教育及管理具有深刻理解的人,这种理解所基于的视角与现在的学校大相径庭,甚至完全相背。

这种自主的教育职业一方面将对被学校拒于门外的许多人持欢迎态度,另一方面也将把被学校认可的许多人拒于门外。建立与操作教育网络将需要一些设计者和管理者,但并不像现在的学校管理一样需要那么多人,也不需要适合于现在学校管理的那些类型的人。我所描述的网络中既不会有维持学生纪律,开展公关宣传,雇佣、监督以及解雇教师等事务,也不会有与之类似的名堂;既不会有课程编制、教科书采购、校园以及设施维修等事务,也不会有校际体育竞赛管理。在教育网络的运行中,也不会像现在的学校那样让教师耗费大量时间去监护儿童、辅导学习计划以及记录日常活动等。操作学习互联网所需要的,是人们现在期待博物馆、图书馆、就业服务机构的职员以及旅馆老板所需具备的某些技能与态度。

如今的教育管理者们所关心的是对教师与学生的控制，以博得其他一些人——学校董事、议会议员以及公司经理们——的满意。而教育网络的建立者与管理者们则必须展现自己的才能，以防止自己与别人成为他人学习道路上的障碍；促进学生、技能展示者和教育指导者之间的相识；促进人们对教育物品的利用。现在被吸引到教师职业中的许多人都存在严重的权威主义倾向，他们难以设想建立教育交换制度这一任务。建立教育交换制度将意味着可以使人们——尤其是年轻人——易于追求自己的目标，而这种目标同交通管理者期望实现的理想状况完全不同。[1]

如果我所描述的网络得以建立，那么，每个学生的教育路径都将成为他自己的独特途径，且唯有在日后回顾时才会理解其独特之处。聪明的学生将会定期寻求专业的建议，比如，在专业人员的帮助下制订新目标、深入分析遇到的困难、在多种可能的方法中进行选择等。即便在今天，大多数人也会承认，教师为他们提供的那些重要帮助，乃是教师在和他们偶然相遇时或对他们进行单独指导时提出的建议或劝告。在一个未被学校化的社会中，教育者也将能发挥自己的才能，并能实现如今那些心灰意懒的教师假装要追求的目标。

网络管理者们将主要致力于建立与保障获取教育资源的各种途径，教育者们则将帮助学生找到能最快实现其目标的路径。假如一个学生想跟一个中国邻居学说广东话，那么，教育者便可对他的口语流利程度加以判断，帮助其选择同他的才能、性格以及可用于学习的时间最相适宜的教科书与学习方法。对于想成为飞机修理技师的学生，教育者可在寻找最合适的见习场所方面提供参考意见。对于想要寻找能和自己一起讨论非洲历史且水平相当的伙伴的学生，教育者则可向他推荐有关书籍。如同网络管理者一样，教育顾问将把自己视为专业教育者。个人可凭借教育票单得到这

---

[1] 在伊利奇看来，交通管理者所追求的理想状况是所有通行者都遵守机械统一的交通规则，服从管制与指挥，显然这同教育交换制度所追求的目标相悖。——译者注

两者中任意一者的服务。

对于教育引导者或教育指导者——也即导师或"真正的"指导者——的角色的理解，比对于专业管理者或教育者的角色的理解要困难一些，原因在于"指导"这一概念本身就难以界定。实际上，假如人们接受某人的引导，并在其不断发现的过程中成为其弟子，那么，这个人就是一个指导者。这里常常带有一种对于全新标准的前瞻性眼光，这些全新标准在今天已很好理解。按照这些全新标准，现在被认为是"错误的"东西将会变成"正确的"。在一个尊重个人通过伙伴选配方式去和他人相识相聚之权利的社会中，人们面对特定主题所具有的获取教育主动权的能力所及范围将和学习本身所及范围一样宽广。然而，一个人为讨论某篇文章而召集一次富有成效的聚会所具有的主动权，同他在系统探讨这篇文章之意涵的过程中予以指导的能力之间无疑有着天壤之别。

指导能力也不取决于指导正确与否。如同库恩业已指出的那样，在范式不断变化的时期里，大多数杰出的指导者后来都必定会被证明是错误的。智性指导所依靠的是优质的智性训练、丰富的联想以及与他人合作共事的意愿。比如，一个学习者可能会认为，美国的反奴隶制运动或古巴革命同纽约市哈莱姆黑人居住区正在发生的事情之间具有相似之处。而一个自身也是历史学家的教育者则会向这个学习者示明如何识别这种类比的缺陷。他可以回顾自己作为一个历史学家的研究历程，可以邀请学习者参加他自己的研究活动。不论采取哪一种方式，他都将训练他的学生去学习在学校中很少能学到、用钱或其他财物换取不到的批判艺术。

导师与弟子的关系并不仅仅存在于智性训练中。文学、物理学、宗教、心理分析以及教育学等领域也存在类似关系。这种关系也适合于登山、银器制作、政治事务、家具制作以及人事管理等活动。所有真正的导师与弟子间关系的共同点在于，导师与弟子都意识到他们之间的关系确实十分珍贵，且都意识到从多种不同意义上来说，这种关系对于他们双方都幸运之至。

可证实的是，庸医、蛊惑人心的政客、变换信仰者、堕落的宗师、买卖僧职的神父、骗子、奇迹编造者以及以救世主自居的人也会假扮指导者的角色，这就表明弟子对于导师的任何依赖都存在着危险。为了防范这些假冒的教师，不同的社会已经采取了各种不同的措施。印度人靠的是种姓制度；东方犹太人靠的是让人们成为拉比[1]的精神门徒；基督教在其全盛时期靠的是将禁欲生活推崇为美德，在其他时期则靠的是等级秩序。而我们现在的社会靠的是学校颁发的文凭。令人生疑的是，依据文凭是否能更有效地甄别真假教师？而假如有人声称可以，那么，我们便可以提出反驳意见：这样做的代价便是导致弟子这种个人身份几乎化为乌有。

实际上，技能教师与上文所辨识的教育指导者之间一直很难区别得一清二楚。而且，完全有理由相信，从那些将学生引导进入自己的探究领域的技能教师中去发现"导师"，便可让学生找到适合于自己的教育指导者。

另一方面，赋予真正的师徒关系以特征的，是这种关系的珍贵品质。亚里士多德将这种品质称为"道德型友情"，"这种品质不受特定条件限制，它使得向他人赠送礼品或对他人做任何事情都像是对朋友所为"。阿奎那谈及这种类型的教育时，说它是爱与慈悲必然产生的一种行为。它对教师而言总是一种享受，且对教师以及他的学生来说，也是一种休闲方式（希腊语是"schole"），即是说，这种类型的教育对于师生双方都是一种有意义的活动，因为他们除此之外别无他图。

显然，即便在我们的社会中，寻找真正的智性指导也必须激发那些有天赋的人产生提供这种指导的愿望，但这在目前还无法成为一项政策。我们首先必须建立这样一个社会，在这个社会中，个人成为他自己将重新获得比制造物品与操控他人更为重要的价值。在这样一个社会中，以探索、发明以及创造为特征的教学将会被合乎逻辑地视为享受"失业"的最理想的方式之一。然而，我们不应坐等理想社会的到来。即便是现在，进行

---

[1] 拉比，希伯来语 "rabbi" 的音译，意为"老师""先生"。原指犹太人对师长的尊称。后指犹太教中学过《圣经》《塔木德》等，负责执行教规、律法并主持宗教仪式的人。基督教信奉的耶稣，有时也被门徒称作"拉比"。——译者注

去学校化努力与提供伙伴选配的各种条件也将产生一些最重要的结果，其中之一便是开创"导师"可把自己中意的弟子收罗于门下之先河。如前所述，它还将向潜在的弟子们提供分享信息或选择导师的充足的机会。

学校并不是因为套装角色（packaging roles）而导致专业化职业出现功能扭曲的唯一制度。医院的存在使得家庭护理越来越无所作为，于是，住院被视为理所当然，其理由是对病人有益。与此同时，医生的合法性和治病能力也变得越来越需要通过他和医院之间的联系来证明，尽管尚未达到像教师那样全面依赖学校的程度。法院也同样如此，由于审理新案件需要经过法律程序，这就使得法院的日程表被排得满而又满，结果便拖延了判决。或者，我们也可以教会为例，教会的成功之处在于它把一种自由职业变成了一种圈养的专业化职业。无论是上述哪一种专业化职业，到头来都是收费高却服务少，而且，能力差者反而收入更高。

只要传统的专业化职业在收入和声誉方面处于支配地位，那就很难对它们进行改革。但学校教师这一职业的改革应该比较容易，这并不仅仅因为这个专业化职业的问世相对而言比较晚。现在，这个专业化职业声称要对教育进行全面垄断，不仅要求拥有对将会进入本行业的见习生进行训练的专有权，而且要求拥有对将会进入其他行业的见习生进行训练的专有权。这种过度膨胀的要求很容易遭到其他专业性职业的批评，这些专业性职业要求收回对将会进入本行业的见习生进行训练的权利。学校教师薪水极低，并因受到学校教育制度的严格控制而心灰意懒。他们当中最富有进取心与才能者或可通过成为专门的技能演示者、网络管理者或指导专家，而找到更合适的工作，获得更多的自主性乃至更高的收入。

最后，学校注册学生对持有许可证的教师的依赖，要比对其他专业人员的依赖——比如，住院病人对医生的依赖——更容易摆脱。假如学校教育不再具有强制性，那么，满足于行使其教育权威的教师们将会发现，只剩下那些喜欢其权威方式的学生愿意留在教室里与其相伴。废除我们现在的专业性职业的结构，可以首先从学生摆脱对学校教师的依赖开始。

废除学校将是不可避免的，且其发生过程也将是异常迅猛的。人们无法长期阻止其发生，但也几无必要强力加剧这一过程，因为这一过程已在进行之中。我们现在值得做的是，努力使它朝充满希望的方向发展。这是因为，这一过程会在两个截然相反的方向中的任意一个方向上发生。

第一个方向是：教育者的权限膨胀，甚至对学校外部社会的控制也日趋增强。由于人们对教育怀有最美好的愿望，且如今学校中诡辩术盛行，因此学校的当下危机会让教育者们找到利用现代社会中的所有网络向我们灌输他们的那些说教的借口，即：都是为了我们好。如此一来便意味着，业已开启而不能停下的去学校化过程将会出现一个由"好心的"、按部就班的教学管理者们所支配的"美丽新世界"[1]。

第二个方向是：随着雇主、纳税人、有见识的教师、学校管理者以及政府当局对于为文凭服务的拾级而上的课程教学之危害性的认识不断提高，将可向广大公众提供大量机会，包括维护自己获取学习工具的平等权利之机会、维护同他人分享自己知晓并相信的学习工具的平等权利之机会。不过，这将需要进行在以下目标指引下的教育革命，包括：

(1) 通过打破现今个人与制度对于物品的教育价值的控制，开放使用物品的机会。

(2) 通过保证传授或运用所需技能的自由，开放分享技能的机会。

(3) 通过把召集与主办聚会的资格——现在这种资格更多地被那些声称代表公众利益的各种制度垄断——还给个人，使人们释放出自己的批判精神与创造精神。

(4) 通过向个人提供汲取同伴的经验以及选择自己信任的教师、引导者、顾问或医生的机会，把个人从不得不根据现存的专业性职业所提供的种种服务去形塑自己的期待这种状况中解放出来。社

---

[1] "美丽新世界"，赫胥黎（Aldous Huxley，1894—1963，英国小说家、散文作家、博物学家）著有科幻小说《美丽新世界》(*Brave New World*)，作者以讽刺的笔法描写他心目中未来的世界。——译者注

会的去学校化必将使经济、教育和政治之间的界限变得模糊起来，而这些界限正是现今国际秩序与国家稳定的基石。

对于教育制度的上述检视，引导我们接下来要对人的形象加以检视。作为学校不可或缺的主顾，人这种创造物现在既无自主权利，也无按己所愿地去成长的动力。我们可以把普及学校教育视为普罗米修斯[1]式伟业的顶峰，并把取而代之的世界称为适合厄庇米修斯[2]式的人居住的世界。尽管我们能够阐明，取代学校灌输渠道的是借助于真正的沟通互联网所形成的通体透明的世界，并且能够十分具体地示明这一切如何得以运转，但我们也只能期盼具有厄庇米修斯特性的人再次出现。对此，我们既无法进行规划，也无法加以炮制。

---

[1] 普罗米修斯（Prometheus），希腊神话中造福人类的神。曾为人类盗取天火，并传授多种技艺，因此触犯主神宙斯，被锁在高加索山崖，每日遭神鹰啄食肝脏，夜间伤口愈合，天明神鹰复来。后神鹰为赫拉克勒斯（Hercules）杀死，他始获解救。——译者注

[2] 厄庇米修斯（Epimetheus），又译为"伊比米修斯"。希腊神话中伊比塔斯（Iapetus）与克里门（Clymene）之子，普罗米修斯之弟，潘多拉（Pandora）之夫。被视为愚笨的神之一，也被称为"后知后觉"。——译者注

# 第七章 "厄庇米修斯式的人"的再生

我们的社会很像我在纽约一家玩具店里见到的一种终端机。那是一个金属小匣子，你按一下开关，匣盖便会啪的一下打开，露出一只机械手来。那镀了铬的手指伸出来抓住匣盖，把它拉回，并从里面把它扣上。这是一个匣子，你或许希望能从中得到些什么，但整个匣子只有用于关上匣盖的机械装置。这个小玩意儿与潘多拉的"盒子"[1]迥然相异。

在最初的神话传说中，潘多拉（Pandora）——即"具有一切天赋的女人"[2]——是史前母权制希腊的大地女神。她把所有的恶都从其携带的罐子（Pythos）中放出，却把希望（Hope）关闭于其中。现代人的历史起始于潘多拉神话的破灭，并在自我封闭的匣子里走向终结。这便是努力建立各种制度以图把四处蔓延的各种罪恶圈闭起来的"普罗米修斯式的人"的历史——是希望破灭的历史，也是期待膨胀的历史。

为了弄清此处所指何意，我们必须重新探明希望与期待的区别。所谓希望，从其积极意义来说，意味着笃信自然的善性；而所谓期待，如同我这里将要指涉的含义那样，意味着依赖人所筹划与控制的结果。希望是一心渴望他人赠予我们翘首以盼的礼物，期待则是从可预见的过程中寻求满

---

[1] 潘多拉的"盒子"（Pandora's "box"），潘多拉为希腊神话中的第一个女人。普罗米修斯盗火给人类后，主神宙斯图谋报复，命火神赫菲斯托斯用黏土做成美女潘多拉，送给普罗米修斯的弟弟厄庇米修斯做妻子。潘多拉私自打开宙斯让她带给厄庇米修斯的一个盒子，于是盒子里的疾病、疯狂、罪恶、嫉妒等祸患一起飞出，只有希望留在盒底。人间因此而充满各种灾祸。"潘多拉的盒子"常用来比喻灾祸的来源。——译者注

[2] "具有一切天赋的女人"，在希腊神话中，这是宙斯给潘多拉起这个名字的含义。——译者注

足，这一过程将产生我们有权要求得到的东西。如今，普罗米修斯精神已遮蔽了希望之光。而人类能否生存则取决于能否重新发现作为社会动力的希望。

在最初的神话传说中，潘多拉被派来地球时所带的罐子中装着所有的恶，而善的东西只有希望。原始人便生活在希望的世界之中，他们依靠大自然的慷慨、诸神的施舍以及其种群延续的生存本能。古希腊人开始用期待取代希望。在他们的传说中，潘多拉把恶与善都从罐子中释放了出来。他们记起潘多拉，主要是因为她放出了恶。而最重要的是，他们忘记了潘多拉这个"具有一切天赋的女人"同时也是希望的守护人。

希腊人中流传着关于普罗米修斯与厄庇米修斯两兄弟的传说。普罗米修斯告诫厄庇米修斯不要去理会潘多拉，而厄庇米修斯却娶了潘多拉。在古希腊，厄庇米修斯这个名字意为"后知后觉"，并被转喻为"笨蛋"或"蠢货"。及至赫西俄德[1]重新恢复这一传说的本来面目时，希腊已经成为尊奉道德准则并厌恶女人的父权制社会，他们一想起人类的第一个女人[2]便感到恐慌。他们建立了一个理性的权威主义社会，设计了用以对付四处蔓延之罪恶的各种制度。他们开始意识到自己具有塑造世界的力量，并能使世界为他们提供各种服务，他们还学会了期待这些服务。他们希望像制造工艺品那样去形塑自己的需要以及其子女的未来需要。他们成了立法者、建筑家和作家；他们制定的法律、建造的城市以及创造的艺术品成为其子孙后代的风范。原始人通过使个人按神话所说的那样参加各种宗教仪式而将社会知识传于个人，而古希腊人则仅仅将那些通过教育而使自己适应于前人建立的各种制度的公民视为真正的人。

神话的演变反映了从一个"解释"愿望的世界转向一个"编造"神谕的世界的变迁。自远古以来，在曾被视为地球中心的帕纳塞斯山[3]的山坡

---

[1] 赫西俄德（Hesiod，约公元前8世纪），古希腊诗人。著有《工作与时日》等。——译者注
[2] 人类的第一个女人，这里指潘多拉。——译者注
[3] 帕纳塞斯山（Mount Parnassus），位于希腊中部，海拔2459米。——译者注

上，一直敬奉着大地女神。坐落在那里的特尔斐[1]（源自"delphys"，意为子宫）是混沌[2]的妹妹盖娅[3]与厄洛斯[4]就寝的地方。一天晚间，月光朦胧，夜露翠滴，盖娅在其儿子皮同[5]的守护下香甜入梦。这时，特洛伊[6]的建造者太阳神阿波罗[7]从东方赶来，杀死了皮同，成为盖娅的山洞的主人。阿波罗的神官们掌管了盖娅的神殿，他们差使一个当地少女，让她坐在位于青烟袅袅的大地正中的一个三角祭坛上，使其昏昏欲睡，然后将其恍惚碎语编成了自我实现预言[8]的六音步诗[9]。从伯罗奔尼撒半岛[10]各地来的人都带着自己的问题来到阿波罗神殿。人们寻求有关社会选择的神谕，诸如怎样消除瘟疫或饥荒，怎样为斯巴达[11]选择正确的宪法，怎样选择吉祥地作为一些

---

[1] 特尔斐（Delphi），古希腊城市，因有阿波罗神殿及其神托所（求神问卜之处）而闻名。——译者注

[2] 混沌（Chaos），又译为"卡俄斯"。在古希腊神话中，指在万物形成之前原始的模糊状态，也称为混沌之神，没有形体，无边无际。其后，由混沌分离出大地之神盖娅（Gaia）、地狱之神塔耳塔洛斯（Tartarus）、黑暗之神俄瑞波斯（Erebus）、黑夜女神尼克斯（Nyx）和爱神厄洛斯（Eros），世界由此开始。——译者注

[3] 盖娅（Gaia），希腊神话中的大地之神，众神之母。传说她从混沌中分离出来后，生出苍天、洼地和海洋。——译者注

[4] 厄洛斯（Eros），希腊神话中的爱神，混沌的弟弟。在罗马神话中被称为丘比特。——译者注

[5] 皮同（Python），希腊神话中居住于特尔斐的巨蟒。阿波罗将皮同杀死后在其占据的地方建起了自己的神庙。——译者注

[6] 特洛伊（Troy），小亚细亚西北部的古城，今土耳其的希沙立克（Hissarlik）。——译者注

[7] 阿波罗（Apollo），希腊神话中的太阳神。主神宙斯之子。主管光明、青春、医药、畜牧、音乐、诗歌，并代表宙斯宣告神旨。——译者注

[8] 自我实现预言，又称"自证预言"。指关于某种个人行为或社会行为的预言。它影响了人们的实际行为，却又被由它造成的后果证实。如谣传某种商品供应不足，多人信以为真而纷纷抢购，以致原来供应充足的商品变为短缺，被用来证实谣传的"真实性"。——译者注

[9] 六音步诗（hexameters），英诗中重读与非重读音节的特殊性组合叫作音步。一个音步的音节数量可能为两个或三个音节，但不能少于两个或多于三个音节，而且其中只有一个必须重读。根据一首英诗组成的音步数量，每一诗行有一个音步的，称"单音步"；每一诗行有两个音步的，称"双音步"；每一诗行有三个音步的，称"三音步"；依此类推，六音步即指每一诗行含有六个音步。——译者注

[10] 伯罗奔尼撒半岛（Peloponnesus），位于希腊南部。——译者注

[11] 斯巴达（Sparta），古希腊城邦。——译者注

城市的所在地，这些吉祥地后来建成了拜占庭[1]与卡尔西登[2]。神箭成了阿波罗的象征，与阿波罗有关的一切都被认为是有意义的、有用的。

柏拉图在其《理想国》（*Republic*）中描绘理想国家时，已将通俗音乐排除在外，只有竖琴与阿波罗的七弦琴才被准予在城中弹奏，理由是只有这两者的和声才能创造出"必然之调与自由之调、不幸之调与幸运之调、勇敢之调与适合于公民的节制之调"。[3] 城市居民则对潘神[4]的笛声及其唤醒人的本能的力量感到惊恐万分，因为只有"羊倌才会吹竖笛，而羊倌只居于乡间"。

于是，人们担负起了制定法律的责任，希望在法律的治理下生活，并担负起了按照自己的想象去塑造环境的责任。由孕育万物的大地把人们带进神话生活的那种原始的导引仪式被公民教育取而代之，而这些公民觉得在广场上讨论事务同其在家中一样无拘无束。

在原始人看来，世界被命运、事实以及必然性支配。普罗米修斯盗取了天火，将事实转变成为问题，对必然性加以怀疑，并向命运发起挑战。古代人为人类视角构建了一种文明语境。他们发现自己能够战胜命中注定的自然环境，但必须自担风险。现代人走得更远，他们试图按照自己的想象创造世界，构筑一个彻头彻尾的人工环境，但其后便会发现，只有不断改变自身、适应环境，才能实现这一企图。现在，我们必须正视人类自身正濒临危境这一事实。

今天，生活在纽约便会对纽约是什么，以及纽约能是什么的问题形成相当独特的看法，若无这种看法，则无法在纽约生活。在纽约街头，儿童

---

[1] 拜占庭（Byzantium），一为东罗马帝国的简称，一为古希腊殖民城市。此处指后者。——译者注

[2] 卡尔西登（Chalcedon），古希腊城市，今为土耳其卡德柯伊市所在地。——译者注

[3] 伊利奇未注明本段引文的具体出处。此处译文参照了侯建的译本（柏拉图. 理想国 [M]. 侯建, 译. 台北：联经出版事业公司，1981：130）。——译者注

[4] 潘神（Pan），希腊神话中的畜牧神。人身羊足，头上有角，住在山林中保护牧人、猎人。爱好音乐，创制排箫，常带领山林女神舞蹈嬉戏。——译者注

接触到的东西无一不是按照科学要求而开发、设计、筹划并出售的。就连行道树所在的位置也是由园林部门决定的。儿童们在电视中听到的那些笑话是耗费巨资制作而成的。哈莱姆黑人居住区街道的儿童们玩耍的那些用废品代替的玩具，是用原本为别人设计生产的已破损的包装物品制作的。甚至连人们的愿望和恐惧也是制度性形塑的产物。权力与暴力都处于有组织、有操控的状态之中，犯罪团伙与警察的对抗即为其例。学习本身被界定为对教材的消费，而教材则是研究、计划和推销项目的产物。不论教材有多好，其都是某些专门机构的产物。想要得到专门机构生产不出来的什么东西，这样的想法会被认为是荒唐可笑的。在制度性过程可能的开发范围之外，城市儿童无法指望得到任何东西，甚至连儿童的想象也被怂恿用来创作科幻小说。儿童只有在接触"肮脏之物"、出现错误或遭到失败后，才会体验到带有诗意的意外惊奇，即是说，阴沟里的橘子皮、街头的水坑、秩序的紊乱、计划的搁浅或机械故障等，唯有这些才会激发儿童的创造性想象。"闲荡"成了儿童仅存的唾手可得的浪漫情调。

由于所有想要得到的东西都是有计划地生产出来的，所以，城市儿童很快便得出一个结论，即：对于每一种需要，我们总是能设计出一种制度来满足它。他们理所当然地认为，过程具有创造价值的力量。不论所确定的目标是想要结识伙伴，还是与邻里和睦相处，或是习得阅读技能，都可以通过预先设计得以实现。一个得知任何所需要的东西均可生产出来的人，很快便会期待所有生产出来的东西都能满足其需要。假如能设计出飞往月球的工具，那么很快便会出现飞往月球的需要。假如一个人不前往能够到达的地方，则会被视为有悖常理。这清楚地表明，关于每一种需要的满足都会产生更大的需要这一假定荒唐透顶。这种见识将可阻挡无节制生产的进程。不去生产具有生产可能性的东西，将可揭示所谓"日益强烈的期待"之定律，乃是对日益增多的不满的一种委婉表达；而这种日益增多的不满乃是以服务和对服务的需要这两者的同时生产为基础而建立起来的社会的原动力。

现代城市居民呈现出来的精神状态只能用神话中"地狱"的模样来形容。一度被与萨纳托斯[1]锁在一起的西西弗斯[2]必须把一块大石头推至地狱之顶,但石头总是在接近地狱之顶时从他手中滑下来。坦塔罗斯[3]被诸神邀去一起进餐,席间,他盗取了能包治百病、可保长生不老的仙果的制作秘密,结果被罚站在长有果树的水中。若他想喝水,水位便会退落,若他想吃果子,树枝便会升高,从而使他永远处于饥渴的状态之中。一个有着无尽需要的世界岂止是不幸,它简直可被称为"地狱"。

由于人无法想象有什么东西是制度不能为他提供的,因此便形成了什么都想要的难填欲壑。人处于他自己制造出来的无所不能的种种工具的包围之中,结果降格为这些工具的工具。对人来说,原本为了驱除人类最初的种种罪恶而建立的每一种制度,现在都成了一种可自动关闭且从不失手的灵柩。人被诱缚于他自己制作的、原本用来关押被潘多拉放出的各种罪恶的盒子之中。现实世界已被我们自己制造的工具所产生的烟雾搅得天昏地暗,转瞬之间,我们发现已掉进自己设下的陷阱之中,伸手不见五指。

现实本身已开始成为人的决策的结果。下令对柬埔寨进行毫无成效的侵略的美国总统,同样也能轻而易举地下令使用原子弹以取得成效。今天,"广岛按钮"[4]已能决定地球的存亡。人类已经获得一种能力,使得混乱和无序颠覆爱和生命。人类所拥有的足以摧毁地球的这种新的力量不断提醒我们:我们的各种制度不仅编造出其自身的目的,而且具有将其自身以及我们都推向末路的能量。军队即为现代制度的荒谬性之典型例证。现代武器得以保护自由、文明和生命的唯一途径却是损毁自由、文明和生命。

---

[1] 萨纳托斯(Thanatos),希腊神话中的死神。他在命运女神所定时间结束之前现身,将人带往冥界。——译者注

[2] 西西弗斯(Sisyphus),希腊神话中的科林斯国王,被罚在冥府把一块巨石推到山上,巨石滚下山后再推上去,永无休止。——译者注

[3] 坦塔罗斯(Tantalus),希腊神话中宙斯的儿子。神话中关于坦塔罗斯的有关内容即如伊利奇本处所述。——译者注

[4] 广岛按钮(Hiroshima switch),1945年8月6日,美国在日本广岛市投下第一颗原子弹,此处意为核武器操控权。——译者注

## 第七章 "厄庇米修斯式的人"的再生

军事术语中的"安全"一词,意味着具有摧毁地球的能力。

存在于非军事制度中的荒谬性同样显而易见。这些制度并没有启动其破坏能力的按钮,但它们根本不需要按钮,就已紧紧扣牢这个世界之灵柩的顶盖。它们制造需要的速度要快于它们能使需要得以满足的速度;它们在试图让它们所制造的各种需要得到满足的过程中吞噬着地球。农业与工业便是如此,医疗与教育亦然。现代农业污染着土地并损耗着土地的肥力。"绿色革命"[1]通过改良种子可使农作物亩产量提高三倍,但这只有借助于大量使用化肥、杀虫剂、水和电力才能实现。如同其他所有物品的生产一样,这些物品的生产污染了海水和空气,毁坏了不可替代的资源。如果我们仍以目前的速度消耗燃料,那么,大气层中的氧气很快便会因来不及再生而消耗殆尽。我们无法相信,用核裂变或核聚变来取代燃料就不会带来同等的乃至更多的危害。现代巫医取代了接生婆,并许诺使人有所改变,即:运用遗传学对人进行设计,运用药理学使患者享受治疗过程并能长期抵抗病魔。当今人们的理想世界是一个保健万能的世界,即是说,在这个世界中,人与人之间以及人与世界之间的所有接触都是预见与操控的产物。学校教育已成为一种对人进行加工,使其适合于在预先设定的世界中生存的有计划的过程,即是说,学校成了把人诱入其自身所设陷阱的主要工具。人们认为学校应当对每一个人进行塑造,使其在这种全球性游戏中胜任一定的角色。人们毫无顾忌地进行各种耕作、采取各种措施、生产各种物品,并通过学校教育将世界导入穷途。

军事制度的荒谬性较为明显,而非军事制度的荒谬性则较难识破。而且,正因为非军事制度的运行毫无顾忌,所以它更让人感到恐惧。我们知道应当控制住哪一个按钮,以避免发生原子弹爆炸的大灾难,可我们却找不到任何按钮能阻止生态大毁灭。

---

[1] 绿色革命,20世纪60年代某些发达国家将高产谷物品种及其农业技术引入发展中国家,以推进粮食生产的技术改革活动。虽曾使某些国家的粮食产量显著增长,但因在化肥、农药以及灌溉方面需要大量投入,故无法普遍推广。后发现还会引起土壤肥力衰退等问题。——译者注

古代人业已发现,世界可以按照人的计划加以塑造。基于这一见解,人们认为世界天生是不安定的、戏剧性的、荒唐可笑的。于是,人们建立了种种民主制度,并认为在这些制度的架构中,人是值得信赖的。由合适的过程所产生的期待与对人的本性的信赖这两者之间可以保持平衡。一些传统的专业化职业逐渐发展起来,同时,这些专业化职业的活动所需要的各种制度也逐渐建立起来。

这样,对于制度性过程的依赖便偷梁换柱地取代了对于个人善意的依赖。世界已失去其人道的层面,再度回到被必然性与命运支配的状况中,而这曾是原始时代的特征。然而,在未开化时代,世界的无序状态是人们假借各种神秘的拟人神(anthropomorphic gods)的名义不断发号施令的结果,而今天,世界之所以成为现在这种状况,只能归因于人的计划安排。人已经成了科学家、工程师以及计划制订者们的玩物。

我们可以在自己与他人身上看到这种逻辑正在发生作用。我知道一个墨西哥村庄,每天经过这个村庄的小汽车顶多只有十二辆。有一天,一个墨西哥人正在他家门前新铺就的硬质路面上玩多米诺骨牌——他或许自幼时起就常坐在自家门口玩耍——这时,一辆小汽车飞驶而过,撞死了他。告诉我这件事的一位美国游客深感不安,但他仍然说:"这个人理应知道这种危险。"

乍看起来,这位美国游客所言同某些原始的布须曼人[1]在谈及其同伴因触犯禁忌而被处死时的所言没有什么两样,但两者具有不同的含义。原始人所言可以是对某种恐怖的、无形的超然存在的埋怨,这位美国游客所言则是对汽车正常行驶这一无情逻辑的畏惧。原始人并未意识到责任,这位美国游客虽然意识到责任,但却否认责任。两者所言均未见有戏剧性事件的传统形式、悲剧风格以及个人努力与叛逆的逻辑。原始人尚未意识到这些,这位美国游客则丧失了对于这些的意识。布须曼原始部落的神话与

---

[1] 布须曼人(bushman),非洲南部的种族,分布在纳米比亚、博茨瓦纳、安哥拉、津巴布韦、南非等地,大多从事狩猎和采集活动,部分在农场做工。——译者注

美国人的神话的产生都源自无生命的、非人类的力量,两者均未遇到颠覆性反抗。在布须曼原始部落的人看来,同伴之死是因为触犯了魔法法则;而在这位美国游客看来,墨西哥人之死则是因为违反了科学规则。对于这位美国游客来说,该事件使其置于机械法则的咒语中,他相信这一法则支配着与身体、社会和心理相关的一切事件。

1971年的气氛有利于在寻求有希望的未来方向上实现重要转变。制度性目标与制度性结果之间总是出现矛盾。消灭贫困的计划反而导致更多的穷人出现;在亚洲进行的战争反而导致更多的越共(Vietcong)出现;技术援助反而导致受援国更加落后;增设节育诊所反而导致生育率上升、人口膨胀;增加学校经费反而导致辍学者增多;控制一种污染通常也会带来另一种污染。

消费者们开始认识到,他们能买到的东西越多,则必定会蒙受更多的欺骗。长期以来,一种看似合乎逻辑的做法是,人们在指责这种广泛蔓延的负功能时,不是将其归咎于技术需要背后的科学发现的失衡,就是将其归咎于种族纷争、意识形态冲突或阶级对抗。而现在,指望科学可以带来人类未来幸福时代与指望用战争去消灭战争这两种不切实际的期待均已降温。

在有经验的消费者看来,没有任何途径可以使人们恢复对于魔术般的科学技术的轻信。相当多的人都曾是计算机神经过敏症、住院感染、无处不在的陆路与空路交通拥堵以及电话久拨不通的不愉快体验者。仅仅在10年之前,人们还普遍期待随着科学发现的增加,人们的生活会更加幸福。而今天,科学家们却使儿童惊恐万分。月球飞船的发射强有力地表明,在那些复杂系统的操控者那里,人类已近乎无所不能。然而,这并不能消除我们对于人类未能根据解决方案抑制失控的消费而产生的忧虑。

对于社会改革者来说,也没有任何途径能重新回到20世纪40年代的设想中去。以为通过大量生产商品便能绕开商品公平分配问题的期待已经破灭,但满足人们的现代趣味的起码所需物品的价格则飞速上涨,而赋予这些趣味以现代特征的那些因素则在这些嗜好尚未得到满足时便已过时。

地球的资源是有限的，这一点已显而易见。无论科学或技术有何重大突破，都不可能向世界上所有的人都提供目前富国中的穷人所能得到的各种商品与服务。比如，若要实现这样的目标，即便使用另行开发的耗费资源最少的技术，也将需要开采相当于目前使用量之一百倍的铁、锡、铜等金属。

终于，教师、医生以及社会工作者们认识到，他们各自提供的不同的专业服务至少都有一个共同点，即：这些专业服务都制造出人们对于他们所提供的制度安排的更多需要，这些需要的增长速度比他们所能提供的服务性制度的增长速度要快。

现在，不仅传统思维的某些方面，而且这种思维的逻辑本身也开始遭到质疑。甚至连各种经济规律似乎也对于超出狭隘参数范围之外的现象缺乏说服力，而这些参数只适用于集中了大部分货币的那些社会与地理区域。不错，货币是一种最易贬值的通货，但这只是对一个适合以货币形式来进行有效测评的经济体来说才能成立。形形色色的资本主义国家与共产主义国家都采用以美元计算的成本—效益比来测量劳动效率，资本主义国家以高生活水准来炫耀其制度的优越性，共产主义国家则宣称将高增长率作为其最后必将取得胜利的标志。但无论在哪一种意识形态下，用以提高劳动效率的总成本都在以几何级数增长。那些规模最大的制度之间进行着最激烈的争夺，以获取未被列入任何资源目录中的那些资源，即空气、海洋、安静、阳光以及健康。当这些竞争引起公众的关注时，这些资源已经被破坏到近乎枯竭的地步。无论走到哪里，都可看到大自然满目疮痍，社会毫无人道，人的精神生活遭到侵犯，个人职业难以为继。

以价值观的制度化为取向的社会将商品及服务的生产，同对商品及服务的需要混为一谈。教育让你对产品产生需要，而教育的费用已被包含在产品的价格之中。学校是一个广告商，它让你相信你需要这个现存社会。

在这个社会中，边际价值[1]不断自行攀升。它驱使一小撮最大的消费者们为获得足以耗尽地球资源的力量而展开争夺，以填塞自己日益膨大的肚子，以便让其他处于弱势的消费者遵守规则，并让那些知足常乐者难以为继。贪得无厌的心态是导致自然环境被破坏、社会两极分化以及心理消极顺从的根本原因。

在现代社会中，当价值观已经在各种有计划的精心安排过程中被制度化了时，人们便会相信好的生活有赖于各种制度，这些制度界定着人们及其社会都认为是必不可少的价值观。特定制度的价值取决于该制度所提供的产品的数量规模，特定制度下的人的相应价值则取决于人消费与损耗制度性产品的能力，以及创造出对制度性产品的新的乃至更强的需要的能力。于是，制度化了的人的价值便取决于其充当焚烧炉的能力。可以这样来形容，人已经成为他亲手制造的物品的偶像。人现在把自己当作熔炉，即用来焚烧由他自己亲手制造的工具所生产出来的各种价值的熔炉。而且，人在这方面的能力没有界限，人把普罗米修斯式的行为发展到了登峰造极的地步。

地球资源的枯竭与污染首先是人的自我形象毁损的结果，是人的意识倒退的产物。有些人喜欢谈论集体意识的转变，认为这种转变导致形成关于人的一种观念，即：人作为一种有机组织更多地依存于制度，而不是依存于自然与个人。这样一种对根本价值观进行的制度化，这样一种对有计划的安排过程最终都能产生受助者期待的结果的盲信，这样一种消费至上的时代精神，可谓普罗米修斯式谬误的要害。

寻求全球环境新平衡的努力能否奏效，取决于能否实现价值观的去制度化。

---

[1] 边际价值（marginal value），原文如此。伊利奇对于概念的使用有时比较随意，如同此前在第六章开头将"卡内基促进教学基金会"或"卡内基基金会"略称为"卡内基委员会"一样，此处疑为"边际产品价值（value of the marginal product）"的略称。所谓边际产品价值，是指在其他条件不变的前提下，厂商增加一单位要素投入所增加的产品收益。——译者注

在资本主义国家、共产主义国家以及发展中国家中，日渐增多的人开始怀疑"工作人[1]"的观点是否存在结构上的问题。这种怀疑是新型社会精英的共同特征。在所有社会阶级、经济收入、宗教信仰以及文明程度各不相同的群体中，都有这种社会精英。他们已开始警惕大多数人所信奉的种种神话，诸如关于科学乌托邦的神话、关于意识形态崇拜的神话、关于期待商品与服务公平分配的神话。同大多数人一样，他们也有落入圈套之感；同大多数人一样，他们也意识到经由广泛赞同而采取的大部分新政策，总是导致产生同政策所声称的目标截然相反的结果。然而，或许将来会到太空生活的大多数普罗米修斯式的人仍在回避社会结构问题，而正在形成的少数精英则对科学机器的神奇、意识形态的灵丹妙药以及对付罪恶的妙招持批判态度。这些少数精英开始表明他们的疑虑：我们总是蒙受欺骗，一直被捆绑在当今的各种制度上，这同普罗米修斯被锁于山崖上有什么两样？我们必须把满怀希望的信赖与传统的嘲弄结合起来，去揭露普罗米修斯式的谬误。

普罗米修斯通常被认为喻指"预见"，有时甚至被认为是"他推动着北极星旋转"。他蒙骗了垄断天火的诸神，从他们那里盗取了天火，并教会人类用火打铁。因此，普罗米修斯成为技术专家们信奉的神，但也因盗取天火而遭铁链锁身。

现在，特尔斐城中的皮提亚[2]已被对芯片版与穿孔卡片上的数据来回运算的计算机取代；六音步诗式的神谕已让位于十六进制编码的计算机指令；曾经是舵手的人已把方舟[3]之舵交由自动控制机来操纵；计算机终端出

---

[1] 工作人（homo faber），也译为"制造的人"。源自瑞士作家马克斯·弗里施（Max Frisch）1957年发表的同名小说《工作人》（*Homo Faber*）。小说中的主人公沃尔特·费伯（Walter Faber）是一名成功的工程师，其世界观建立在逻辑、概率和技术之上，相信一切都是可能的，技术可以让人们控制他们生活的各个方面。——译者注
[2] 皮提亚（Pythia），希腊神话中在阿波罗神殿里宣示阿波罗神谕的女祭司。——译者注
[3] 方舟，犹太教、基督教《圣经》中挪亚为躲避洪水而制造的长方木柜形大船。西方人常以（挪亚）方舟喻作避难处所。——译者注

## 第七章 "厄庇米修斯式的人"的再生

现在人类面前,指示着我们的命运;孩子们则幻想着乘坐太空飞船驶离浑浊不清的地球。

从"月球人"的视角来看,普罗米修斯恐怕会认为我们现在这个蓝光闪烁的地球就是希望的星球,就是人类的方舟。现在,对于地球的有限性的新感受和对于昔日时光的新怀恋,能使我们看清当初普罗米修斯的弟弟厄庇米修斯为何要选择娶潘多拉为妻在地球生活。

就这一点来看,希腊神话便成了充满希望的预言,因为它告诉我们,普罗米修斯的儿子是丢卡利翁[1]。如同挪亚[2]驾方舟冲出洪水一样,丢卡利翁也是方舟的舵手,他是新人类之父,他同厄庇米修斯与潘多拉的女儿匹娜一起,用地球之土创造了新人类。我们逐渐深刻认识到,潘多拉从诸神那里得到的那个"罐子"的含义与人们一直以来所理解的"潘多拉盒子"的含义刚好相反;这个"罐子"乃是我们的救生之船,我们的避难方舟。

我们现在需要为那些把希望看得比期待更重要的人正名,需要为那些热爱人甚于热爱产品的人正名,需要为那些信奉如下观点的人正名——

> 凡人皆有其趣,
> 人之命运犹如星辰秘史;
> 凡人皆有特点,
> 恰如星斗各各相异。

---

[1] 丢卡利翁(Deucalion),希腊神话中普罗米修斯之子,传说主神宙斯因对人类行恶不满,降洪水为灾。丢卡利翁造一方舟,与其妻匹娜(Pyrrha,一译"皮拉")一同脱险。后奉神谕将"大地母亲的骨头"向后投掷,以再生新人。两人猜知"大地母亲的骨头"系指石头,遂即照办,石头果然变为男男女女,从而重新创造了人类。——译者注

[2] 挪亚(Noah),也译"诺亚""诺厄"。《圣经》中洪水灭世后的人类新始祖。据《创世纪》记载,上帝虽因对人类行恶不满而降洪水为灾,但念挪亚一家行善,维护正义,故命挪亚制造方舟,率全家并选取所有禽兽各一对避难,因而使人类得以存续。——译者注

我们需要为那些热爱地球的人正名，在这个地球上，每个人都可同他人相识，而且——

一个人若悄然生活于世，
不为人知，
且于悄然中交友，
那悄然也饶有乐趣。

我们需要为这样一些人正名，他们与普罗米修斯兄弟携手点火打铁，而他们这样做的目的在于增强自己关怀、照料以及陪伴他人的能力，他们懂得——

凡人皆有自己的世界，
这世界中美好的瞬间、
悲惨的瞬间，
皆为他自己的瞬间。[1]

我建议将这些满怀希望的兄弟姐妹称为"厄庇米修斯式的人"。

---

[1] 这三段引文源自叶夫图申科所著《诗选》（Selected Poems）中的"人（People）"这一部分。该书由米尔纳-古兰德（Robin Milner-Gulland）与利瓦伊（Peter Levi）翻译并作序。经译者同意，由企鹅图书（Penguin Books）1962年再版发行。——作者注（叶夫图申科，Yergeny Yevtushenko, 1933—2017, 苏联诗人，著有《诗选》等。——译者注）

# 译 后 记

笔者对伊万·伊利奇（Ivan Illich）的激进主义教育思想的最初了解，是在1982年春天。当时，南京师范大学鲁洁教授在为我们78级本科生开设的"教育社会学"课程中，专门介绍了伊利奇的 Deschooling Society 这本书。在连义务教育制度都八字未见一撇的当年，得知西方学者竟然将学校教育制度视为一种祸害，对于这种制度及其服务的社会进行尖锐的、近乎尖刻的批判，思想上所受的震撼自然非同一般。笔者当时就萌生了一个心愿，希望什么时候英文水平提高了，能有机会把这本书译成中文，并希望在此之前最好不要有其他什么人也有翻译的念头并付诸行动。

未曾料到，这个心愿在12年后竟然真的实现了。20世纪90年代前半期，台湾桂冠图书公司筹划出版一套"当代思潮系列丛书"，其中就有伊利奇的这本 Deschooling Society。经李锦旭博士（现供职于台湾屏东大学人文社会学院）牵线，该书由笔者担纲翻译，并于1994年在台湾出版了中文繁体译本（以下简称"繁体译本"），书名为《非学校化社会》。时至今日，笔者还清楚地记得当时的感激与兴奋。

据笔者所知，该译本虽为繁体，且在台湾出版，但在大陆学人中，尤其是在青年学子中较受欢迎。但也正因为是繁体，且在台湾出版，所以在大陆，不只书市未见出售，就连图书馆也极少收藏，这就给读者的购买与借阅带来了诸多不便。于是，笔者就又有了一个心愿，希望大陆什么时候能出版该书的中文简体译本（以下简称"简体译本"）。

同样未曾料到，22年后，机会再次降临。中国轻工业出版社"万千教育"编辑部计划出版一套双语版教育名著，伊利奇的这本 *Deschooling Society* 也列于其中。在此之前，曾有数家出版社希望能出版该书的简体译本，并为此做过努力，但都因种种原因而功亏一篑。而中国轻工业出版社的意愿似乎更强烈一些，意志似乎也更坚定一些。经过不懈努力，在最终获得该书的汉英双语版版权之后，"万千教育"总策划石铁先生随即于2016年5月下旬联系笔者，请笔者翻译该书。这自然同样让笔者感激与兴奋，想都没想就承接了下来。

原以为完成这个任务实属小事一桩，因为毕竟有自己20多年前的繁体译本做基础，只需重新阅读一下，仔细校对一遍，适当修改一些，便可大功告成。可当笔者真正静下心来认真对照英文原著，逐字逐句检查繁体译本时，才发现事情远非预想的那么简单。限于20多年前对教育发展的历史进程及其与社会之间关系的片面理解，限于20多年前对该书所涉发达国家与贫困国家的学校教育及社会现实的表浅了解，限于20多年前对该书所涉教育学科之外其他诸多学科知识的零碎吸收，当然也限于20多年前还相当稚嫩的英文翻译能力，同时还有当时一心想着译著能早早问世，以至多少有点赶时间的缘故，导致繁体译本在信、达、雅三方面都存在诸多问题，留下较多遗憾。笔者想借这篇"译后记"，向此前曾阅读过该书繁体译本的读者深表歉意。

因此，笔者也就十分珍惜这次中文简体译本翻译的宝贵机会。希望繁体译本存在的种种不当之处，能在这个简体译本中得到纠正。

这里就书中几个重要词语的翻译做一简要说明。

1. deschooling

在繁体译本中，"deschooling"被译为"非学校化"，诸如"非学校化社会""非学校化教育"等。现在看来，这个译法不太恰当。因为，在伊利奇看来，美国社会已经被学校化了，对于这样一个已经被学校化了的美国社会，必须进行"deschooling"，也即"去学校化"。鉴于此，简体译本将

"deschooling"统一改译为"去学校化",于是便有"去学校化社会""去学校化教育"等。其实,迄今已有大陆学人在述及伊利奇的"deschooling"这一概念时,所使用的中文表达就是"去学校化",而不是"非学校化"。

事实上,伊利奇在书中倒是使用了另一个词来专门表达"非学校化"这层含义,即"nonschooled",尽管这个词在全书中只出现过一次。伊利奇用它来组成的概念是"nonschooled learning(非学校化学习)"。

此外,伊利奇在书中还使用了"unschooled(未被学校化的)"这个词,尽管这个词在全书中也只出现过一次。伊利奇用它来组成的概念是"unschooled society(未被学校化的社会)"。

另可顺便提及的是,在大陆,有学人将该书书名 *Deschooling Society* 译为"贬抑学校教育的社会";在台湾,则有人译为"解除学校教育的社会"。

## 2. institutional

伊利奇在书中频繁使用"institutional"这个词,多半用来指称社会事项(如教会、目标、管理等)的性质。大陆学人在述及伊利奇的教育思想时,常把伊利奇用"institutional"来修饰的社会事项称为"制度化××",诸如"制度化常识""制度化过程""制度化商品"等。

其实,对于"制度化"这层意涵,伊利奇在书中专门使用了另外几个词,如:institutionalization——institutionalization of values(价值观的制度化);institutionalized——institutionalized values(制度化了的价值观),institutionalized man(制度化了的人),institutionalized learning(制度化了的学习);institutionalize——institutionalize the skill exchange(使技能交换制度化);deinstitutionalization——deinstitutionalization of values(价值观的去制度化)。

为此,在中文简体译本中,"institutional"一般都译为"制度性"或"制度性的",如制度性的宗教、制度性常识、制度性计划、制度性目标、制度性过程、制度性分等、制度性操控,等等。

### 3. skill exchange

"技能交换"是伊利奇在书中使用较多的一个概念。对于这个概念，伊利奇用了两个不同的短语来表达：一是"skill exchange(s)"（7次）；二是"exchange of skills"（3次）。译为中文自然无法也无须区别。繁体译本中都译为"技能交换"，而其他学人在述及伊利奇的这一概念时，也有称之为"技艺交流"的。这就涉及对"skill"与"exchange"这两个词的理解，似可略加讨论。

首先是对"skill"的理解。伊利奇在书中所说的"skill"的涵盖范围很广，几乎无所不包，诸如无线电密码的转译、第二及第三语言的阅读与写作、代数运算、计算机程序设计、化学分析、会计系统操作、水压起重机操作、车辆驾驶、数据录入打字、钟表制作、管道铺设、线路安装、电视机修理、驾驶、舞蹈乃至跳水等，应有尽有。而在中文里，"技能"与"技艺"相比，"技能"的涵盖范围显然要更广一些，也近乎无所不包；"技艺"的意涵则相对窄一些，它更多地是同"表演艺术"或"手艺"有关，"技巧性"色彩较浓。因此，在中文简体译本中，仍将"skill"译为"技能"。

其次是对"exchange"的理解。根据所指意涵不同，"exchange"可译为"交换"，也可译为"交流"。在中文里，"交换"与"交流"的共同之处是双方各拿出自己的给予对方。不同之处在于"交换"是在拿出自己的给予对方的同时，还希望有所回报，且回报通常是给予的前提；而"交流"虽然也是"互相"的，即所谓"互相交流"，但并不特别强调回报是给予的前提。

如此来看，本书中的"skill exchange"就宜译为"技能交换"了。这是因为，在伊利奇那里，作为推动"skill exchange"的必要措施，"技能演示者"的"给予"与"回报"这两者缺一不可。伊利奇认为，一方面，"为了保证任何人都有机会进行有效的技能交换……更为激进的办法是建立一种为技能交换服务的'银行'。每个国民均可得到一笔用于习得一些基本技能的基本贷款。除此之外，技能传授者还将获得更多贷款，不论其演示技能的场所是在有组织的技能中心，还是在自己家中，或者是在学校操场上。只有对他人进行了一定时间的技能传授，才有权提出让更高层次的技能教师对自己进行同等时间的技能传授"；另一方面，"在技能传授中，除了给予技能教师教学酬金外，还需对其予以其他激励……为了使技能交换得以正常开展，就需要向技能教师发放技能教学酬金、技能教学贷款或其他有形的物质奖励，哪怕技能教师进行技能交换的目的就是为了挣得酬金"。显然，对于这样一种"skill exchange"，译为"技能交流"或"技艺交流"就较难准确表达出伊利奇所说之意了。

翻译总是一件遗憾的事情。由于各种各样的原因，这个中文简体译本一定存有不当之处，真诚期待读者批评。

最后，对中国轻工业出版社"万千教育"总策划石铁先生的决策与支持深表感谢！在翻译过程中，笔者向周采教授和秦志宁女士请教了有关美国教育的若干问题，对于她们的热情帮助，在此一并致谢！

吴康宁<br>
2017年5月8日于金陵天地居

# Deschooling Society

# 去学校化社会
（英文版）

Ivan Illich

# INTRODUCTION

I owe my interest in public education to Everett Reimer. Until we first met in Puerto Rico in 1958, I had never questioned the value of extending obligatory schooling to all people. Together we have come to realize that for most men the right to learn is curtailed by the obligation to attend school. The essays given at CIDOC and gathered in this book grew out of memoranda which I submitted to him, and which we discussed during 1970, the thirteenth year of our dialogue. The last chapter contains my afterthoughts on a conversation with Erich Fromm on Bachofen's *Mutterrecht.*

Since 1967 Reimer and I have met regularly at the Center for Intercultural Documentation (CIDOC) in Cuernavaca, Mexico. Valentine Borremans, the director of the Center, also joined our dialogue, and constantly urged me to test our thinking against the realities of Latin America and Africa. This book reflects her conviction that the ethos, not just the institutions, of society ought to be "deschooled."

Universal education through schooling is not feasible. It would be no more feasible if it were attempted by means of alternative institutions built on the style of present schools. Neither new attitudes of teachers toward their pupils nor the proliferation of educational hardware or software (in classroom or bedroom), nor finally the attempt to expand the pedagogue's responsibility until it engulfs his pupils' lifetimes will deliver universal education. The current search for new educational *funnels* must be reversed into the search for their institutional inverse: educational *webs* which heighten the opportunity for each one to transform each moment of his living into one of learning, sharing, and caring. We hope to contribute concepts needed

Deschooling Society

by those who conduct such counterfoil research on education—and also to those who seek alternatives to other established service industries.

On Wednesday mornings, during the spring and summer of 1970, I submitted the various parts of this book to the participants in our CIDOC programs in Cuernavaca. Dozens of them made suggestions or provided criticisms. Many will recognize their ideas in these pages, especially Paulo Freire, Peter Berger, and José María Bulnes, as well as Joseph Fitzpatrick, John Holt, Angel Quintero, Layman Allen, Fred Goodman, Gerhard Ladner, Didier Piveteau, Joel Spring, Augusto Salazar Bondy, and Dennis Sullivan. Among my critics, Paul Goodman most radically obliged me to revise my thinking. Robert Silvers provided me with brilliant editorial assistance on Chapters 1, 3, and 6, which have appeared in *The New York Review of Books*.

Reimer and I have decided to publish separate views of our joint research. He is working on a comprehensive and documented exposition, which will be subjected to several months of further critical appraisal and be published late in 1971 by Doubleday & Company. Dennis Sullivan, who acted as secretary at the meetings between Reimer and myself, is preparing a book for publication in the spring of 1972 which will place my argument in the context of current debate about public schooling in the United States. I offer this volume of essays now in the hope that it will provoke additional critical contributions to the sessions of a seminar on "Alternatives in Education" planned at CIDOC in Cuernavaca for 1972 and 1973.

I intend to discuss some perplexing issues which are raised once we embrace the hypothesis that society can be deschooled; to search for criteria which may help us distinguish institutions which merit development because they support learning in a deschooled milieu; and to clarify those personal goals which would foster the advent of an Age of Leisure (*schole*) as opposed to an economy dominated by service industries.

Ivan Illich<br>
CIDOC<br>
Cuernavaca, Mexico<br>
*November, 1970*

# 1. WHY WE MUST DISESTABLISH SCHOOL

Many students, especially those who are poor, intuitively know what the schools do for them. They school them to confuse process and substance. Once these become blurred, a new logic is assumed: the more treatment there is, the better are the results; or, escalation leads to success. The pupil is thereby "schooled" to confuse teaching with learning, grade advancement with education, a diploma with competence, and fluency with the ability to say something new. His imagination is "schooled" to accept service in place of value. Medical treatment is mistaken for health care, social work for the improvement of community life, police protection for safety, military poise for national security, the rat race for productive work. Health, learning, dignity, independence, and creative endeavor are defined as little more than the performance of the institutions which claim to serve these ends, and their improvement is made to depend on allocating more resources to the management of hospitals, schools, and other agencies in question.

In these essays, I will show that the institutionalization of values leads inevitably to physical pollution, social polarization, and psychological impotence: three dimensions in a process of global degradation and modernized misery. I will explain how this process of degradation is accelerated when nonmaterial needs are transformed into demands for commodities; when health, education, personal mobility, welfare, or psychological healing are defined as the result of services or "treatments." I do this because I believe that most of the research now going on about the future tends to advocate further increases in the institutionalization of values and that we must define conditions which would permit precisely the contrary to happen. We need research on the possible use of technology to create institutions which serve personal, creative, and autonomous interaction and the emergence of values which cannot be substantially controlled by technocrats. We need counterfoil research to current futurology.

I want to raise the general question of the mutual definition of man's nature and the nature of modern institutions which characterizes our world view and language. To do so, I have chosen the school as my paradigm, and I therefore deal only indirectly with other bureaucratic agencies of the corporate state: the consumer-family, the party, the army, the church, the media. My analysis of the hidden curriculum of school should make it evident that public education would profit from the deschooling of society, just as family life, politics, security, faith, and communication would profit from an analogous process.

I begin my analysis, in this first essay, by trying to convey what the deschooling of a schooled society might mean. In this context, it should be easier to understand my choice of the five specific aspects relevant to this process with which I deal in the subsequent chapters.

Not only education but social reality itself has become schooled. It costs roughly the same to school both rich and poor in the same dependency. The yearly expenditure per pupil in the slums and in the rich suburbs of any one of twenty U.S. cities lies in the same range—and sometimes is favorable to the poor.[1] Rich and poor alike depend on schools and hospitals which guide their lives, form their world view, and define for them what is legitimate and what is not. Both view doctoring oneself as irresponsible, learning on one's own as unreliable, and community organization, when not paid for by those in authority, as a form of aggression or subversion. For both groups the reliance on institutional treatment renders independent accomplishment suspect. The progressive underdevelopment of self- and community-reliance is even more typical in Westchester than it is in the northeast of Brazil.

---

[1] Penrose B. Jackson, *Trends in Elementary and Secondary Education Expenditures: Central City and Suburban Comparisons 1965 to 1968*, U.S. Office of Education, Office of Program and Planning Evaluation, June 1969.

# 1. Why We Must Disestablish School

Everywhere not only education but society as a whole needs "deschooling."

Welfare bureaucracies claim a professional, political, and financial monopoly over the social imagination, setting standards of what is valuable and what is feasible. This monopoly is at the root of the modernization of poverty. Every simple need to which an institutional answer is found permits the invention of a new class of poor and a new definition of poverty. Ten years ago in Mexico it was the normal thing to be born and to die in one's own home and to be buried by one's friends. Only the soul's needs were taken care of by the institutional church. Now to begin and end life at home become signs either of poverty or of special privilege. Dying and death have come under the institutional management of doctors and undertakers.

Once basic needs have been translated by a society into demands for scientifically produced commodities, poverty is defined by standards which the technocrats can change at will. Poverty then refers to those who have fallen behind an advertised ideal of consumption in some important respect. In Mexico the poor are those who lack three years of schooling, and in New York they are those who lack twelve.

The poor have always been socially powerless. The increasing reliance on institutional care adds a new dimension to their helplessness: psychological impotence, the inability to fend for themselves. Peasants on the high plateau of the Andes are exploited by the landlord and the merchant—once they settle in Lima they are, in addition, dependent on political bosses, and disabled by their lack of schooling. Modernized poverty combines the lack of power over circumstances with a loss of personal potency. This modernization of poverty is a world-wide phenomenon, and lies at the root of contemporary underdevelopment. Of course it appears under different guises in rich and in poor countries.

It is probably most intensely felt in U.S. cities. Nowhere else is poverty treated at greater cost. Nowhere else does the treatment of poverty produce so much dependence, anger, frustration, and further demands. And nowhere else should it be so evident that poverty—once it has become modernized—has become resistant to treatment with dollars alone and requires an institutional revolution.

Today in the United States the black and even the migrant can aspire to a level of professional treatment which would have been unthinkable two generations ago, and which seems grotesque to most people in the Third World. For instance, the U.S. poor can count on a truant officer to return their children to school until they reach seventeen, or on a doctor to assign them to a hospital bed which costs sixty dollars per day—the equivalent of three months' income for a majority of the people in the world. But such care only makes them dependent on more treatment, and renders them increasingly incapable of organizing their own lives around their own experiences and resources within their own communities.

The poor in the United States are in a unique position to speak about the predicament which threatens all the poor in a modernizing world. They are making the discovery that no amount of dollars can remove the inherent destructiveness of welfare institutions, once the professional hierarchies of these institutions have convinced society that their ministrations are morally necessary. The poor in the U.S. inner city can demonstrate from their own experience the fallacy on which social legislation in a "schooled" society is built.

Supreme Court Justice William O. Douglas observed that "the only way to establish an institution is to finance it." The corollary is also true. Only by channeling dollars away from the institutions which now treat health, education, and welfare can the further impoverishment resulting from their disabling side effects be stopped.

This must be kept in mind when we evaluate federal aid programs. As a case in point, between 1965 and 1968 over three billion dollars were spent in U.S. schools to offset the disadvantages of about six million children. The program is known as Title One. It is the most expensive compensatory program ever attempted anywhere in education, yet no significant improvement can be detected in the learning of these "disadvantaged" children. Compared with their classmates from middle-income homes, they have fallen further behind. Moreover, in the course of this program, professionals discovered an additional ten million children laboring under economic and educational handicaps. More reasons for claiming more federal funds are now at hand.

This total failure to improve the education of the poor despite more costly treatment can be explained in three ways:

1. Three billion dollars are insufficient to improve the performance of six million children by a measurable amount; or
2. The money was incompetently spent: different curricula, better administration, further concentration of the funds on the poor child, and more research are needed and would do the trick; or
3. Educational disadvantage cannot be cured by relying on education within the school.

The first is certainly true so long as the money has been spent through the school budget. The money indeed went to the schools which contained most of the disadvantaged children, but it was not spent on the poor children themselves. These children for whom the money was intended comprised only about half of those who were attending the schools that added the federal subsidies to their budgets. Thus the money was spent for custodial care, indoctrination and the selection of social roles, as well as education, all of which functions are inextricably mingled in the physical plants, curricula, teachers, administrators, and other key components of these schools, and, therefore, in their budgets.

The added funds enabled schools to cater disproportionately to the satisfaction of the relatively richer children who were "disadvantaged" by having to attend school in the company of the poor. At best a small fraction of each dollar intended to remedy a poor child's disadvantages in learning could reach the child through the school budget.

It might be equally true that the money was incompetently spent. But even unusual incompetence cannot beat that of the school system. Schools by their very structure resist the concentration of privilege on those otherwise disadvantaged. Special curricula, separate classes, or longer hours only constitute more discrimination at a higher cost.

Taxpayers are not yet accustomed to permitting three billion dollars to vanish from HEW as if it were the Pentagon. The present Administration may believe that it can afford the wrath of educators. Middle-class Americans have nothing to lose if the program is cut. Poor parents think they do, but, even more, they are demanding control of the funds meant for their children. A logical way of cutting the budget and, one hopes, of increasing benefits is a system of tuition grants such as that proposed by Milton Friedman and others. Funds would be channeled to the beneficiary, enabling him to buy his share of the schooling of his choice. If such credit were limited to purchases which fit into a school curriculum, it would tend to provide greater equality of treatment, but would not thereby increase the equality of social claims.

It should be obvious that even with schools of equal quality a poor child can seldom catch up with a rich one. Even if they attend equal schools and begin at the same age, poor children lack most of the educational opportunities which are casually available to the middle-class child. These advantages range from conversation and books in the home to vacation travel and a different sense of oneself, and apply, for the child who enjoys them, both in and out of school. So the poorer student will generally fall behind so long as he depends on school for advancement or learning. The poor need funds to enable them to learn, not to get certified for the treatment of their alleged disproportionate deficiencies.

All this is true in poor nations as well as in rich ones, but there it appears under a different guise. Modernized poverty in poor nations affects more people more visibly but also—for the moment—more superficially. Two-thirds of all children in Latin America leave school before finishing the fifth grade, but these *"desertores"* are not therefore as badly off as they would be in the United States.

Few countries today remain victims of classical poverty, which was stable and less disabling. Most countries in Latin America have reached the "take-off" point toward economic development and competitive consumption, and thereby toward modernized poverty: their citizens have learned to think rich and live poor. Their laws make six to ten years of school obligatory. Not only in Argentina but also in Mexico or Brazil the average citizen defines an adequate education by North American standards, even though the chance of getting such prolonged schooling is limited to a tiny minority. In these countries the majority is already hooked on school, that is, they are schooled in a sense of inferiority toward the better-schooled. Their fanaticism in favor of school makes it possible to exploit them doubly: it permits increasing allocation of public funds for the education of a few and increasing acceptance of social control by the many.

Paradoxically, the belief that universal schooling is absolutely necessary is most firmly held in those countries where the fewest people have been —and will be—served by schools. Yet in Latin America different paths toward education could still be taken by the majority of parents and children. Proportionately, national savings invested in schools and teachers might be higher than in rich countries, but these investments are totally insufficient to serve the majority by making even four years of school attendance possible. Fidel Castro talks as if he wanted to go in the direction of deschooling when he promises that by 1980 Cuba will be able to dissolve its university since all of life in Cuba will be an educational experience. At the grammar-school and high-school level, however, Cuba, like all other Latin-American countries, acts as though passage through a period defined as the "school age" were an unquestionable goal for all, delayed merely by a temporary shortage of resources.

The twin deceptions of increased treatment, as actually provided in the United States—and as merely promised in Latin America—complement each other. The Northern poor are being disabled by the same twelve-year treatment whose lack brands the Southern poor as hopelessly backward. Neither in North America nor in Latin America do the poor get equality from obligatory schools. But in both places the mere existence of school discourages and disables the poor from taking control of their own learning.

All over the world the school has an antieducational effect on society: school is recognized as the institution which specializes in education. The failures of school are taken by most people as a proof that education is a very costly, very complex, always arcane, and frequently almost impossible task.

School appropriates the money, men, and good will available for education and in addition discourages other institutions from assuming educational tasks. Work, leisure, politics, city living, and even family life depend on schools for the habits and knowledge they presuppose, instead of becoming themselves the means of education. Simultaneously both schools and the other institutions which depend on them are priced out of the market.

In the United States the per capita costs of schooling have risen almost as fast as the cost of medical treatment. But increased treatment by both doctors and teachers has shown steadily declining results. Medical expenses concentrated on those above forty-five have doubled several times over a period of forty years with a resulting 3 percent increase in life expectancy in men. The increase in educational expenditures has produced even stranger results; otherwise President Nixon could not have been moved this spring to promise that every child shall soon have the "Right to Read" before leaving school.

In the United States it would take eighty billion dollars per year to provide what educators regard as equal treatment for all in grammar and high school. This is well over twice the $36 billion now being spent. Independent cost projections prepared at HEW and the University of Florida indicate that by 1974 the comparable figures will be $107 billion as against the $45 billion now projected, and these figures wholly omit the enormous costs of what is called "higher education," for which demand is growing even faster. The United States, which spent nearly eighty billion dollars in 1969 for "defense" including its deployment in Vietnam, is obviously too poor to provide equal schooling. The President's committee for the study of school finance should ask not how to support or how to trim such increasing costs, but how they

# 1. Why We Must Disestablish School

can be avoided.

Equal obligatory schooling must be recognized as at least economically unfeasible. In Latin America the amount of public money spent on each graduate student is between 350 and 1,500 times the amount spent on the median citizen (that is, the citizen who holds the middle ground between the poorest and the richest). In the United States the discrepancy is smaller, but the discrimination is keener. The richest parents, some 10 percent, can afford private education for their children and help them to benefit from foundation grants. But in addition they obtain ten times the per capita amount of public funds if this is compared with the per capita expenditure made on the children of the 10 percent who are poorest. The principal reasons for this are that rich children stay longer in school, that a year in a university is disproportionately more expensive than a year in high school, and that most private universities depend—at least indirectly—on tax-derived finances.

Obligatory schooling inevitably polarizes a society; it also grades the nations of the world according to an international caste system. Countries are rated like castes whose educational dignity is determined by the average years of schooling of its citizens, a rating which is closely related to per capita gross national product, and much more painful.

The paradox of the schools is evident: increased expenditure escalates their destructiveness at home and abroad. This paradox must be made a public issue. It is now generally accepted that the physical environment will soon be destroyed by biochemical pollution unless we reverse current trends in the production of physical goods. It should also be recognized that social and personal life is threatened equally by HEW pollution, the inevitable by-product of obligatory and competitive consumption of welfare.

The escalation of the schools is as destructive as the escalation of weapons but less visibly so. Everywhere in the world school costs have risen faster than enrollments and faster than the GNP; everywhere expenditures on school fall even further behind the expectations of parents, teachers, and pupils. Everywhere this situation discourages both the motivation and the financing for large-scale planning for nonschooled learning. The United States is proving to the world that no country can be rich enough to afford a school system that meets the demands this same system creates simply by existing, because a successful school system schools parents and pupils to the supreme value of a larger school system, the cost of which increases disproportionately as higher grades are in demand and become scarce.

Rather than calling equal schooling temporarily unfeasible, we must recognize that it is, in principle, economically absurd, and that to attempt it is intellectually emasculating, socially polarizing, and destructive of the credibility of the political system which promotes it. The ideology of obligatory schooling admits of no logical limits. The White House recently provided a good example. Dr. Hutschnecker, the "psychiatrist" who treated Mr. Nixon before he was qualified as a candidate, recommended to the President that all children between six and eight be professionally examined to ferret out those who have destructive tendencies, and that obligatory treatment be provided for them. If necessary, their re-education in special institutions should be required. This memorandum from his doctor the President sent for evaluation to HEW. Indeed, preventive concentration camps for predelinquents would be a logical improvement over the school system.

Equal educational opportunity is, indeed, both a desirable and a feasible goal, but to equate this with obligatory schooling is to confuse salvation with the Church. School has become the world religion of a modernized proletariat, and makes futile promises of salvation to the poor of the technological age. The nation-state has adopted it, drafting all citizens into a graded curriculum leading to sequential diplomas not unlike the initiation rituals and hieratic promotions of former times. The modern state has assumed the duty of enforcing the judgment of its educators through well-meant truant officers and job requirements, much as did the Spanish kings who enforced the judgments of their theologians through the conquistadors and the Inquisition.

# 1. Why We Must Disestablish School

Two centuries ago the United States led the world in a movement to disestablish the monopoly of a single church. Now we need the constitutional disestablishment of the monopoly of the school, and thereby of a system which legally combines prejudice with discrimination. The first article of a bill of rights for a modern, humanist society would correspond to the First Amendment to the U.S. Constitution: "The State shall make no law with respect to the establishment of education." There shall be no ritual obligatory for all.

To make this disestablishment effective, we need a law forbidding discrimination in hiring, voting, or admission to centers of learning based on previous attendance at some curriculum. This guarantee would not exclude performance tests of competence for a function or role, but would remove the present absurd discrimination in favor of the person who learns a given skill with the largest expenditure of public funds or—what is equally likely—has been able to obtain a diploma which has no relation to any useful skill or job. Only by protecting the citizen from being disqualified by anything in his career in school can a constitutional disestablishment of school become psychologically effective.

Neither learning nor justice is promoted by schooling because educators insist on packaging instruction with certification. Learning and the assignment of social roles are melted into schooling. Yet to learn means to acquire a new skill or insight, while promotion depends on an opinion which others have formed. Learning frequently is the result of instruction, but selection for a role or category in the job market increasingly depends on mere length of attendance.

Instruction is the choice of circumstances which facilitate learning. Roles are assigned by setting a curriculum of conditions which the candidate must meet if he is to make the grade. School links instruction—but not learning—to these roles. This is neither reasonable nor liberating. It is not reasonable because it does not link relevant qualities or competences to roles, but rather the process by which such qualities are supposed to be acquired. It is not liberating or educational because school reserves instruction to those whose every step in learning fits previously approved measures of social control.

Curriculum has always been used to assign social rank. At times it could be prenatal: karma ascribes you to a caste and lineage to the aristocracy. Curriculum could take the form of a ritual, of sequential sacred ordinations, or it could consist of a succession of feats in war or hunting, or further advancement could be made to depend on a series of previous princely favors. Universal schooling was meant to detach role assignment from personal life history: it was meant to give everybody an equal chance to any office. Even now many people wrongly believe that school ensures the dependence of public trust on relevant learning achievements. However, instead of equalizing chances, the school system has monopolized their distribution.

To detach competence from curriculum, inquiries into a man's learning history must be made taboo, like inquiries into his political affiliation, church attendance, lineage, sex habits, or racial background. Laws forbidding discrimination on the basis of prior schooling must be enacted. Laws, of course, cannot stop prejudice against the unschooled—nor are they meant to force anyone to intermarry with an autodidact—but they can discourage unjustified discrimination.

A second major illusion on which the school system rests is that most learning is the result of teaching. Teaching, it is true, may contribute to certain kinds of learning under certain circumstances. But most people acquire most of their knowledge outside school, and in school only insofar as school, in a few rich countries, has become their place of confinement during an increasing part of their lives.

Most learning happens casually, and even most intentional learning is not the result of programmed instruction. Normal children learn their first language casually, although faster if their parents pay attention to them. Most people who learn a second language well do so as a result of odd circumstances and not of sequential teaching. They go to live with their grandparents, they travel, or they fall in love with a foreigner. Fluency in reading is also more often than not a result of such extracurricular activities. Most people who read widely, and with pleasure, merely believe that they learned to do so in school; when challenged, they easily discard this illusion.

But the fact that a great deal of learning even now seems to happen casually and as a by-product of some other activity defined as work or leisure does not mean that planned learning does not benefit from planned instruction and that both do not stand in need of improvement. The strongly motivated student who is faced with the task of acquiring a new and complex skill may benefit greatly from the discipline now associated with the old-fashioned schoolmaster who taught reading, Hebrew, catechism, or multiplication by rote. School has now made this kind of drill teaching rare and disreputable, yet there are many skills which a motivated student with normal aptitude can master in a matter of a few months if taught in this traditional way. This is as true of codes as of their encipherment; of second and third languages as of reading and writing; and equally of special languages such as algebra, computer programming, chemical analysis, or of manual skills like typing, watchmaking, plumbing, wiring, TV repair; or for that matter dancing, driving, and diving.

In certain cases acceptance into a learning program aimed at a specific skill might presuppose competence in some other skill, but it should certainly not be made to depend upon the process by which such prerequisite skills were acquired. TV repair presupposes literacy and some math; diving, good swimming; and driving, very little of either.

Progress in learning skills is measurable. The optimum resources in time and materials needed by an average motivated adult can be easily estimated. The cost of teaching a second Western European language to a high level of fluency ranges between four and six hundred dollars in the United States, and for an Oriental tongue the time needed for instruction might be doubled. This would still be very little compared with the cost of twelve years of schooling in New York City (a condition for acceptance of a worker into the Sanitation Department)—almost fifteen thousand dollars. No doubt not only the teacher but also the printer and the pharmacist protect their trades through the public illusion that training for them is very expensive.

At present schools pre-empt most educational funds. Drill instruction which costs less than comparable schooling is now a privilege of those rich enough to bypass the schools, and those whom either the army or big business sends through in-service training. In a program of progressive deschooling of U.S. education, at first the resources available for drill training would be limited. But ultimately there should be no obstacle for anyone at any time of his life to be able to choose instruction among hundreds of definable skills at public expense.

Right now educational credit good at any skill center could be provided in limited amounts for people of all ages, and not just to the poor. I envisage such credit in the form of an educational passport or an "edu-credit card" provided to each citizen at birth. In order to favor the poor, who probably would not use their yearly grants early in life, a provision could be made that interest accrued to later users of cumulated "entitlements." Such credits would permit most people to acquire the skills most in demand, at their convenience, better, faster, cheaper, and with fewer undesirable side effects than in school.

Potential skill teachers are never scarce for long because, on the one hand, demand for a skill grows only with its performance within a community and, on the other, a man exercising a skill could also teach it. But, at present, those using skills which are in demand and do require a human teacher are discouraged from sharing these skills with others. This is done either by teachers who monopolize the licenses or by unions which protect their trade interests. Skill centers which would be judged by customers on their results, and not on the personnel they employ or the process they use, would open unsuspected working opportunities, frequently even for those who are now considered unemployable. Indeed, there is no reason why such skill centers should not be at the work place itself, with the employer and his work force supplying instruction as well as jobs to those who choose to use their educational credits in this way.

# 1. Why We Must Disestablish School

In 1956 there arose a need to teach Spanish quickly to several hundred teachers, social workers, and ministers from the New York Archdiocese so that they could communicate with Puerto Ricans. My friend Gerry Morris announced over a Spanish radio station that he needed native speakers from Harlem. Next day some two hundred teen-agers lined up in front of his office, and he selected four dozen of them—many of them school dropouts. He trained them in the use of the U.S. Foreign Service Institute (FSI) Spanish manual, designed for use by linguists with graduate training, and within a week his teachers were on their own-each in charge of four New Yorkers who wanted to speak the language. Within six months the mission was accomplished. Cardinal Spellman could claim that he had 127 parishes in which at least three staff members could communicate in Spanish. No school program could have matched these results.

Skill teachers are made scarce by the belief in the value of licenses. Certification constitutes a form of market manipulation and is plausible only to a schooled mind. Most teachers of arts and trades are less skillful, less inventive, and less communicative than the best craftsmen and tradesmen. Most high-school teachers of Spanish or French do not speak the language as correctly as their pupils might after half a year of competent drills. Experiments conducted by Angel Quintero in Puerto Rico suggest that many young teen-agers, if given the proper incentives, programs, and access to tools, are better than most schoolteachers at introducing their peers to the scientific exploration of plants, stars, and matter, and to the discovery of how and why a motor or a radio functions.

Opportunities for skill-learning can be vastly multiplied if we open the "market." This depends on matching the right teacher with the right student when he is highly motivated in an intelligent program, without the constraint of curriculum.

Free and competing drill instruction is a subversive blasphemy to the orthodox educator. It dissociates the acquisition of skills from "humane" education, which schools package together, and thus it promotes unlicensed learning no less than unlicensed teaching for unpredictable purposes.

There is currently a proposal on record which seems at first to make a great deal of sense. It has been prepared by Christopher Jencks of the Center for the Study of Public Policy and is sponsored by the Office of Economic Opportunity. It proposes to put educational "entitlements" or tuition grants into the hands of parents and students for expenditure in the schools of their choice. Such individual entitlements could indeed be an important step in the right direction. We need a guarantee of the right of each citizen to an equal share of tax-derived educational resources, the right to verify this share, and the right to sue for it if denied. It is one form of a guarantee against regressive taxation.

The Jencks proposal, however, begins with the ominous statement that "conservatives, liberals, and radicals have all complained at one time or another that the American educational system gives professional educators too little incentive to provide high quality education to most children." The proposal condemns itself by proposing tuition grants which would have to be spent on schooling.

This is like giving a lame man a pair of crutches and stipulating that he use them only if the ends are tied together. As the proposal for tuition grants now stands, it plays into the hands not only of the professional educators but of racists, promoters of religious schools, and others whose interests are socially divisive. Above all, educational entitlements restricted to use within schools play into the hands of all those who want to continue to live in a society in which social advancement is tied not to proven knowledge but to the learning pedigree by which it is supposedly acquired. This discrimination in favor of schools which dominates Jencks's discussion on refinancing education could discredit one of the most critically needed principles for educational reform: the return of initiative and accountability for learning to the learner or his most immediate tutor.

The deschooling of society implies a recognition of the twofaced nature of learning. An insistence on skill drill alone could be a disaster; equal emphasis must be placed on other kinds of learning. But if schools are the wrong places for learning a skill, they are even worse places for getting

## 1. Why We Must Disestablish School

an education. School does both tasks badly, partly because it does not distinguish between them. School is inefficient in skill instruction especially because it is curricular. In most schools a program which is meant to improve one skill is chained always to another irrelevant task. History is tied to advancement in math, and class attendance to the right to use the playground.

Schools are even less efficient in the arrangement of the circumstances which encourage the open-ended, exploratory use of acquired skills, for which I will reserve the term "liberal education." The main reason for this is that school is obligatory and becomes schooling for schooling's sake: an enforced stay in the company of teachers, which pays off in the doubtful privilege of more such company. Just as skill instruction must be freed from curritular restraints, so must liberal education be dissociated from obligatory attendance. Both skill-learning and education for inventive and creative behavior can be aided by institutional arrangement, but they are of a different, frequently opposed nature.

Most skills can be acquired and improved by drills, because skill implies the mastery of definable and predictable behavior. Skill instruction can rely, therefore, on the simulation of circumstances in which the skill will be used. Education in the exploratory and creative use of skills, however, cannot rely on drills. Education can be the outcome of instruction, though instruction of a kind fundamentally opposed to drill. It relies on the relationship between partners who already have some of the keys which give access to memories stored in and by the community. It relies on the critical intent of all those who use memories creatively. It relies on the surprise of the unexpected question which opens new doors for the inquirer and his partner.

The skill instructor relies on the arrangement of set circumstances which permit the learner to develop standard responses. The educational guide or master is concerned with helping matching partners to meet so that learning can take place. He matches individuals starting from their own, unresolved questions. At the most he helps the pupil to formulate his puzzlement since only a clear statement will give him the power to find his match, moved like him, at the moment, to explore the same issue in the same context.

Matching partners for educational purposes initially seems more difficult to imagine than finding skill instructors and partners for a game. One reason is the deep fear which school has implanted in us, a fear which makes us censorious. The unlicensed exchange of skills—even undesirable skills—is more predictable and therefore seems less dangerous than the unlimited opportunity for meeting among people who share an issue which for them, at the moment, is socially, intellectually, and emotionally important.

The Brazilian teacher Paulo Freire knows this from experience. He discovered that any adult can begin to read in a matter of forty hours if the first words he deciphers are charged with political meaning. Freire trains his teachers to move into a village and to discover the words which designate current important issues, such as the access to a well or the compound interest on the debts owed to the *patron*. In the evening the villagers meet for the discussion of these key words. They begin to realize that each word stays on the blackboard even after its sound has faded. The letters continue to unlock reality and to make it manageable as a problem. I have frequently witnessed how discussants grow in social awareness and how they are impelled to take political action as fast as they learn to read. They seem to take reality into their hands as they write it down.

I remember the man who complained about the weight of pencils: they were difficult to handle because they did not weigh as much as a shovel; and I remember another who on his way to work stopped with his companions and wrote the word they were discussing with his hoe on the ground: "*agua.*" Since 1962 my friend Freire has moved from exile to exile, mainly because he refuses to conduct his sessions around words which are preselected by approved educators, rather than those which his discussants bring to the class.

The educational matchmaking among people who have been successfully schooled is a different task. Those who do not need such assistance are a minority, even among the readers of serious journals. The majority cannot and should not be rallied for discussion around a slogan, a word, or a picture. But the idea remains the same: they should be able to meet around a problem chosen and defined by their own initiative. Creative, exploratory learning requires peers currently puzzled about the same terms or problems. Large universities make the futile attempt to match them by multiplying their courses, and they generally fail since they are bound to curriculum, course structure, and bureaucratic administration. In schools, including universities, most resources are spent to purchase the time and motivation of a limited number of people to take up predetermined problems in a ritually defined setting. The most radical alternative to school would be a network or service which gave each man the same opportunity to share his current concern with others motivated by the same concern.

Let me give, as an example of what I mean, a description of how an intellectual match might work in New York City. Each man, at any given moment and at a minimum price, could identify himself to a computer with his address and telephone number, indicating the book, article, film, or recording on which he seeks a partner for discussion. Within days he could receive by mail the list of others who recently had taken the same initiative. This list would enable him by telephone to arrange for a meeting with persons who initially would be known exclusively by the fact that they requested a dialogue about the same subject.

Matching people according to their interest in a particular title is radically simple. It permits identification only on the basis of a mutual desire to discuss a statement recorded by a third person, and it leaves the initiative of arranging the meeting to the individual. Three objections are usually raised against this skeletal purity. I take them up not only to clarify the theory that I want to illustrate by my proposal—for they highlight the deep seated resistance to deschooling education, to separating learning from social control—but also because they may help to suggest existing resources which are not now used for learning purposes.

The first objection is: Why cannot self-identification be based also on an *idea* or an issue? Certainly such subjective terms could also be used in a computer system. Political parties, churches, unions, clubs, neighborhood centers, and professional societies already organize their educational activities in this way and in effect they act as schools. They all match people in order to explore certain "themes"; and these are dealt with in courses, seminars, and curricula in which presumed "common interests" are prepackaged. Such theme-matching is by definition teacher- centered: it requires an authoritarian presence to define for the participants the starting point for their discussion.

By contrast, matching by the title of a book, film, etc., in its pure form leaves it to the author to define the special language, the terms, and the framework within which a given problem or fact is stated; and it enables those who accept this starting point to identify themselves to one another. For instance, matching people around the idea of "cultural revolution" usually leads either to confusion or to demagoguery. On the other hand, matching those interested in helping each other understand a specific article by Mao, Marcuse, Freud, or Goodman stands in the great tradition of liberal learning from Plato's Dialogues, which are built around presumed statements by Socrates, to Aquinas's commentaries on Peter the Lombard. The idea of matching by title is thus radically different from the theory on which the "Great Books" clubs, for example, were built: instead of relying on the selection by some Chicago professors, any two partners can choose any book for further analysis.

The second objection asks: Why not let the identification of match seekers include information on age, background, world view, competence, experience, or other defining characteristics? Again, there is no reason why such discriminatory restrictions could not and should not be built into some of the many universities—with or without walls—which could use title-matching as their basic organizational device. I could conceive of a system designed to encourage meetings of interested persons at which the author of the book chosen would be present or represented; or a system which guaranteed the presence of a competent adviser; or one to which only students registered in a department or school had access; or one which permitted meetings only between people who defined their special

## 1. Why We Must Disestablish School

approach to the title under discussion. Advantages for achieving specific goals of learning could be found for each of these restrictions. But I fear that, more often than not, the real reason for proposing such restrictions is contempt arising from the presumption that people are ignorant: educators want to avoid the ignorant meeting the ignorant around a text which they may not understand and which they read *only* because they are interested in it.

The third objection: Why not provide match seekers with incidental assistance that will facilitate their meetings—with space, schedules, screening, and protection? This is now done by schools with all the inefficiency characterizing large bureaucracies. If we left the initiative for meetings to the match seekers themselves, organizations which nobody now classifies as educational would probably do the job much better. I think of restaurant owners, publishers, telephone-answering services, department store managers, and even commuter train executives who could promote their services by rendering them attractive for educational meetings.

At a first meeting in a coffee shop, say, the partners might establish their identities by placing the book under discussion next to their cups. People who took the initiative to arrange for such meetings would soon learn what items to quote to meet the people they sought. The risk that the self-chosen discussion with one or several strangers might lead to a loss of time, disappointment, or even unpleasantness is certainly smaller than the same risk taken by a college applicant. A computer-arranged meeting to discuss an article in a national magazine, held in a coffee shop off Fourth Avenue, would obligate none of the participants to stay in the company of his new acquaintances for longer than it took to drink a cup of coffee, nor would he have to meet any of them ever again. The chance that it would help to pierce the opaqueness of life in a modern city and further new friendship, self-chosen work, and critical reading is high. (The fact that a record of personal readings and meetings could be obtained thus by the FBI is undeniable; that this should still worry anybody in 1970 is only amusing to a free man, who willy-nilly contributes his share in order to drown snoopers in the irrele vancies they gather.)

Both the exchange of skills and matching of partners are based on the assumption that education for all means education by all. Not the draft into a specialized institution but only the mobilization of the whole population can lead to popular culture. The equal right of each man to exercise his competence to learn and to instruct is now pre-empted by certified teachers. The teachers' competence, in turn, is restricted to what may be done in school. And, further, work and leisure are alienated from each other as a result: the spectator and the worker alike are supposed to arrive at the work place all ready to fit into a routine prepared for them. Adaptation in the form of a product's design, instruction, and publicity shapes them for their role as much as formal education by schooling. A radical alternative to a schooled society requires not only new formal mechanisms for the formal acquisition of skills and their educational use. A deschooled society implies a new approach to incidental or informal education.

Incidental education cannot any longer return to the forms which learning took in the village or the medieval town. Traditional society was more like a set of concentric circles of meaningful structures, while modern man must learn how to find meaning in many structures to which he is only marginally related. In the village, language and architecture and work and religion and family customs were consistent with one another, mutually explanatory and reinforcing. To grow into one implied a growth into the others. Even specialized apprenticeship was a by-product of specialized activities, such as shoemaking or the singing of psalms. If an apprentice never became a master or a scholar, he still contributed to making shoes or to making church services solemn. Education did not compete for time with either work or leisure. Almost all education was complex, lifelong, and unplanned.

Contemporary society is the result of conscious designs, and educational opportunities must be designed into them. Our reliance on specialized, full-time instruction through school will now decrease, and we must find more ways to learn and teach: the educational quality of all institutions must increase again. But this is a very ambiguous forecast. It could mean that men in the modern city will be increasingly the victims of an effective process of total instruction and manipulation once they are deprived of even the tenuous pretense of critical independence which liberal schools now provide for at least some of their pupils.

It could also mean that men will shield themselves less behind certificates acquired in school and thus gain in courage to "talk back" and thereby control and instruct the institutions in which they participate. To ensure the latter we must learn to estimate the social value of work and leisure by the educational give-and-take for which they offer opportunity. Effective participation in the politics of a street, a work place, the library, a news program, or a hospital is therefore the best measuring stick to evaluate their level as educational institutions.

I recently spoke to a group of junior-high-school students in the process of organizing a resistance movement to their obligatory draft into the next class. Their slogan was "participation—not simulation." They were disappointed that this was understood as a demand for less rather than for more education, and reminded me of the resistance which Karl Marx put up against a passage in the Gotha program which—one hundred years ago—wanted to outlaw child labor. He opposed the proposal in the interest of the education of the young, which could happen only at work. If the greatest fruit of man's labor should be the education he receives from it and the opportunity which work gives him to initiate the education of others, then the alienation of modern society in a pedagogical sense is even worse than its economic alienation.

The major obstacle on the way to a society that truly educates was well defined by a black friend of mine in Chicago, who told me that our imagination was "all schooled up." We permit the state to ascertain the universal educational deficiencies of its citizens and establish one specialized agency to treat them. We thus share in the delusion that we can distinguish between what is necessary education for others and what is not, just as former generations established laws which defined what was sacred and what was profane.

Durkheim recognized that this ability to divide social reality into two realms was the very essence of formal religion. There are, he reasoned, religions without the supernatural and religions without gods, but none which does not subdivide the world into things and times and persons that are sacred and others that as a consequence are profane. Durkheim's insight can be applied to the sociology of education, for school is radically divisive in a similar way.

The very existence of obligatory schools divides any society into two realms: some time spans and processes and treatments and professions are "academic" or "pedagogic," and others are not. The power of school thus to divide social reality has no boundaries: education becomes unworldly and the world becomes noneducational.

Since Bonhoeffer contemporary theologians have pointed to the confusions now reigning between the Biblical message and institutionalized religion. They point to the experience that Christian freedom and faith usually gain from secularization. Inevitably their statements sound blasphemous to many churchmen. Unquestionably, the educational process will gain from the deschooling of society even though this demand sounds to many schoolmen like treason to the enlightenment. But it is enlightenment itself that is now being snuffed out in the schools.

The secularization of the Christian faith depends on the dedication to it on the part of Christians rooted in the Church. In much the same way, the deschooling of education depends on the leadership of those brought up in the schools. Their curriculum cannot serve them as an alibi for the task: each of us remains responsible for what has been made of him, even though he may be able to do no more than accept this responsibility and serve as a warning to others.

## 2. PHENOMENOLOGY OF SCHOOL

Some words become so flexible that they cease to be useful. "School" and "teaching" are such terms. Like an amoeba they fit into almost any interstice of the language. ABM will teach the Russians, IBM will teach Negro children, and the army can become the school of a nation.

The search for alternatives in education must therefore start with an agreement on what it is we mean by "school." This might be done in several ways. We could begin by listing the latent functions performed by modern school systems, such as custodial care, selection, indoctrination, and learning. We could make a client analysis and verify which of these latent functions render a service or a disservice to teachers, employers, children, parents, or the professions. We could survey the history of Western culture and the information gathered by anthropology in order to find institutions which played a role like that now performed by schooling. We could, finally, recall the many normative statements which have been made since the time of Comenius, or even since Quintilian, and discover which of these the modern school system most closely approaches. But any of these approaches would oblige us to start with certain assumptions about a relationship between school and education. To develop a language in which we can speak about school without such constant recourse to education, I have chosen to begin with something that might be called a phenomenology of public school. For this purpose I shall define "school" as the age-specific, teacher-related process requiring full-time attendance at an obligatory curriculum.

*1. Age* School groups people according to age. This grouping rests on three unquestioned premises. Children belong in school. Children learn in school. Children can be taught only in school. I think these unexamined premises deserve serious questioning.

We have grown accustomed to children. We have decided that they should go to school, do as they are told, and have neither income nor families of their own. We expect them to know their place and behave like children. We remember, whether nostalgically or bitterly, a time when we were children, too. We are expected to tolerate the childish behavior of children. Mankind, for us, is a species both afflicted and blessed with the task of caring for children. We forget, however, that our present concept of "childhood" developed only recently in Western Europe and more recently still in the Americas.[1]

Childhood as distinct from infancy, adolescence, or youth was unknown to most historical periods. Some Christian centuries did not even have an eye for its bodily proportions. Artists depicted the infant as a miniature adult seated on his mother's arm. Children appeared in Europe along with the pocket watch and the Christian moneylenders of the Renaissance. Before our century neither the poor nor the rich knew of children's dress, children's games, or the child's immunity from the law. Childhood belonged to the bourgeoisie. The worker's child, the peasant's child, and the nobleman's child all dressed the way their fathers dressed, played the way their fathers played, and were hanged by the neck as were their fathers. After the discovery of "childhood" by the bourgeoisie all this changed. Only some churches continued to respect for some time the dignity and maturity of the young. Until the Second Vatican Council, each child was instructed that a Christian reaches moral discernment and freedom at the age of seven, and from then on is capable of committing sins for which he may be punished by an eternity in Hell. Toward the middle of this century, middle-class parents began to try to spare their children the impact of this doctrine, and their thinking about children now prevails in the practice of

---

[1] For parallel histories of modern capitalism and modern childhood see Philippe Aries, *Centuries of Childhood*, Knopf, 1962.

## 2. Phenomenology of School

the Church.

Until the last century, "children" of middle-class parents were made at home with the help of preceptors and private schools. Only with the advent of industrial society did the mass production of "childhood" become feasible and come within the reach of the masses. The school system is a modern phenomenon, as is the childhood it produces.

Since most people today live outside industrial cities, most people today do not experience childhood. In the Andes you till the soil once you have become "useful." Before that, you watch the sheep. If you are well nourished, you should be useful by eleven, and otherwise by twelve. Recently, I was talking to my night watchman, Marcos, about his eleven-year-old son who works in a barbershop. I noted in Spanish that his son was still a *"niño."* Marcos, surprised, answered with a guileless smile: "Don Ivan, I guess you're right." Realizing that until my remark the father had thought of Marcos primarily as his "son," I felt guilty for having drawn the curtain of childhood between two sensible persons. Of course if I were to tell the New York slum-dweller that his working son is still a "child," he would show no surprise. He knows quite well that his eleven-year-old son should be allowed childhood, and resents the fact that he is not. The son of Marcos has yet to be afflicted with the yearning for childhood; the New Yorker's son feels deprived.

Most people around the world, then, either do not want or cannot get modern childhood for their offspring. But it also seems that childhood is a burden to a good number of those few who are allowed it. Many of them are simply forced to go through it and are not at all happy playing the child's role. Growing up through childhood means being condemned to a process of inhuman conflict between self-awareness and the role imposed by a society going through its own school age. Neither Stephen Daedalus nor Alexander Portnoy enjoyed childhood, and neither, I suspect, did many of us like to be treated as children.

If there were no age-specific and obligatory learning institution, "childhood" would go out of production. The youth of rich nations would be liberated from its destructiveness, and poor nations would cease attempting

## Deschooling Society

to rival the childishness of the rich. If society were to outgrow its age of childhood, it would have to become livable for the young. The present disjunction between an adult society which pretends to be humane and a school environment which mocks reality could no longer be maintained.

The disestablishment of schools could also end the present discrimination against infants, adults, and the old in favor of children throughout their adolescence and youth. The social decision to allocate educational resources preferably to those citizens who have outgrown the extraordinary learning capacity of their first four years and have not arrived at the height of their self-motivated learning will, in retrospect, probably appear as bizarre.

Institutional wisdom tells us that children need school. Institutional wisdom tells us that children learn in school. But this institutional wisdom is itself the product of schools because sound common sense tells us that only children can be taught in school. Only by segregating human beings in the category of childhood could we ever get them to submit to the authority of a schoolteacher.

*2. Teachers and Pupils*   By definition, children are pupils. The demand for the milieu of childhood creates an unlimited market for accredited teachers. School is an institution built on the axiom that learning is the result of teaching. And institutional wisdom continues to accept this axiom, despite overwhelming evidence to the contrary.

We have all learned most of what we know outside school. Pupils do most of their learning without, and often despite, their teachers. Most tragically, the majority of men are taught their lesson by schools, even though they never go *to* school.

Everyone learns how to live outside school. We learn to speak, to think, to love, to feel, to play, to curse, to politick, and to work without interference from a teacher. Even children who are under a teacher's care day and night are no exception to the rule. Orphans, idiots, and schoolteachers' sons learn most of what they learn outside the "educational" process planned for them. Teachers have made a poor showing in their attempts at increasing learning among the poor. Poor parents who want their children to go to school are less concerned about what they will learn than about the certificate and money they will earn. And middle-class parents commit their children to a teacher's care to keep them from learning what the poor learn on the streets. Increasingly educational research demonstrates that children learn most of what teachers pretend to teach them from peer groups, from comics, from chance observations, and above all from mere participation in the ritual of school. Teachers, more often than not, obstruct such learning of subject matters as goes on in school.

Half of the people in our world never set foot in school. They have no contact with teachers, and they are deprived of the privilege of becoming dropouts. Yet they learn quite effectively the message which school teaches: that they should have school, and more and more of it. School instructs them in their own inferiority through the tax Collector who makes them pay for it, or through the demagogue who raises their expectations of it, or through their children once the latter are hooked on it. So the poor are robbed of their self-respect by subscribing to a creed that grants salvation only through the school. At least the Church gave them a chance to repent at the hour of death. School leaves them with the expectation (a counterfeit hope) that their grandchildren will make it. That expectation is of course still more learning which comes from school but not from teachers.

Pupils have never credited teachers for most of their learning. Bright and dull alike have always relied on rote, reading, and wit to pass their exams, motivated by the stick or by the carrot of a desired career.

Adults tend to romanticize their schooling. In retrospect, they attribute their learning to the teacher whose patience they learned to admire. But the same adults would worry about the mental health of a child who rushed home to tell them what he learned from his every teacher.

Schools create jobs for schoolteachers, no matter what their pupils learn from them.

*3. Full-Time Attendance*   Every month I see another list of proposals made by some U.S. industry to AID, suggesting the replacement of Latin-American "classroom practitioners" either by disciplined systems administrators or just by TV. In the United States teaching as a team enterprise of educational researchers, designers, and technicians is gaining acceptance. But, no matter whether the teacher is a schoolmarm or a team of men in white coats, and no matter whether they succeed in teaching the subject matter listed in the catalogue or whether they fail, the professional teacher creates a sacred milieu.

Uncertainty about the future of professional teaching puts the classroom into jeopardy. Were educational professionals to specialize in promoting learning, they would have to abandon a system which calls for between 750 and 1,000 gatherings a year. But of course teachers do a lot more. The institutional wisdom of schools tells parents, pupils, and educators that the teacher, if he is to teach, must exercise his authority in a sacred precinct. This is true even for teachers whose pupils spend most of their school time in a classroom without walls.

School, by its very nature, tends to make a total claim on the time and energies of its participants. This, in turn, makes the teacher into custodian, preacher, and therapist.

In each of these three roles the teacher bases his authority on a different claim. The *teacher-as-custodian* acts as a master of ceremonies, who guides his pupils through a drawn-out labyrinthine ritual. He arbitrates the observance of rules and administers the intricate rubrics of initiation to life. At his best, he sets the stage for the acquisition of some skill as schoolmasters always have. Without illusions of producing any profound learning, he drills his pupils in some basic routines.

The *teacher-as-moralist* substitutes for parents, God, or the state. He indoctrinates the pupil about what is right or wrong, not only in school but also in society at large. He stands *in loco parentis* for each one and thus ensures that all feel themselves children of the same state.

The *teacher-as-therapist* feels authorized to delve into the personal life of his pupil in order to help him grow as a person. When this function is exercised by a custodian and preacher, it usually means that he persuades the pupil to submit to a domestication of his vision of truth and his sense of what is right.

The claim that a liberal society can be founded on the modern school is paradoxical. The safeguards of individual freedom are all canceled in the dealings of a teacher with his pupil. When the schoolteacher fuses in his person the functions of judge, ideologue, and doctor, the fundamental style of society is perverted by the very process which should prepare for life. A teacher who combines these three powers contributes to the warping of the child much more than the laws which establish his legal or economic minority, or restrict his right to free assembly or abode.

Teachers are by no means the only professionals who offer therapy. Psychiatrists, guidance counselors, and job counselors, even lawyers, help their clients to decide, to develop their personalities, and to learn. Yet common sense tells the client that such professionals should abstain from imposing their opinion of what is right or wrong, or from forcing anyone to follow their advice. Schoolteachers and ministers are the only professionals who feel entitled to pry into the private affairs of their clients at the same time as they preach to a captive audience.

Children are protected by neither the First nor the Fifth Amendment when they stand before that secular priest, the teacher. The child must confront a man who wears an invisible triple crown, like the papal tiara, the symbol of triple authority combined in one person. For the child, the teacher pontificates as pastor, prophet, and priest—he is at once guide, teacher, and administrator of a sacred ritual. He combines the claims of medieval popes in a society constituted under the guarantee that these claims shall never be exercised together by one established and obligatory institution—church or state.

Defining children as full-time pupils permits the teacher to exercise a kind of power over their persons which is much less limited by constitutional and consuetudinal restrictions than the power wielded by the guardians of other social enclaves. Their chronological age disqualifies children from safeguards which are routine for adults in a modern asylum—madhouse, monastery, or jail.

Under the authoritative eye of the teacher, several orders of value collapse into one. The distinctions between morality, legality, and personal worth are blurred and eventually eliminated. Each transgression is made to be felt as a multiple offense. The offender is expected to feel that he has broken a rule, that he has behaved immorally, and that he has let himself down. A pupil who adroitly obtains assistance on an exam is told that he is an outlaw, morally corrupt, and personally worthless.

Classroom attendance removes children from the everyday world of Western culture and plunges them into an environment far more primitive, magical, and deadly serious. School could not create such an enclave within which the rules of ordinary reality are suspended, unless it physically incarcerated the young during many successive years on sacred territory. The attendance rule makes it possible for the schoolroom to serve as a magic womb, from which the child is delivered periodically at the schoolday's and school year's completion until he is finally expelled into adult life. Neither universal extended childhood nor the smothering atmosphere of the classroom could exist without schools. Yet schools, as compulsory channels for learning, could exist without either and be more repressive and destructive than anything we have come to know. To understand what it means to deschool society, and not just to reform the educational establishment, we must now focus on the hidden curriculum of schooling. We are not concerned here, directly, with the hidden curriculum of the ghetto streets which brands the poor or with the hidden curriculum of the drawing room which benefits the rich. We are rather concerned to call attention to the fact that the ceremonial or ritual of schooling itself constitutes such a hidden curriculum. Even the best of teachers cannot entirely protect his pupils from it. Inevitably, this hidden curriculum of schooling adds prejudice and guilt to the discrimination which a society practices against some of its members and compounds the privilege of others with a new title to condescend to the majority. Just as inevitably, this hidden curriculum serves as a ritual of initiation into a growth-oriented consumer society for rich and poor alike.

## 3. RITUALIZATION OF PROGRESS

The university graduate has been schooled for selective service among the rich of the world. Whatever his or her claims of solidarity with the Third World, each American college graduate has had an education costing an amount five times greater than the median life income of half of humanity. A Latin American student is introduced to this exclusive fraternity by having at least 350 times as much public money spent on his education as on that of his fellow citizens of median income. With very rare exceptions, the university graduate from a poor country feels more comfortable with his North American and European colleagues than with his nonschooled compatriots, and all students are academically processed to be happy only in the company of fellow consumers of the products of the educational machine.

The modern university confers the privilege of dissent on those who have been tested and classified as potential money-makers or power-holders. No one is given tax funds for the leisure in which to educate himself or the right to educate others unless at the same time he can also be certified for achievement. Schools select for each successive level those who have, at earlier stages in the game, proved themselves good risks for the established order. Having a monopoly on both the resources for learning and the investiture of social roles, the university coopts the discoverer and the potential dissenter. A degree always leaves its indelible price tag on the curriculum of its consumer. Certified college graduates fit only into a world which puts a price tag on their heads, thereby giving them the power to define the level of expectations in their society. In each country the amount of consumption by the college graduate sets the standard for all others; if

## Deschooling Society

they would be civilized people on or off the job, they will aspire to the style of life of college graduates.

The university thus has the effect of imposing consumer standards at work and at home, and it does so in every part of the world and under every political system. The fewer university graduates there are in a country, the more their cultivated demands are taken as models by the rest of the population. The gap between the consumption of the university graduate and that of the average citizen is even wider in Russia, China, and Algeria than in the United States. Cars, airplane trips, and tape recorders confer more visible distinction in a socialist country, where only a degree, and not just money, can procure them.

The ability of the university to fix consumer goals is something new. In many countries the university acquired this power only in the sixties, as the delusion of equal access to public education began to spread. Before that the university protected an individual's freedom of speech, but did not automatically convert his knowledge into wealth. To be a scholar in the Middle Ages meant to be poor, even a beggar. By virtue of his calling, the medieval scholar learned Latin, became an outsider worthy of the scorn as well as the esteem of peasant and prince, burgher and cleric. To get ahead in the world, the scholastic first had to enter it by joining the civil service, preferably that of the Church. The old university was a liberated zone for discovery and the discussion of ideas both new and old. Masters and students gathered to read the texts of other masters, now long dead, and the living words of the dead masters gave new perspective to the fallacies of the present day. The university was then a community of academic quest and endemic unrest.

In the modern multiversity this community has fled to the fringes, where it meets in a pad, a professor's office, or the chaplain's quarters. The structural purpose of the modern university has little to do with the traditional quest. Since Gutenberg, the exchange of disciplined, critical inquiry has, for the most part, moved from the "chair" into print. The modern university has forfeited its chance to provide a simple setting

## 3. Ritualization of Progress

for encounters which are both autonomous and anarchic, focused yet unplanned and ebullient, and has chosen instead to manage the process by which so-called research and instruction are produced.

The American university, since Sputnik, has been trying to catch up with the body count of Soviet graduates. Now the Germans are abandoning their academic tradition and are building "campuses" in order to catch up with the Americans. During the present decade they want to increase their expenditure for grammar and high schools from 14 to 59 billion DM, and more than triple expenditures for higher learning. The French propose by 1980 to raise to 10 percent of their GNP the amount spent on schools, and the Ford Foundation has been pushing poor countries in Latin America to raise per capita expenses for "respectable" graduates toward North American levels. Students see their studies as the investment with the highest monetary return, and nations see them as a key factor in development.

For the majority who primarily seek a college degree, the university has lost no prestige, but since 1968 it has visibly lost standing among its believers. Students refuse to prepare for war, pollution, and the perpetuation of prejudice. Teachers assist them in their challenge to the legitimacy of the government, its foreign policy, education, and the American way of life. More than a few reject degrees and prepare for a life in a counter culture, outside the certified society. They seem to choose the way of medieval Fraticelli and Alumbrados of the Reformation, the hippies and dropouts of their day. Others recognize the monopoly of the schools over the resources which they need to build a countersociety. They seek support from each other to live with integrity while submitting to the academic ritual. They form, so to speak, hotbeds of heresy right within the hierarchy.

Large parts of the general population, however, regard the modern mystic and the modern heresiarch with alarm. They threaten the consumer economy, democratic privilege, and the self-image of America. But they cannot be wished away. Fewer and fewer can be reconverted by patience or coopted by subtlety—for instance, by appointing them to teach their heresy. Hence the search for means which would make it possible either to get rid of dissident individuals or to reduce the importance of the university which serves them as a base for protest.

The students and faculty who question the legitimacy of the university, and do so at high personal cost, certainly do not feel that they are setting consumer standards or abetting a production system. Those who have founded such groups as the Committee of Concerned Asian Scholars and the North American Congress on Latin America (NACLA) have been among the most effective in changing radically the perceptions of the realities of foreign countries for millions of young people. Still others have tried to formulate Marxian interpretations of American society or have been among those responsible for the flowering of communes. Their achievements add new strength to the argument that the existence of the university is necessary to guarantee continued social criticism.

There is no question that at present the university offers a unique combination of circumstances which allows some of its members to criticize the whole of society. It provides time, mobility, access to peers and information, and a certain impunity—privileges not equally available to other segments of the population. But the university provides this freedom only to those who have already been deeply initiated into the consumer society and into the need for some kind of obligatory public schooling.

The school system today performs the threefold function common to powerful churches throughout history. It is simultaneously the repository of society's myth, the institutionalization of that myth's contradictions, and the locus of the ritual which reproduces and veils the disparities between myth and reality. Today the school system, and especially the university, provides ample opportunity for criticism of the myth and for rebellion against its institutional perversions. But the ritual which demands tolerance of the fundamental contradictions between myth and institution still goes largely unchallenged, for neither ideological criticism nor social action can bring about a new society. Only disenchantment with and detachment from the central social ritual and reform of that ritual can bring about radical change.

## 3. Ritualization of Progress

The American university has become the final stage of the most all-encompassing initiation rite the world has ever known. No society in history has been able to survive without ritual or myth, but ours is the first which has needed such a dull, protracted, destructive, and expensive initiation into its myth. The contemporary world civilization is also the first one which has found it necessary to rationalize its fundamental initiation ritual in the name of education. We cannot begin a reform of education unless we first understand that neither individual learning nor social equality can be enhanced by the ritual of schooling. We cannot go beyond the consumer society unless we first understand that obligatory public schools inevitably reproduce such a society, no matter what is taught in them.

The project of demythologizing which I propose cannot be limited to the university alone. Any attempt to reform the university without attending to the system of which it is an integral part is like trying to do urban renewal in New York City from the twelfth story up. Most current college-level reform looks like the building of high-rise slums. Only a generation which grows up without obligatory schools will be able to recreate the university.

### The Myth of Institutionalized Values

School initiates, too, the Myth of Unending Consumption. This modern myth is grounded in the belief that process inevitably produces something of value and, therefore, production necessarily produces demand. School teaches us that instruction produces learning. The existence of schools produces the demand for schooling. Once we have learned to need school, all our activities tend to take the shape of client relationships to other specialized institutions. Once the self-taught man or woman has been discredited, all nonprofessional activity is rendered suspect. In school we are taught that valuable learning is the result of attendance; that the value of learning increases with the amount of input; and, finally, that this value can be measured and documented by grades and certificates.

In fact, learning is the human activity which least needs manipulation by others. Most learning is not the result of instruction. It is rather the result of unhampered participation in a meaningful setting. Most people learn best by being "with it," yet school makes them identify their personal, cognitive growth with elaborate planning and manipulation.

Once a man or woman has accepted the need for school, he or she is easy prey for other institutions. Once young people have allowed their imaginations to be formed by curricular instruction, they are conditioned to institutional planning of every sort. "Instruction" smothers the horizon of their imaginations. They cannot be betrayed, but only short-changed, because they have been taught to substitute expectations for hope. They will no longer be surprised, for good or ill, by other people, because they have been taught what to expect from every other person who has been taught as they were. This is true in the case of another person or in the case of a machine.

This transfer of responsibility from self to institution guarantees social regression, especially once it has been accepted as an obligation. So rebels against Alma Mater often "make it" into her faculty instead of growing into the courage to infect others with their personal teaching and to assume responsibility for the results. This suggests the possibility of a new Oedipus story—Oedipus the Teacher, who "makes" his mother in order to engender children with her. The man addicted to being taught seeks his security in compulsive teaching. The woman who experiences her knowledge as the result of a process wants to reproduce it in others.

## The Myth of Measurement of Values

The institutionalized values school instills are quantified ones. School initiates young people into a world where everything can be measured, including their imaginations, and, indeed, man himself.

But personal growth is not a measurable entity. It is growth in disciplined dissidence, which cannot be measured against any rod, or any curriculum, nor compared to someone else's achievement. In such learning one can

## 3. Ritualization of Progress

emulate others only in imaginative endeavor, and follow in their footsteps rather than mimic their gait. The learning I prize is immeasurable re-creation.

School pretends to break learning up into subject "matters," to build into the pupil a curriculum made of these prefabricated blocks, and to gauge the result on an international scale. People who submit to the standard of others for the measure of their own personal growth soon apply the same ruler to themselves. They no longer have to be put in their place, but put themselves into their assigned slots, squeeze themselves into the niche which they have been taught to seek, and, in the very process, put their fellows into their places, too, until everybody and everything fits.

People who have been schooled down to size let unmeasured experience slip out of their hands. To them, what cannot be measured becomes secondary, threatening. They do not have to be robbed of their creativity. Under instruction, they have unlearned to "do" their thing or "be" themselves, and value only what has been made or could be made.

Once people have the idea schooled into them that values can be produced and measured, they tend to accept all kinds of rankings. There is a scale for the development of nations, another for the intelligence of babies, and even progress toward peace can be calculated according to body count. In a schooled world the road to happiness is paved with a consumer's index.

### The Myth of Packaging Values

School sells curriculum—a bundle of goods made according to the same process and having the same structure as other merchandise. Curriculum production for most schools begins with allegedly scientific research, on whose basis educational engineers predict future demand and tools for the assembly line, within the limits set by budgets and taboos. The distributor-teacher delivers the finished product to the consumer-pupil, whose reactions are carefully studied and charted to provide research data for the preparation of the next model, which may be "ungraded," "student-designed," "team-taught," "visually-aided," or "issue-centered."

The result of the curriculum production process looks like any other modern staple. It is a bundle of planned meanings, a package of values, a commodity whose "balanced appeal" makes it marketable to a sufficiently large number to justify the cost of production. Consumer-pupils are taught to make their desires conform to marketable values. Thus they are made to feel guilty if they do not behave according to the predictions of consumer research by getting the grades and certificates that will place them in the job category they have been led to expect.

Educators can justify more expensive curricula on the basis of their observation that learning difficulties rise proportionately with the cost of the curriculum. This is an application of Parkinson's Law that work expands with the resources available to do it. This law can be verified on all levels of school: for instance, reading difficulties have been a major issue in French schools only since their per capita expenditures have approached U.S. levels of 1950—when reading difficulties became a major issue in U.S. schools.

In fact, healthy students often redouble their resistance to teaching as they find themselves more comprehensively manipulated. This resistance is due not to the authoritarian style of a public school or the seductive style of some free schools, but to the fundamental approach common to all schools —the idea that one person's judgment should determine what and when another person must learn.

## The Myth of Self-Perpetuating Progress

Even when accompanied by declining returns in learning, paradoxically, rising per capita instructional costs increase the value of the pupil in his or her own eyes and on the market. At almost any cost, school pushes the pupil up to the level of competitive curricular consumption, into progress to ever higher levels. Expenditures to motivate the student to stay on in school skyrocket as he climbs the pyramid. On higher levels they are disguised as new football stadiums, chapels, or programs called International Education. If it teaches nothing else, school teaches the value of escalation: the value of the American way of doing things.

The Vietnam war fits the logic of the moment. Its success has been measured by the numbers of persons effectively treated by cheap bullets delivered at immense cost, and this brutal calculus is unashamedly called "body count." Just as business is business, the never-ending accumulation of money, so war is killing, the never-ending accumulation of dead bodies. In like manner, education is schooling, and this open-ended process is counted in pupil-hours. The various processes are irreversible and self-justifying. By economic standards the country gets richer and richer. By death-accounting standards the nation goes on winning its war forever. And by school standards the population becomes increasingly educated.

School programs hunger for progressive intake of instruction, but even if the hunger leads to steady absorption, it never yields the joy of knowing something to one's satisfaction. Each subject comes packaged with the instruction to go on consuming one "offering" after another, and last year's wrapping is always obsolete for this year's consumer. The textbook racket builds on this demand. Educational reformers promise each new generation the latest and the best, and the public is schooled into demanding what they offer. Both the dropout who is forever reminded of what he missed and the graduate who is made to feel inferior to the new breed of student know exactly where they stand in the ritual of rising deceptions and continue to support a society which euphemistically calls the widening frustration gap a "revolution of rising expectations."

But growth conceived as open-ended consumption—eternal progress—can never lead to maturity. Commitment to unlimited quantitative increase vitiates the possibility of organic development.

## Ritual Game and the New World Religion

The school-leaving age in developed nations outpaces the rise in life expectancy. The two curves will intersect in a decade and create a problem for Jessica Mitford and professionals concerned with "terminal education." I am reminded of the late Middle Ages, when the demand for Church services outgrew a lifetime, and "Purgatory" was created to purify souls under the pope's control before they could enter eternal peace. Logically, this led first to a trade in indulgences and then to an attempt at Reformation. The Myth of Unending Consumption now takes the place of belief in life everlasting.

Arnold Toynbee has pointed out that the decadence of a great culture is usually accompanied by the rise of a new World Church which extends hope to the domestic proletariat while serving the needs of a new warrior class. School seems eminently suited to be the World Church of our decaying culture. No institution could better veil from its participants the deep discrepancy between social principles and social reality in today's world. Secular, scientific, and death-denying, it is of a piece with the modern mood. Its classical, critical veneer makes it appear pluralist if not antireligious. Its curriculum both defines science and is itself defined by so-called scientific research. No one completes school—yet. It never closes its doors on anyone without first offering him one more chance: at remedial, adult, and continuing education.

School serves as an effective creator and sustainer of social myth because of its structure as a ritual game of graded promotions. Introduction into this gambling ritual is much more important than what or how something is taught. It is the game itself that schools, that gets into the blood and becomes a habit. A whole society is initiated into the Myth of Unending Consumption of services. This happens to the degree that token participation in the open-ended ritual is made compulsory and compulsive everywhere. School directs ritual rivalry into an international game which obliges competitors to blame the world's ills on those who cannot or will not play. School is a ritual of initiation which introduces the neophyte to the sacred race of progressive consumption, a ritual of propitiation whose academic priests mediate between the faithful and the gods of privilege and power, a ritual of expiation which sacrifices its dropouts, branding them as scapegoats of underdevelopment.

Even those who spend at best a few years in school—and this is the overwhelming majority in Latin America, Asia, and Africa—learn to feel guilty because of their underconsumption of schooling. In Mexico six grades of school are legally obligatory. Children born into the lower economic third have only two chances in three to make it into the first grade. If they make it, they have four chances in one hundred to finish obligatory schooling by the sixth grade. If they are born into the middle third group, their chances increase to twelve out of a hundred. With these rules, Mexico is more successful than most of the other twenty-five Latin American republics in providing public education.

Everywhere, all children know that they were given a chance, albeit an unequal one, in an obligatory lottery, and the presumed equality of the international standard now compounds their original poverty with the self-inflicted discrimination accepted by the dropout. They have been schooled to the belief in rising expectations and can now rationalize their growing frustration outside school by accepting their rejection from scholastic grace. They are excluded from Heaven because, once baptized, they did not go to church. Born in original sin, they are baptized into first grade, but go to Gehenna (which in Hebrew means "slum") because of their personal faults. As Max Weber traced the social effects of the belief that salvation belonged to those who accumulated wealth, we can now observe that grace is reserved for those who accumulate years in school.

## The Coming Kingdom:
## The Universalization of Expectations

School combines the expectations of the consumer expressed in its claims with the beliefs of the producer expressed in its ritual. It is a liturgical expression of a world-wide "cargo cult," reminiscent of the cults which swept Melanesia in the forties, which injected cultists with the belief that if they but put on a black tie over their naked torsos, Jesus would arrive in a steamer bearing an icebox, a pair of trousers, and a sewing machine for each believer.

School fuses the growth in humiliating dependence on a master with the growth in the futile sense of omnipotence that is so typical of the pupil who wants to go out and teach all nations to save themselves. The ritual is tailored to the stern work habits of the hardhats, and its purpose is to celebrate the myth of an earthly paradise of never-ending consumption, which is the only hope for the wretched and dispossessed.

Epidemics of insatiable this-worldly expectations have occurred throughout history, especially among colonized and marginal groups in all cultures. Jews in the Roman Empire had their Essenes and Jewish messiahs, serfs in the Reformation their Thomas Münzer, dispossessed Indians from Paraguay to Dakota their infectious dancers. These sects were always led by a prophet, and limited their promises to a chosen few. The school- induced expectation of the kingdom, on the other hand, is impersonal rather than prophetic, and universal rather than local. Man has become the engineer of his own messiah and promises the unlimited rewards of science to those who submit to progressive engineering for his reign.

## The New Alienation

School is not only the New World Religion. It is also the world's fastest-growing labor market. The engineering of consumers has become the economy's principal growth sector. As production costs decrease in rich nations, there is an increasing concentration of both capital and labor in the vast enterprise of equipping man for disciplined consumption. During the past decade capital investments directly related to the school system rose even faster than expenditures for defense. Disarmament would only accelerate the process by which the learning industry moves to the center of the national economy. School gives unlimited opportunity for legitimated waste, so long as its destructiveness goes unrecognized and the cost of palliatives goes up.

If we add those engaged in full-time teaching to those in full-time attendance, we realize that this so-called superstructure has become society's major employer. In the United States sixty-two million people are in school and eighty million at work else-where. This is often forgotten by neo-Marxist analysts who say that the process of deschooling must be postponed or bracketed until other disorders, traditionally understood as more fundamental, are corrected by an economic and political revolution. Only if school is understood as an industry can revolutionary strategy be planned realistically. For Marx, the cost of producing demands for commodities was barely significant. Today most human labor is engaged in the production of demands that can be satisfied by industry which makes intensive use of capital. Most of this is done in school.

Alienation, in the traditional scheme, was a direct consequence of work's becoming wage-labor which deprived man of the opportunity to create and be recreated. Now young people are prealienated by schools that isolate them while they pretend to be both producers and consumers of their own knowledge, which is conceived of as a commodity put on the market in school. School makes alienation preparatory to life, thus depriving education of reality and work of creativity. School prepares for the alienating institutionalization of life by teaching the need to be taught. Once this lesson is learned, people lose their incentive to grow in independence; they no longer find relatedness attractive, and close themselves off to the surprises which life offers when it is not predetermined by institutional definition. And school directly or indirectly employs a major portion of the population. School either keeps people for life or makes sure that they will fit into some institution.

The New World Church is the knowledge industry, both purveyor of opium and the workbench during an increasing number of the years of an individual's life. Deschooling is, therefore, at the root of any movement for human liberation.

## The Revolutionary Potential of Deschooling

Of course, school is not, by any means, the only modern institution which has as its primary purpose the shaping of man's vision of reality. The hidden curriculum of family life, draft, health care, so-called professionalism, or of the media play an important part in the institutional manipulation of man's world—vision, language, and demands. But school enslaves more profoundly and more systematically, since only school is credited with the principal function of forming critical judgment, and, paradoxically, tries to do so by making learning about oneself, about others, and about nature depend on a prepackaged process. School touches us so intimately that none of us can expect to be liberated from it by something else.

Many self-styled revolutionaries are victims of school. They see even "liberation" as the product of an institutional process. Only liberating oneself from school will dispel such illusions. The discovery that most learning requires no teaching can be neither manipulated nor planned. Each of us is personally responsible for his or her own deschooling, and only we have the power to do it. No one can be excused if he fails to liberate himself from schooling. People could not free themselves from the Crown until at least some of them had freed themselves from the established Church. They cannot free themselves from progressive consumption until they free themselves from obligatory school.

We are all involved in schooling, from both the side of production and that of consumption. We are superstitiously convinced that good learning can and should be produced in us—and that we can produce it in others. Our attempt to withdraw from the concept of school will reveal the resistance we find in ourselves when we try to renounce limitless consumption and the pervasive presumption that others can be manipulated for their own good. No one is fully exempt from the exploitation of others in the schooling process.

School is both the largest and the most anonymous employer of all. Indeed, the school is the best example of a new kind of enterprise, succeeding the guild, the factory, and the corporation. The multinational corporations which have dominated the economy are now being complemented, and may one day be replaced, by supernationally planned service agencies. These enterprises present their services in ways that make all men feel

## 3. Ritualization of Progress

obliged to consume them. They are internationally standardized, redefining the value of their services periodically and everywhere at approximately the same rhythm.

"Transportation" relying on new cars and superhighways serves the same institutionally packaged need for comfort, prestige, speed, and gadgetry, whether its components are produced by the state or not. The apparatus of "medical care" defines a peculiar kind of health, whether the service is paid for by the state or by the individual. Graded promotion in order to obtain diplomas fits the student for a place on the same international pyramid of qualified manpower, no matter who directs the school.

In all these cases employment is a hidden benefit: the driver of a private automobile, the patient who submits to hospitalization, or the pupil in the schoolroom must now be seen as part of a new class of "employees." A liberation movement which starts in school, and yet is grounded in the awareness of teachers and pupils as simultaneously exploiters and exploited, could fore shadow the revolutionary strategies of the future; for a radical program of deschooling could train youth in the new style of revolution needed to challenge a social system featuring obligatory "health," "wealth," and "security."

The risks of a revolt against school are unforeseeable, but they are not as horrible as those of a revolution starting in any other major institution. School is not yet organized for self-protection as effectively as a nation-state, or even a large corporation. Liberation from the grip of schools could be bloodless. The weapons of the truant officer and his allies in the courts and employment agencies might take very cruel measures against the individual offender, especially if he or she were poor, but they might turn out to be powerless against the surge of a mass movement.

School has become a social problem; it is being attacked on all sides, and citizens and their governments sponsor unconventional experiments all over the world. They resort to unusual statistical devices in order to keep faith and save face. The mood among some educators is much like the mood among Catholic bishops after the Vatican Council. The curricula of so-called "free schools" resemble the liturgies of folk and rock masses. The demands of high-school students to have a say in choosing their teachers are as strident as those of parishioners demanding to select their pastors. But the stakes for society are much higher if a significant minority loses its faith in schooling. This would endanger the survival not only of the economic order built on the coproduction of goods and demands, but equally of the political order built on the nation-state into which students are delivered by the school.

Our options are clear enough. Either we continue to believe that institutionalized learning is a product which justifies unlimited investment or we rediscover that legislation and planning and investment, if they have any place in formal education, should be used mostly to tear down the barriers that now impede opportunities for learning, which can only be a personal activity.

If we do not challenge the assumption that valuable knowledge is a commodity which under certain circumstances may be forced into the consumer, society will be increasingly dominated by sinister pseudo schools and totalitarian managers of information. Pedagogical therapists will drug their pupils more in order to teach them better, and students will drug themselves more to gain relief from the pressures of teachers and the race for certificates. Increasingly larger numbers of bureaucrats will presume to pose as teachers. The language of the schoolman has already been coopted by the adman. Now the general and the policeman try to dignify their professions by masquerading as educators. In a schooled society, warmaking and civil repression find an educational rationale. Pedagogical warfare in the style of Vietnam will be increasingly justified as the only way of teaching people the superior value of unending progress.

Repression will be seen as a missionary effort to hasten the coming of the mechanical Messiah. More and more countries will resort to the pedagogical torture already implemented in Brazil and Greece. This pedagogical torture is not used to extract information or to satisfy the psychic needs of sadists. It relies on random terror to break the integrity of an entire population and make it plastic material for the teachings invented by technocrats. The totally destructive and constantly progressive nature of obligatory instruction will fulfill its ultimate logic unless we begin to liberate ourselves right now from our pedagogical hubris, our belief that man can do what God cannot, namely, manipulate others for their own salvation.

Many people are just awakening to the inexorable destruction which present production trends imply for the environment, but individuals have only very limited power to change these trends. The manipulation of men and women begun in school has also reached a point of no return, and most people are still unaware of it. They still encourage school reform, as Henry Ford III proposes less poisonous automobiles.

Daniel Bell says that our epoch is characterized by an extreme disjunction between cultural and social structures, the one being devoted to apocalyptic attitudes, the other to technocratic decision-making. This is certainly true for many educational reformers, who feel impelled to condemn almost everything which characterizes modern schools—and at the same time propose new schools.

In his *The Structure of Scientific Revolutions*, Thomas Kuhn argues that such dissonance inevitably precedes the emergence of a new cognitive paradigm. The facts reported by those who observed free fall, by those who returned from the other side of the earth, and by those who used the new telescope did not fit the Ptolemaic world view. Quite suddenly, the Newtonian paradigm was accepted. The dissonance which characterizes many of the young today is not so much cognitive as a matter of attitudes— a feeling about what a tolerable society can *not* be like. What is surprising about this dissonance is the ability of a very large number of people to tolerate it.

The capacity to pursue incongruous goals requires an explanation. According to Max Gluckman, all societies have procedures to hide such dissonances from their members. He suggests that this is the purpose of ritual. Rituals can hide from their participants even discrepancies and conflicts between social principle and social organization. As long as an individual is not explicitly conscious of the ritual character of the process through which he was initiated to the forces which shape his cosmos, he cannot break the spell and shape a new cosmos. As long as we are not aware of the ritual through which school shapes the progressive consumer —the economy's major resource—we cannot break the spell of this economy and shape a new one.

## 4. INSTITUTIONAL SPECTRUM

Most utopian schemes and futuristic scenarios call for new and costly technologies, which would have to be sold to rich and poor nations alike. Herman Kahn has found pupils in Venezuela, Argentina, and Colombia. The pipe dreams of Sergio Bernardes for his Brazil of the year 2000 sparkle with more new machinery than is now possessed by the United States, which by then will be weighted down with the antiquated missile sites, jetports, and cities of the sixties and seventies. Futurists inspired by Buckminster Fuller would depend on cheaper and more exotic devices. They count on the acceptance of a new but possible technology that would apparently allow us to make more with less—lightweight monorails rather than supersonic transport; vertical living rather than horizontal sprawling. All of today's futuristic planners seek to make economically feasible what is technically possible while refusing to face the inevitable social consequence: the increased craving of all men for goods and services that will remain the privilege of a few.

I believe that a desirable future depends on our deliberately choosing a life of action over a life of consumption, on our engendering a life style which will enable us to be spontaneous, independent, yet related to each other, rather than maintaining a life style which only allows us to make and unmake, produce and consume—a style of life which is merely a way station on the road to the depletion and pollution of the environment. The future depends more upon our choice of institutions which support a life of action than on our developing new ideologies and technologies. We need a set of criteria which will permit us to recognize those institutions which support personal growth rather than addiction, as well as the will to invest our technological resources preferentially in such institutions of growth.

The choice is between two radically opposed institutional types, both of which are exemplified in certain existing institutions, although one type so characterizes the contemporary period as to almost define it. This dominant type I would propose to call the manipulative institution. The other type also exists, but only precariously. The institutions which fit it are humbler and less noticeable; yet I take them as models for a more desirable future. I call them "convivial" and suggest placing them at the left of an institutional spectrum, both to show that there are institutions which fall between the extremes and to illustrate how historical institutions can change color as they shift from facilitating activity to organizing production.

Generally, such a spectrum, moving from left to right, has been used to characterize men and their ideologies, not our social institutions and their styles. This categorization of men, whether as individuals or in groups, often generates more heat than light. Weighty objections can be raised against using an ordinary convention in an unusual fashion, but by doing so I hope to shift the terms of the discussion from a sterile to a fertile plane. It will become evident that men of the left are not always characterized by their opposition to the manipulative institutions, which I locate to the right on the spectrum.

The most influential modern institutions crowd up at the right of the spectrum. Law enforcement has moved there, as it has shifted from the hands of the sheriff to those of the FBI and the Pentagon. Modern warfare has become a highly professional enterprise whose business is killing. It has reached the point where its efficiency is measured in body counts. Its peace-keeping potential depends on its ability to convince friend and foe of the nation's unlimited death-dealing power. Modern bullets and chemicals are so effective that a few cents' worth, properly delivered to the intended "client," unfailingly kill or maim. But delivery costs rise vertiginously; the cost of a dead Vietnamese went from $360,000 in 1967 to $450,000 in 1969. Only economies on a scale approaching race suicide would render modern warfare economically efficient. The boomerang effect in war is becoming

## 4. Institutional Spectrum

more obvious: the higher the body count of dead Vietnamese, the more enemies the United States acquires around the world; likewise, the more the United States must spend to create another manipulative institution—cynically dubbed "pacification"—in a futile effort to absorb the side effects of war.

At this same extreme on the spectrum we also find social agencies which specialize in the manipulation of their clients. Like the military, they tend to develop effects contrary to their aims as the scope of their operations increases. These social institutions are equally counterproductive, but less obviously so. Many assume a therapeutic and compassionate image to mask this paradoxical effect. For example, jails, up until two centuries ago, served as a means of detaining men until they were sentenced, maimed, killed, or exiled, and were sometimes deliberately used as a form of torture. Only recently have we begun to claim that locking people up in cages will have a beneficial effect on their character and behavior. Now quite a few people are beginning to understand that jail increases both the quality and the quantity of criminals, that, in fact, it often creates them out of mere nonconformists. Far fewer people, however, seem to understand that mental hospitals, nursing homes, and orphan asylums do much the same thing. These institutions provide their clients with the destructive self-image of the psychotic, the overaged, or the waif, and provide a rationale for the existence of entire professions, just as jails produce income for wardens. Membership in the institutions found at this extreme of the spectrum is achieved in two ways, both coercive: by forced commitment or by selective service.

At the opposite extreme of the spectrum lie institutions distinguished by spontaneous use—the "convivial" institutions. Telephone link-ups, subway lines, mail routes, public markets and exchanges do not require hard or soft sells to induce their clients to use them. Sewage systems, drinking water, parks, and sidewalks are institutions men use without having to be institutionally convinced that it is to their advantage to do so. Of course, all institutions require some regulation. But the operation of institutions which exist to be used rather than to produce something requires rules of an entirely different nature from those required by treatment-institutions, which are manipulative. The rules which govern institutions for use have mainly the purpose of avoiding abuses which would frustrate their general accessibility. Sidewalks must be kept free of obstructions, the industrial use of drinking water must be held within limits, and ball playing must be restricted to special areas within a park. At present we need legislation to limit the abuse of our telephone lines by computers, the abuse of mail service by advertisers, and the pollution of our sewage systems by industrial wastes. The regulation of convivial institutions sets limits to their use; as one moves from the convivial to the manipulative end of the spectrum, the rules progressively call for unwilling consumption or participation. The different cost of acquiring clients is just one of the characteristics which distinguish convivial from manipulative institutions.

At both extremes of the spectrum we find service institutions, but on the right the service is imposed manipulation, and the client is made the victim of advertising, aggression, indoctrination, imprisonment, or electroshock. On the left the service is amplified opportunity within formally defined limits, while the client remains a free agent. Right-wing institutions tend to be highly complex and costly production processes in which much of the elaboration and expense is concerned with convincing consumers that they cannot live without the product or the treatment offered by the institution. Left-wing institutions tend to be networks which facilitate client-initiated communication or cooperation.

The manipulative institutions of the right are either socially or psychologically "addictive." Social addiction, or escalation, consists in the tendency to prescribe increased treatment if smaller quantities have not yielded the desired results. Psychological addiction, or habituation, results when consumers become hooked on the need for more and more of the process or product. The self-activated institutions of the left tend to be self-limiting. Unlike production processes which identify satisfaction with the mere act of consumption, these networks serve a purpose beyond their own repeated

## 4. Institutional Spectrum

use. An individual picks up the telephone when he wants to say something to someone else, and hangs up when the desired communication is over. He does not, teen-agers excepted, use the telephone for the sheer pleasure of talking into the receiver. If the telephone is not the best way to get in touch, people will write a letter or take a trip. Right-wing institutions, as we can see clearly in the case of schools, both invite compulsively repetitive use and frustrate alternative ways of achieving similar results.

Toward, but not at, the left on the institutional spectrum, we can locate enterprises which compete with others in their own field, but have not begun notably to engage in advertising. Here we find hand laundries, small bakeries, hairdressers, and—to speak of professionals—some lawyers and music teachers. Characteristically left of center, then, are self-employed persons who have institutionalized their services but not their publicity. They acquire clients through their personal touch and the comparative quality of their services.

Hotels and cafeterias are somewhat closer to the center. The big chains like Hilton—which spend huge amounts on selling their image—often behave as if they were running institutions of the right. Yet Hilton and Sheraton enterprises do not usually offer anything more—in fact, they often give less—than similarly priced, independently managed lodgings. Essentially, a hotel sign beckons to a traveler in the manner of a road sign. It says, "Stop, here is a bed for you," rather than, "You should prefer a hotel bed to a park bench!"

The producers of staples and most perishable consumer goods belong in the middle of our spectrum. They fill generic demands and add to the cost of production and distribution whatever the market will bear in advertising costs for publicity and special packaging. The more basic the product—be it goods or services—the more does competition tend to limit the sales cost of the item.

Most manufacturers of consumer goods have moved much further to the right. Both directly and indirectly, they produce demands for accessories which boost real purchase price far beyond production cost. General

Motors and Ford produce means of transportation, but they also, and more importantly, manipulate public taste in such a way that the need for transportation is expressed as a demand for private cars rather than public buses. They sell the desire to control a machine, to race at high speeds in luxurious comfort, while also offering the fantasy at the end of the road. What they sell, however, is not just a matter of uselessly big motors, superfluous gadgetry, or the new extras forced on the manufacturers by Ralph Nader and the clean-air lobbyists. The list price includes souped-up engines, air-conditioning, safety belts, and exhaust controls; but other costs not openly declared to the driver are also involved: the corporation's advertising and sales expenses, fuel, maintenance and parts, insurance, interest on credit, as well as less tangible costs like loss of time, temper, and breathable air in our traffic-congested cities.

An especially interesting corollary to our discussion of socially useful institutions is the system of "public" highways. This major element of the total cost of automobiles deserves lengthier treatment, since it leads directly to the rightist institution in which I am most interested, namely, the school.

## False Public Utilities

The highway system is a network for locomotion across relatively large distances. As a network, it appears to belong on the left of the institutional spectrum. But here we must make a distinction which will clarify both the nature of highways and the nature of true public utilities. Genuinely all-purpose roads are true public utilities. Superhighways are private preserves, the cost of which has been partially foisted upon the public.

Telephone, postal, and highway systems are all networks, and none of them is free. Access to the telephone network is limited by time charges on each call. These rates are relatively small and could be reduced without changing the nature of the system. Use of the telephone system is not in the least limited by what is transmitted, although it is best used by those who can speak coherent sentences in the language of the other party—an ability universally possessed by those who wish to use the network. Postage is usually cheap. Use of the postal system is slightly limited by the price of pen and paper, and somewhat more by the ability to write. Still, when someone who does not know how to write has a relative or friend to whom he can dictate a letter, the postal system is at his service, as it is if he wants to ship a recorded tape.

The highway system does not similarly become available to someone who merely learns to drive. The telephone and postal networks exist to serve those who wish to use them, while the highway system mainly serves as an accessory to the private automobile. The former are true public utilities, whereas the latter is a public service to the owners of cars, trucks, and buses. Public utilities exist for the sake of communication among men; highways, like other institutions of the right, exist for the sake of a product. Auto manufacturers, we have already observed, *produce* simultaneously both cars and the demand for cars. They also *produce* the demand for multilane highways, bridges, and oilfields. The private car is the focus of a cluster of right-wing institutions. The high cost of each element is dictated by elaboration of the basic product, and to sell the basic product is to "hook" society on the entire package.

To plan a highway system as a true public utility would discriminate against those for whom velocity and individualized comfort are the primary transportation values, in favor of those who value fluidity and destination. It is the difference between a far-flung network with maximum access for travelers and one which offers only privileged access to restricted areas.

Transferring a modern institution to the developing nations provides the acid test of its quality. In very poor countries roads are usually just good enough to permit transit by special, high-axle trucks loaded with groceries, livestock, or people. This kind of country should use its limited resources to build a spiderweb of trails extending to every region and should restrict imports to two or three different models of highly durable vehicles which can manage all trails at low speed. This would simplify maintenance and the stocking of spare parts, permit the operation of these vehicles around the clock, and provide maximum fluidity and choice of destination to all citizens. This would require the engineering of all-purpose vehicles with the simplicity of the Model T, making use of the most modern alloys to guarantee durability, with a built-in speed limit of not more than fifteen miles per hour, and strong enough to run on the roughest terrain. Such vehicles are not on the market because there is no demand for them. As a matter of fact, such a demand would have to be cultivated, quite possibly under the protection of strict legislation. At present, whenever such a demand is even slightly felt, it is quickly snuffed out by counterpublicity aimed at universal sales of the machines which currently extract from U.S. taxpayers the money needed for building superhighways.

In order to "improve" transportation, all countries—even the poorest—now plan highway systems designed for the passenger cars and high-speed trailers which fit the velocity-conscious minority of producers and consumers in the elite classes. This approach is frequently rationalized as a saving of the most precious resource of a poor country: the time of the doctor, the school inspector, or the public administrator. These men, of course, serve almost exclusively the same people who have, or hope one day to have, a car. Local taxes and scarce international exchange are wasted on *false public utilities.*

"Modern" technology transferred to poor countries falls into three large categories: goods, factories which make them, and service institutions—principally schools—which make men into modern producers and consumers. Most countries spend by far the largest proportion of their budget on schools. The school-made graduates then create a demand for other conspicuous utilities, such as industrial power, paved highways, modern hospitals, and airports, and these in turn create a market for the goods made for rich countries and, after a while, the tendency to import obsolescent factories to produce them.

Of all "false utilities," school is the most insidious. Highway systems produce only a demand for cars. Schools create a demand for the entire set of modern institutions which crowd the right end of the spectrum. A man who questioned the need for highways would be written off as a romantic; the man who questions the need for school is immediately attacked as either heartless or imperialist.

## Schools as False Public Utilities

Like highways, schools, at first glance, give the impression of being equally open to all comers. They are, in fact, open only to those who consistently renew their credentials. Just as highways create the impression that their present level of cost per year is necessary if people are to move, so schools are presumed essential for attaining the competence required by a society which uses modern technology. We have exposed speedways as spurious public utilities by noting their dependence on private automobiles. Schools are based upon the equally spurious hypothesis that learning is the result of curricular teaching.

Highways result from a perversion of the desire and need for mobility into the demand for a private car. Schools themselves pervert the natural inclination to grow and learn into the demand for instruction. Demand for manufactured maturity is a far greater abnegation of self-initiated activity than the demand for manufactured goods. Schools are not only to the right of highways and cars; they belong near the extreme of the institutional spectrum occupied by total asylums. Even the producers of body counts kill only bodies. By making men abdicate the responsibility for their own growth, school leads many to a kind of spiritual suicide.

Highways are paid for in part by those who use them, since tolls and gasoline taxes are extracted only from drivers. School, on the other hand, is a perfect system of regressive taxation, where the privileged graduates ride on the back of the entire paying public. School puts a head tax on promotion. The underconsumption of highway mileage is not nearly so costly as the underconsumption of schooling. The man who does not own a car in Los Angeles may be almost immobilized, but if he can somehow manage to reach a work place, he can get and hold a job. The school dropout has no alternative route. The suburbanite with his new Lincoln and his country cousin who drives a beat-up jalopy get essentially the same use out of the highway, even though one man's car costs thirty times more than the other's. The value of a man's schooling is a function of the number of years he has completed and of the costliness of the schools he has attended. The law compels no one to drive, whereas it obliges everyone to go to school.

The analysis of institutions according to their present placement on a left-right continuum enables me to clarify my belief that fundamental social change must begin with a change of consciousness about institutions and to explain why the dimension of a viable future turns on the rejuvenation of institutional style.

During the sixties institutions born in different decades since the French Revolution simultaneously reached old age; public school systems founded in the time of Jefferson or of Atatürk, along with others which started after World War II, all became bureaucratic, self-justifying, and manipulative. The same thing happened to systems of social security, to labor unions, major churches and diplomacies, the care of the aged, and the disposal of the dead.

Today, for instance, the school systems of Colombia, Britain, the U.S.S.R., and the U.S. resemble each other more closely than U.S. schools of the late 1890's resembled either today's or their contemporaries in Russia. Today all schools are obligatory, open-ended, and competitive. The same convergence in institutional style affects health care, merchandising, personnel administration, and political life. All these institutional processes tend to pile up at the manipulative end of the spectrum.

A merger of world bureaucracies results from this convergence of institutions. The style, the ranking systems, and the paraphernalia (from textbook to computer) are standardized on the planning boards of Costa Rica or Afghanistan after the model of Western Europe.

Everywhere these bureaucracies seem to focus on the same task: promoting the growth of institutions of the right. They are concerned with the making of things, the making of ritual rules, and the making—and reshaping—of "executive truth," the ideology or fiat which establishes the current value which should be attributed to their product. Technology provides these bureaucracies with increasing power on the right hand of society. The left hand of society seems to wither, not because technology is less capable of increasing the range of human action, and providing time for the play of individual imagination and personal creativity, but because such use of technology does not increase the power of an elite which administers it. The postmaster has no control over the substantive use of the mails, the switchboard operator or Bell Telephone executive has no power to stop adultery, murder, or subversion from being planned over his network.

At stake in the choice between the institutional right and left is the very nature of human life. Man must choose whether to be rich in things or in the freedom to use them. He must choose between alternate styles of life and related production schedules.

Aristotle had already discovered that "making and acting" are different, so different, in fact, that one never includes the other. "For neither is acting a way of making—nor making a way of truly acting. Architecture [*techne*] is a way of making ... of bringing something into being whose origin is in the maker and not in the thing. Making has always an end other than itself, action not; for good action itself is its end. Perfection in making is an art, perfection in acting is a virtue."[1] The word which Aristotle employed for making was "*poesis*," and the word he employed for doing, "*praxis*." A move to the right implies that an institution is being restructured to increase its ability to "make," while as it moves to the left, it is being restructured to allow increased "doing" or "*praxis*." Modern technology has increased the ability of man to relinquish the "making" of things to machines, and his potential time for "acting" has increased. "Making" the necessities of life has ceased to take up his time. Unemployment is the result of this modernization: it is the idleness of a man for whom there is nothing to "make"

---

[1] *Nichomachean Ethics,* 1140.

and who does not know what to "do"—that is, how to "act." Unemployment is the sad idleness of a man who, contrary to Aristotle, believes that making things, or working, is virtuous and that idleness is bad. Unemployment is the experience of the man who has succumbed to the Protestant ethic. Leisure, according to Weber, is necessary for man to be able to work. For Aristotle, work is necessary for man to have leisure.

Technology provides man with discretionary time he can fill either with making or with doing. The choice between sad unemployment and joyful leisure is now open for the entire culture. It depends on the institutional style the culture chooses. This choice would have been unthinkable in an ancient culture built either on peasant agriculture or on slavery. It has become inevitable for postindustrial man.

One way to fill available time is to stimulate increased demands for the consumption of goods and, simultaneously, for the production of services. The former implies an economy which provides an ever-growing array of ever newer things which can be made, consumed, wasted, and recycled. The latter implies the futile attempt to "make" virtuous actions into the products of "service" institutions. This leads to the identification of schooling and education, of medical service and health, of program-watching and entertainment, of speed and effective locomotion. This first option now goes under the name of development.

The radically alternative way to fill available time is a limited range of more durable goods and to provide access to institutions which can increase the opportunity and desirability of human interaction.

A durable-goods economy is precisely the contrary of an economy based on planned obsolescence. A durable-goods economy means a constraint on the bill of goods. Goods would have to be such that they provided the maximum opportunity to "do" something with them: items made for self-assembly, self-help, reuse, and repair.

The complement to a durable, repairable, and reusable bill of goods is not an increase of institutionally produced services, but rather an institutional framework which constantly educates to action, participation, and self-help.

## 4. Institutional Spectrum

The movement of our society from the present—in which all institutions gravitate toward post-industrial bureaucracy—to a future of postindustrial conviviality—in which the intensity of action would prevail over production—must begin with a renewal of style in the service institutions—and, first of all, with a renewal of education. A future which is desirable and feasible depends on our willingness to invest our technological know-how into the growth of convivial institutions. In the field of educational research, this amounts to the request for a reversal of present trends.

# 5. IRRATIONAL CONSISTENCIES[1]

I believe that the contemporary crisis of education demands that we review the very idea of publicly prescribed learning, rather than the methods used in its enforcement. The dropout rate—especially of junior-high-school students and elementary-school teachers—points to a grass-roots demand for a completely fresh look. The "classroom practitioner" who considers himself a liberal teacher is increasingly attacked from all sides. The free-school movement, confusing discipline with indoctrination, has painted him into the role of a destructive authoritarian. The educational technologist consistently demonstrates the teacher's inferiority at measuring and modifying behavior. And the school administration for which he works forces him to bow to both Summerhill and Skinner, making it obvious that compulsory learning cannot be a liberal enterprise. No wonder that the desertion rate of teachers is overtaking that of their students.

America's commitment to the compulsory education of its young now reveals itself to be as futile as the pretended American commitment to compulsory democratization of the Vietnamese. Conventional schools obviously cannot do it. The free-school movement entices unconventional educators, but ultimately does so in support of the conventional ideology of schooling. And the promises of educational technologists, that their research and development—if adequately funded—can offer some kind of final solution to the resistance of youth to compulsory learning, sound as confident and prove as fatuous as the analogous promises made by the military technologists.

---

[1] This chapter was presented originally at a meeting of the American Educational Research Association, in New York City, February 6, 1971.

## Deschooling Society

The criticism directed at the American school system by the behaviorists and that coming from the new breed of radical educators seem radically opposed. The behaviorists apply educational research to the "induction of autotelic instruction through individualized learning packages." Their style clashes with the nondirective cooption of youth into liberated communes established under the supervision of adults. Yet, in historical perspective, these two are just contemporary manifestations of the seemingly contradictory yet really complementary goals of the public school system. From the beginning of this century, the schools have been protagonists of social control on the one hand and free cooperation on the other, both placed at the service of the "good society," conceived of as a highly organized and smoothly working corporate structure. Under the impact of intense urbanization, children became a natural resource to be molded by the schools and fed into the industrial machine. Progressive politics and the cult of efficiency converged in the growth of the U.S. public school.[1] Vocational guidance and the junior high school were two important results of this kind of thinking.

It appears, therefore, that the attempt to produce specified behavioral changes which can be measured and for which the processor can be held accountable is just one side of a coin, whose other side is the pacification of the new generation within specially engineered enclaves which will seduce them into the dream world of their elders. These pacified in society are well described by Dewey, who wants us to "make each one of our schools an embryonic community life, active with types of occupations that reflect the life of the larger society, and *permeate* it with the *spirit* of art, history and science." In this historical perspective, it would be a grave mistake to interpret the current three-cornered controversy between the school establishment, the educational technologists and the free schools as the prelude to a revolution in education. This controversy reflects rather a

---

[1] See Joel Spring, *Education and the Rise of the Corporate State*, Cuaderno No. 50, Centro Intercultural de Documentación, Cuernavaca, Mexico, 1971.

## 5. Irrational Consistencies

stage of an attempt to escalate an old dream into fact, and to finally make all valuable learning the result of professional teaching. Most educational alternatives proposed converge toward goals which are immanent in the production of the cooperative man whose individual needs are met by means of his specialization in the American system: They are oriented toward the improvement of what—for lack of a better phrase—I call the schooled society. Even the seemingly radical critics of the school system are not willing to abandon the idea that they have an obligation to the young, especially to the poor, an obligation to process them, whether by love or by fear, into a society which needs disciplined specialization as much from its producers as from its consumers and also their full commitment to the ideology which puts economic growth first.

Dissent veils the contradictions inherent in the very idea of school. The established teachers unions, the technological wizards, and the educational liberation movement reinforce the commitment of the entire society to the fundamental axioms of a schooled world, somewhat in the manner in which many peace and protest movements reinforce the commitments of their members—be they black, female, young, or poor—to seek justice through the growth of the gross national income.

Some of the tenets which now go unchallenged are easy to list. There is, first, the shared belief that behavior which has been acquired in the sight of a pedagogue is of special value to the pupil and of special benefit to society. This is related to the assumption that social man is born only in adolescence, and properly born only if he matures in the school-womb, which some want to gentle by permissiveness, others to stuff with gadgets, and still others to varnish with a liberal tradition. And there is, finally, a shared view of youth which is psychologically romantic and politically conservative. According to this view, changes in society must be brought about by burdening the young with the responsibility of transforming it—but only after their eventual release from school. It is easy for a society founded on such tenets to build up a sense of its responsibility for the education of the new generation, and this inevitably means that some men may set, specify, and evaluate the personal goals of others. In a "passage from an imaginary Chinese encyclopedia," Jorge Luis Borges tries to evoke the sense of giddiness such an attempt must produce. He tells us that animals are divided into the following classes: " (a) those belonging to the emperor, (b) those that are embalmed, (c) those that are domesticated, (d) the suckling pigs, (e) the sirens, (f) fabulous ones, (g) the roaming dogs, (h) those included in the present classification, (i) those that drive themselves crazy, (j) innumerable ones, (k) those painted with a very fine brush of camel hair, (l) et cetera, (m) those who have just broken the jug, (n) those who resemble flies from afar." Now, such a taxonomy does not come into being unless somebody feels it can serve his purpose: in this case, I suppose, that somebody was a tax collector. For him, at least, this taxonomy of beasts *must* have made sense, the same way in which the taxonomy of educational objectives makes sense to scientific authors.

In the peasant, the vision of men with such inscrutable logic, empowered to assess his cattle, must have induced a chilling sense of impotence. Students, for analogous reasons, tend to feel paranoiac when they seriously submit to a curriculum. Inevitably they are even more frightened than my imaginary Chinese peasant, because it is their life goals rather than their livestock which is being branded with an inscrutable sign.

This passage of Borges is fascinating, because it evokes the logic of *irrational consistency* which makes Kafka's and Koestler's bureaucracies so sinister yet so evocative of everyday life. Irrational consistency mesmerizes accomplices who are engaged in mutually expedient and disciplined exploitation. It is the logic generated by bureaucratic behavior. And it becomes the logic of a society which demands that the managers of its educational institutions be held publicly accountable for the behavioral modification they produce in their clients. Students who can be motivated to value the educational packages which their teachers obligate them to consume are comparable to Chinese peasants who can fit their flocks into the tax form provided by Borges.

At some time during the last two generations a commitment to therapy

## 5. Irrational Consistencies

triumphed in American culture, and teachers came to be regarded as the therapists whose ministrations all men need, if they wish to enjoy the equality and freedom with which, according to the Constitution, they are born. Now the teacher-therapists go on to propose life-long educational treatment as the next step. The *style* of this treatment is under discussion: Should it take the form of continued adult classroom attendance? Electronic ecstasy? Or periodic sensitivity sessions? All educators are ready to conspire to push out the walls of the classroom, with the goal of transforming the entire culture into a school.

The American controversy over the future of education, behind its rhetoric and noise, is more conservative than the discourse in other areas of public policy. On foreign affairs, at least, an organized minority constantly reminds us that the United States must renounce its role as the world's policeman. Radical economists, and now even their less radical teachers, question aggregate growth as a desirable goal. There are lobbies for prevention over cure in medicine and others in favor of fluidity over speed in transportation. Only in the field of education do the articulate voices demanding a radical deschooling of society remain so dispersed. There is a lack of cogent argument and of mature leadership aiming at the disestablishment of any and all institutions which serve the purpose of compulsory *learning*. For the moment, the radical deschooling of society is still a cause without a party. This is especially surprising in a time of growing, though chaotic, resistance to all forms of institutionally planned instruction on the part of those aged twelve to seventeen.

Educational innovators still assume that educational institutions function like funnels for the programs they package. For my argument it is irrelevant whether these funnels take the form of a classroom, a TV transmitter, or a "liberated zone." It is equally irrelevant whether the packages purveyed are rich or poor, hot or cold, hard and measurable (like Math III), or impossible to assess (like sensitivity). What counts is that education is assumed to be the result of an institutional process managed by the educator. As long as the relations continue to be those between a supplier and a consumer, educational research will remain a circular process. It will amass scientific evidence in support of the need for more educational packages and for their more deadly accurate delivery to the individual customer, just as a certain brand of social science can prove the need for the delivery of more military treatment.

An educational revolution depends on a twofold inversion: a new orientation for research and a new understanding of the educational style of an emerging counterculture.

Operational research now seeks to optimize the efficiency of an inherited framework—a framework which is itself never questioned. This framework has the syntactic structure of a funnel for teaching packages. The syntactic alternative to it is an educational network or web for the autonomous assembly of resources under the personal control of each learner. This alternative structure of an educational institution now lies within the conceptual blind spot of our operational research. If research were to focus on it, this would constitute a true scientific revolution.

The blind spot of educational research reflects the cultural bias of a society in which technological growth has been confused with technocratic control. For the technocrat the value of an environment increases as more contacts between each man and his milieu can be programmed. In this world the choices which are manageable for the observer or planner converge with the choices possible for the observed so-called beneficiary. Freedom is reduced to a selection among packaged commodities.

The emerging counterculture reaffirms the values of semantic content above the efficiency of increased and more rigid syntax. It values the wealth of connotation above the power of syntax to produce wealth. It values the unpredictable outcome of self-chosen personal encounter above the certified quality of professional instruction. This reorientation toward personal surprise rather than institutionally engineered values will be disruptive of the established order until we dissociate the increasing availability of technological tools which facilitate encounter from the increasing control of the technocrat of what happens when people meet.

## 5. Irrational Consistencies

Our present educational institutions are at the service of the teacher's goals. The relational structures we need are those which will enable each man to define himself by learning and by contributing to the learning of others.

# 6. LEARNING WEBS

In a previous chapter I discussed what is becoming a common complaint about schools, one that is reflected, for example, in the recent report of the Carnegie Commission: In school registered students submit to certified teachers in order to obtain certificates of their own; both are frustrated and both blame insufficient resources—money, time, or buildings—for their mutual frustration.

Such criticism leads many people to ask whether it is possible to conceive of a different style of learning. The same people, paradoxically, when pressed to specify how they acquired what they know and value, will readily admit that they learned it more often outside than inside school. Their knowledge of facts, their understanding of life and work came to them from friendship or love, while viewing TV, or while reading, from examples of peers or the challenge of a street encounter. Or they may have learned what they know through the apprenticeship ritual for admission to a street gang or the initiation to a hospital, newspaper city room, plumber's shop, or insurance office. The alternative to dependence on schools is not the use of public resources for some new device which "makes" people learn; rather it is the creation of a new style of educational relationship between man and his environment. To foster this style, attitudes toward growing up, the tools available for learning, and the quality and structure of daily life will have to change concurrently.

Attitudes are already changing. The proud dependence on school is gone. Consumer resistance increases in the knowledge industry. Many teachers and pupils, taxpayers and employers, economists and policemen would prefer not to depend any longer on schools. What prevents their frustration from shaping new institutions is a lack not only of imagination but frequently also of appropriate language and of enlightened self-interest. They cannot visualize either a deschooled society or educational institutions in a society which has disestablished school.

In this chapter I intend to show that the inverse of school is possible: that we can depend on self-motivated learning instead of employing teachers to bribe or compel the student to find the time and the will to learn; that we can provide the learner with new links to the world instead of continuing to funnel all educational programs through the teacher. I shall discuss some of the general characteristics which distinguish schooling from learning and outline four major categories of educational institutions which should appeal not only to many individuals but also to many existing interest groups.

## An Objection: Who Can Be Served by Bridges to Nowhere?

We are used to considering schools as a variable, dependent on the political and economic structure. If we can change the style of political leadership, or promote the interests of one class or another, or switch from private to public ownership of the means of production, we assume the school system will change as well. The educational institutions I will propose, however, are meant to serve a society which does not now exist, although the current frustration with schools is itself potentially a major force to set in motion change toward new social arrangements. An obvious objection has been raised to this approach: Why channel energy to build bridges to nowhere, instead of marshaling it first to change not the schools but the political and economic system?

This objection, however, underestimates the fundamental political and economic nature of the school system itself, as well as the political potential inherent in any effective challenge to it.

In a basic sense, schools have ceased to be dependent on the ideology professed by any government or market organization. Other basic institutions might differ from one country to another: family, party, church, or press.

## 6. Learning Webs

But everywhere the school system has the same structure, and everywhere its hidden curriculum has the same effect. Invariably, it shapes the consumer who values institutional commodities above the nonprofessional ministration of a neighbor.

Everywhere the hidden curriculum of schooling initiates the citizen to the myth that bureaucracies guided by scientific knowledge are efficient and benevolent. Everywhere this same curriculum instills in the pupil the myth that increased production will provide a better life. And everywhere it develops the habit of self-defeating consumption of services and alienating production, the tolerance for institutional dependence, and the recognition of institutional rankings. The hidden curriculum of school does all this in spite of contrary efforts undertaken by teachers and no matter what ideology prevails.

In other words, schools are fundamentally alike in all countries, be they fascist, democratic or socialist, big or small, rich or poor. This identity of the school system forces us to recognize the profound world-wide identity of myth, mode of production, and method of social control, despite the great variety of mythologies in which the myth finds expression.

In view of this identity, it is illusory to claim that schools are, in any profound sense, dependent variables. This means that to hope for fundamental change in the school system as an effect of conventionally conceived social or economic change is also an illusion. Moreover, this illusion grants the school—the reproductive organ of a consumer society—almost unquestioned immunity.

It is at this point that the example of China becomes important. For three millennia, China protected higher learning through a total divorce between the process of learning and the privilege conferred by mandarin examinations. To become a world power and a modern nation-state, China had to adopt the international style of schooling.

Even the piecemeal creation of new educational agencies which were the inverse of school would be an attack on the most sensitive link of a pervasive phenomenon, which is organized by the state in all countries. A political program which does not explicitly recognize the need for deschooling is not revolutionary; it is demagoguery calling for more of the same. Any major political program of the seventies should be evaluated by this measure: How clearly does it state the need for deschooling—and how clearly does it provide guidelines for the educational quality of the society for which it aims?

The struggle against domination by the world market and big-power politics might be beyond some poor communities or countries, but this weakness is an added reason for emphasizing the importance of liberating each society through a reversal of its educational structure, a change which is not beyond any society's means.

## General Characteristics of New Formal Educational Institutions

A good educational system should have three purposes: it should provide all who want to learn with access to available resources at any time in their lives; empower all who want to share what they know to find those who want to learn it from them; and, finally, furnish all who want to present an issue to the public with the opportunity to make their challenge known. Such a system would require the application of constitutional guarantees to education. Learners should not be forced to submit to an obligatory curriculum, or to discrimination based on whether they possess a certificate or a diploma. Nor should the public be forced to support, through a regressive taxation, a huge professional apparatus of educators and buildings which in fact restricts the public's chances for learning to the services the profession is willing to put on the market. It should use modern technology to make free speech, free assembly, and a free press truly universal and, therefore, fully educational.

Schools are designed on the assumption that there is a secret to everything in life; that the quality of life depends on knowing that secret; that secrets can be known only in orderly successions; and that only teachers can properly reveal these secrets. An individual with a schooled mind conceives of the world as a pyramid of classified packages accessible only to those who carry the proper tags. New educational institutions would break apart this pyramid. Their purpose must be to facilitate access for the learner: to allow him to look into the windows of the control room or the parliament, if he cannot get in by the door. Moreover, such new institutions should be channels to which the learner would have access without credentials or pedigree—public spaces in which peers and elders outside his immediate horizon would become available.

I believe that no more than four—possibly even three—distinct "channels" or learning exchanges could contain all the resources needed for real learning. The child grows up in a world of things, surrounded by people who serve as models for skills and values. He finds peers who challenge him to argue, to compete, to cooperate, and to understand; and if the child is lucky, he is exposed to confrontation or criticism by an experienced elder who really cares. Things, models, peers, and elders are four resources each of which requires a different type of arrangement to ensure that everybody has ample access to it.

I will use the words "opportunity web" for "network" to designate specific ways to provide access to each of four sets of resources. "Network" is often used, unfortunately, to designate the channels reserved to material selected by others for indoctrination, instruction, and entertainment. But it can also be used for the telephone or the postal service, which are primarily accessible to individuals who want to send messages to one another. I wish we had another word to designate such reticular structures for mutual access, a word less evocative of entrapment, less degraded by current usage and more suggestive of the fact that any such arrangement includes legal, organizational, and technical aspects. Not having found such a term, I will try to redeem the one which is available, using it as a synonym of "educational web".

What are needed are new networks, readily available to the public and designed to spread equal opportunity for learning and teaching.

To give an example: The same level of technology is used in TV and in tape recorders. All Latin-American countries now have introduced TV: in Bolivia the government has financed a TV station, which was built six years ago, and there are no more than seven thousand TV sets for four million citizens. The money now tied up in TV installations throughout Latin America could have provided every fifth adult with a tape recorder. In addition, the money would have sufficed to provide an almost unlimited library of prerecorded tapes, with outlets even in remote villages, as well as an ample supply of empty tapes.

This network of tape recorders, of course, would be radically different from the present network of TV. It would provide opportunity for free expression: literate and illiterate alike could record, preserve, disseminate, and repeat their opinions. The present investment in TV, instead, provides bureaucrats, whether politicians or educators, with the power to sprinkle the continent with institutionally produced programs which they—or their sponsors—decide are good for or in demand by the people.

Technology is available to develop either independence and learning or bureaucracy and teaching.

## Four Networks

The planning of new educational institutions ought not to begin with the administrative goals of a principal or president, or with the teaching goals of a professional educator, or with the learning goals of any hypothetical class of people. It must not start with the question, "What should someone learn?" but with the question, "What kinds of things and people might learners want to be in contact with in order to learn?"

Someone who wants to learn knows that he needs both information and critical response to its use from somebody else. Information can be stored in things and in persons. In a good educational system access to things ought to be available at the sole bidding of the learner, while access to informants requires, in addition, others' consent. Criticism can also come from two directions: from peers or from elders, that is, from fellow learners

## 6. Learning Webs

whose immediate interests match mine, or from those who will grant me a share in their superior experience. Peers can be colleagues with whom to raise a question, companions for playful and enjoyable (or arduous) reading or walking, challengers at any type of game. Elders can be consultants on which skill to learn, which method to use, what company to seek at a given moment. They can be guides to the right questions to be raised among peers and to the deficiency of the answers they arrive at. Most of these resources are plentiful. But they are neither conventionally perceived as educational resources, nor is access to them for learning purposes easy, especially for the poor. We must conceive of new relational structures which are deliberately set up to facilitate access to these resources for the use of anybody who is motivated to seek them for his education. Administrative, technological, and especially legal arrangements are required to set up such web-like structures.

Educational resources are usually labeled according to educators' curricular goals. I propose to do the contrary, to label four different approaches which enable the student to gain access to any educational resource which may help him to define and achieve his own goals:

1. Reference Services to Educational Objects—which facilitate access to things or processes used for formal learning. Some of these things can be reserved for this purpose, stored in libraries, rental agencies, laboratories, and showrooms like museums and theaters; others can be in daily use in factories, airports, or on farms, but made available to students as apprentices or on off- hours.

2. Skill Exchanges—which permit persons to list their skills, the conditions under which they are willing to serve as models for others who want to learn these skills, and the addresses at which they can be reached.

3. Peer-Matching—a communications network which permits persons to describe the learning activity in which they wish to engage, in the hope of finding a partner for the inquiry.

4. Reference Services to Educators-at-Large—who can be listed in a directory giving the addresses and self-descriptions of professionals,

paraprofessionals, and free-lancers, along with conditions of access to their services. Such educators, as we will see, could be chosen by polling or consulting their former clients.

### Reference Services to Educational Objects

Things are basic resources for learning. The quality of the environment and the relationship of a person to it will determine how much he learns incidentally. Formal learning requires special access to ordinary things, on the one hand, or, on the other, easy and dependable access to special things made for educational purposes. An example of the former is the special right to operate or dismantle a machine in a garage. An example of the latter is the general right to use an abacus, a computer, a book, a botanical garden, or a machine withdrawn from production and placed at the full disposal of students.

At present, attention is focused on the disparity between rich and poor children in their access to things and in the manner in which they can learn from them. OEO and other agencies, following this approach, concentrate on equalizing chances, by trying to provide more educational equipment for the poor. A more radical point of departure would be to recognize that in the city rich and poor alike are artificially kept away from most of the things that surround them. Children born into the age of plastics and efficiency experts must penetrate two barriers which obstruct their understanding: one built into things and the other around institutions. Industrial design creates a world of things that resist insight into their nature, and schools shut the learner out of the world of things in their meaningful setting.

After a short visit to New York, a woman from a Mexican village told me she was impressed by the fact that stores sold "only wares heavily made up with cosmetics." I understood her to mean that industrial products "speak" to their customers about their allurements and not about their nature. Industry has surrounded people with artifacts whose inner workings only specialists are allowed to understand. The nonspecialist is discouraged from figuring out what makes a watch tick, or a telephone ring, or an electric typewriter work, by being warned that it will break if he tries. He can be told what makes a transistor radio work, but he cannot find out for himself. This type of design tends to reinforce a noninventive society in which the experts find it progressively easier to hide behind their expertise and beyond evaluation.

The man-made environment has become as inscrutable as nature is for the primitive. At the same time, educational materials have been monopolized by school. Simple educational objects have been expensively packaged by the knowledge industry. They have become specialized tools for professional educators, and their cost has been inflated by forcing them to stimulate either environments or teachers.

The teacher is jealous of the textbook he defines as his professional implement. The student may come to hate the lab because he associates it with schoolwork. The administrator rationalizes his protective attitude toward the library as a defense of costly public equipment against those who would play with it rather than learn. In this atmosphere the student too often uses the map, the lab, the encyclopedia, or the microscope only at the rare moments when the curriculum tells him to do so. Even the great classics become part of "sophomore year" instead of marking a new turn in a person's life. School removes things from everyday use by labeling them educational tools.

If we are to deschool, both tendencies must be reversed. The general physical environment must be made accessible, and those physical learning resources which have been reduced to teaching instruments must become generally available for self-directed learning. Using things only as part of a curriculum can have an even worse effect than just removing them from the general environment. It can corrupt the attitudes of pupils.

Games are a case in point. I do not mean the "games" of the physical education department (such as football and basketball), which the schools use to raise income and prestige and in which they have made a substantial capital investment. As the athletes themselves are well aware, these enterprises, which take the form of warlike tournaments, have undermined the playfulness of sports and are used to reinforce the competitive nature of schools. Rather I have in mind the educational games which can provide a unique way to penetrate formal systems. Set theory, linguistics, propositional logic, geometry, physics, and even chemistry reveal themselves with little effort to certain persons who play these games. A friend of mine went to a Mexican market with a game called "Wff'n Proof," which consists of some dice on which twelve logical symbols are imprinted. He showed children which two or three combinations constituted a well-formed sentence, and inductively within the first hour some onlookers also grasped the principle. Within a few hours of playfully conducting formal logical proofs, some children are capable of introducing others to the fundamental proofs of propositional logic. The others just walk away.

In fact, for some children such games are a special form of liberating education, since they heighten their awareness of the fact that formal systems are built on changeable axioms and that conceptual operations have a gamelike nature. They are also simple, cheap, and—to a large extent—can be organized by the players themselves. Used outside the curriculum such games provide an opportunity for identifying and developing unusual talent, while the school psychologist will often identify those who have such talent as in danger of becoming antisocial, sick, or unbalanced. Within school, when used in the form of tournaments, games are not only removed from the sphere of leisure; they often become tools used to translate playfulness into competition, a lack of abstract reasoning into a sign of inferiority. An exercise which is liberating for some character types becomes a strait jacket for others.

The control of school over educational equipment has still another effect. It increases enormously the cost of such cheap materials. Once their use is restricted to scheduled hours, professionals are paid to supervise their acquisition, storage, and use. Then students vent their anger against the school on the equipment, which must be purchased once again.

Paralleling the untouchability of teaching tools is the impenetrability

## 6. Learning Webs

of modern junk. In the thirties any self-respecting boy knew how to repair an automobile, but now car makers multiply wires and withhold manuals from everyone except specialized mechanics. In a former era an old radio contained enough coils and condensers to build a transmitter that would make all the neighborhood radios scream in feedback. Transistor radios are more portable, but nobody dares to take them apart. To change this in the highly industrialized countries will be immensely difficult; but at least in the Third World we must insist on built-in educational qualities.

To illustrate my point, let me present a model: By spending ten million dollars it would be possible to connect forty thousand hamlets in a country like Peru with a spiderweb of six-foot-wide trails and maintain these, and, in addition, provide the country with 200,000 three-wheeled mechanical donkeys—five on the average for each hamlet. Few poor countries of this size spend less than this yearly on cars and roads, both of which are now restricted mainly to the rich and their employees, while poor people remain trapped in their villages. Each of these simple but durable little vehicles would cost $125—half of which would pay for transmission and a six-horsepower motor. A "donkey" could make 15 mph, and it can carry loads of 850 pounds (that is, most things besides tree trunks and steel beams which are ordinarily moved).

The political appeal of such a transportation system to a peasantry is obvious. Equally obvious is the reason why those who hold power—and thereby automatically have a car—are not interested in spending money on trails and in clogging roads with engine driven donkeys. The universal donkey could work only if a country's leaders were willing to impose a national speed limit of, say, twenty-five miles an hour and adapt its public institutions to this. The model could not work if conceived only as a stopgap.

This is not the place to elaborate on the political, social, economic, financial, and technical feasibility of this model. I wish only to indicate that educational considerations may be of prime importance when choosing such an alternative to capital-intensive transport. By raising the unit cost per donkey by some 20 percent it would become possible to plan the production of all its parts in such a manner that, as far as possible, each future owner would spend a month or two making and understanding his machine and would be able to repair it. With this additional cost it would also be possible to decentralize production into dispersed plants. The added benefits would result not only from including educational costs in the construction process. Even more significantly, a durable motor which practically anyone could learn to repair and which could be used as a plow and pump by somebody who understood it would provide much higher educational benefits than the inscrutable engines of the advanced countries.

Not only the junk but also the supposedly public places of the modern city have become impenetrable. In American society, children are excluded from most things and places on the grounds that they are private. But even in societies which have declared an end to private property children are kept away from the same places and things because they are considered the special domain of professionals and dangerous to the uninitiated. Since the last generation the railroad yard has become as inaccessible as the fire station. Yet with a little ingenuity it should not be difficult to provide for safety in such places. To deschool the artifacts of education will require making the artifacts and processes available—and recognizing their educational value. Certainly, some workers would find it inconvenient to be accessible to learners; but this inconvenience must be balanced against the educational gains.

Private cars could be banned from Manhattan. Five years ago it was unthinkable. Now certain New York streets are closed off at odd hours, and this trend will probably continue. Indeed, most cross-streets should be closed to automotive traffic and parking should be forbidden everywhere. In a city opened up to people, teaching materials which are now locked up in storerooms and laboratories could be dispersed into independently operated storefront depots which children and adults could visit without the danger of being run over.

If the goals of learning were no longer dominated by schools and schoolteachers, the market for learners would be much more various and the definition of "educational artifacts" would be less restrictive. There could be tool shops, libraries, laboratories, and gaming rooms. Photo labs and offset presses would allow neighborhood newspapers to flourish. Some storefront learning centers could contain viewing booths for closed-circuit television, others could feature office equipment for use and for repair. The jukebox or the record player would be commonplace, with some specializing in classical music, others in international folk tunes, others in jazz. Film clubs would compete with each other and with commercial television. Museum outlets could be networks for circulating exhibits of works of art, both old and new, originals and reproductions, perhaps administered by the various metropolitan museums.

The professional personnel needed for this network would be much more like custodians, museum guides, or reference librarians than like teachers. From the corner biology store, they could refer their clients to the shell collection in the museum or indicate the next showing of biology videotapes in a certain viewing booth. They could furnish guides for pest control, diet, and other kinds of preventive medicine. They could refer those who needed advice to "elders" who could provide it.

Two distinct approaches can be taken to financing a network of "learning objects." A community could determine a maximum budget for this purpose and arrange for all parts of the network to be open to all visitors at reasonable hours. Or the community could decide to provide citizens with limited entitlements, according to their age group, which would give them special access to certain materials which are both costly and scarce, while leaving other, simpler materials available to everyone.

Finding resources for materials made specifically for education is only one—and perhaps the least costly—aspect of building an educational world. The money now spent on the sacred paraphernalia of the school ritual could be freed to provide all citizens with greater access to the real life of the city. Special tax incentives could be granted to those who employed children between the ages of eight and fourteen for a couple of hours each day if the conditions of employment were humane ones. We should return to the tradition of the bar mitzvah or confirmation. By this I mean we should first restrict, and later eliminate, the disenfranchisement of the young and permit a boy of twelve to become a man fully responsible for his participation in the life of the community. Many "school-age" people know more about their neighborhood than social workers or councilmen. Of course, they also ask more embarrassing questions and propose solutions which threaten the bureaucracy. They should be allowed to come of age so that they could put their knowledge and fact-finding ability to work in the service of a popular government.

Until recently the dangers of school were easily underestimated in comparison with the dangers of an apprenticeship in the police force, the fire department, or the entertainment industry. It was easy to justify schools at least as a means to protect youth. Often this argument no longer holds. I recently visited a Methodist church in Harlem occupied by a group of armed Young Lords in protest against the death of Julio Rodan, a Puerto Rican youth found hanged in his prison cell. I knew the leaders of the group, who had spent a semester in Cuernavaca. When I wondered why one of them, Juan, was not among them, I was told that he had "gone back on heroin and to the State University."

Planning, incentives, and legislation can be used to unlock the educational potential within our society's huge investment in plants and equipment. Full access to educational objects will not exist so long as business firms are allowed to combine the legal protections which the Bill of Rights reserves to the privacy of individuals with the economic power conferred upon them by their millions of customers and thousands of employees, stockholders, and suppliers. Much of the world's know-how and most of its productive processes and equipment are locked within the walls of business firms, away from their customers, employees, and stockholders, as well as from the general public, whose laws and facilities allow them to function. Money now spent on advertising in capitalist countries could be redirected toward education in and by General Electric, NBC-TV, or Budweiser beer. That is, the plants and offices should be reorganized so that their daily operations could be more accessible to the public in ways that would make learning possible; and, indeed, ways might be found to pay the companies for the learning people acquired from them.

An even more valuable body of scientific objects and data may be withheld from general access—and even from qualified scientists—under the guise of national security. Until recently science was the one forum which functioned like an anarchist's dream. Each man capable of doing research had more or less the same opportunity of access to its tools and to a hearing by the community of peers. Now bureaucratization and organization have placed much of science beyond public reach. Indeed, what used to be an international network of scientific information has been splintered into an arena of competing teams. The members as well as the artifacts of the scientific community have been locked into national and corporate programs oriented toward practical achievement, to the radical impoverishment of the men who support these nations and corporations.

In a world which is controlled and owned by nations and corporations, only limited access to educational objects will ever be possible. But increased access to those objects which can be shared for educational purposes may enlighten us enough to help us to break through these ultimate political barriers. Public schools transfer control over the educational uses of objects from private to professional hands. The institutional inversion of schools could empower the individual to reclaim the right to use them for education. A truly public kind of ownership might begin to emerge if private or corporate control over the educational aspect of "things" were brought to the vanishing point.

## Skill Exchanges

A guitar teacher, unlike a guitar, can be neither classified in a museum nor owned by the public nor rented from an educational warehouse. Teachers of skills belong to a different class of resources from objects needed to learn a skill. This is not to say that they are indispensable in every case. I can rent not only a guitar but also taped guitar lessons and illustrated chord charts, and with these things I can teach myself to play the guitar. Indeed, this arrangement may have advantages—if the available tapes are better than the available teachers, or if the only time I have for learning the guitar is late at night, or if the tunes I wish to play are unknown in my country, or if I am shy and prefer to fumble along in privacy.

Skill teachers must be listed and contacted through a different kind of channel from that of things. A thing is available at the bidding of the user—or could be—whereas a person formally becomes a skill resource only when he consents to do so, and he can also restrict time, place, and method as he chooses.

Skill teachers must be also distinguished from peers from whom one would learn. Peers who wish to pursue a common inquiry must start from common interests and abilities; they get together to exercise or improve a skill they share: basketball, dancing, constructing a camp site, or discussing the next election. The first transmission of a skill, on the other hand, involves bringing together someone who has the skill and someone who does not have it and wants to acquire it.

A "skill model" is a person who possesses a skill and is willing to demonstrate its practice. A demonstration of this kind is frequently a necessary resource for a potential learner. Modern inventions permit us to incorporate demonstration into tape, film, or chart; yet one would hope personal demonstration will remain in wide demand, especially in communication skills. Some ten thousand adults have learned Spanish at our Center at Cuernavaca—mostly highly motivated persons who wanted to acquire

## 6. Learning Webs

near-native fluency in a second language. When they are faced with a choice between carefully programmed instruction in a lab or drill sessions with two other students and a native speaker following a rigid routine, most choose the second.

For most widely shared skills, a person who demonstrates the skill is the only human resource we ever need or get. Whether in speaking or driving, in cooking or in the use of communication equipment, we are often barely conscious of formal instruction and learning, especially after our first experience of the materials in question. I see no reason why other complex skills, such as the mechanical aspects of surgery and playing the fiddle, of reading or the use of directories and catalogues, could not be learned in the same way.

A well-motivated student who does not labor under a specific handicap often needs no further human assistance than can be provided by someone who can demonstrate on demand how to do what the learner wants to learn to do. The demand made of skilled people that before demonstrating their skill they be certified as pedagogues is a result of the insistence either that people learn what they do not want to know or that all people—even those with a special handicap—learn certain things, at a given moment in their lives, and preferably under specified circumstances.

What makes skills scarce on the present educational market is the institutional requirement that those who can demonstrate them may not do so unless they are given public trust, through a certificate. We insist that those who help others acquire a skill should also know how to diagnose learning difficulties and be able to motivate people to aspire to learn skills. In short, we demand that they be pedagogues. People who can demonstrate skills will be plentiful as soon as we learn to recognize them outside the teaching profession.

Where princelings are being taught, the parents' insistence that the teacher and the person with skills be combined in one person is understandable, if no longer defensible. But for all parents to aspire to have Aristotle for their Alexander is obviously self-defeating. The person who can both inspire students and demonstrate a technique is so rare, and so hard to recognize, that even princelings more often get a sophist than a true philosopher.

A demand for scarce skills can be quickly filled even if there are only small numbers of people to demonstrate them; but such people must be easily available. During the forties radio repairmen, most of them with no schooling in their work, were no more than two years behind radios in penetrating the interior of Latin America. There they stayed until transistor radios, which are cheap to purchase and impossible to repair, put them out of business. Technical schools now fail to accomplish what repairmen of equally useful, more durable radios could do as a matter of course.

Converging self-interests now conspire to stop a man from sharing his skill. The man who has the skill profits from its scarcity and not from its reproduction. The teacher who specializes in transmitting the skill profits from the artisan's unwillingness to launch his own apprentice into the field. The public is indoctrinated to believe that skills are valuable and reliable only if they are the result of formal schooling. The job market depends on making skills scarce and on keeping them scarce, either by proscribing their unauthorized use and transmission or by making things which can be operated and repaired only by those who have access to tools or information which are kept scarce.

Schools thus produce shortages of skilled persons. A good example is the diminishing number of nurses in the United States, owing to the rapid increase of four-year B.S. programs in nursing. Women from poorer families, who would formerly have enrolled in a two- or three-year program, now stay out of the nursing profession altogether.

Insisting on the certification of teachers is another way of keeping skills scarce. If nurses were encouraged to train nurses, and if nurses were employed on the basis of their proven skill at giving injections, filling out charts, and giving medicine, there would soon be no lack of trained nurses. Certification now tends to abridge the freedom of education by converting the civil right to share one's knowledge into the privilege of academic freedom, now conferred only on the employees of a school. To guarantee access to an effective exchange of skills, we need legislation which generalizes academic freedom. The right to teach any skill should come under the protection of freedom of speech. Once restrictions on teaching are removed, they will quickly be removed from learning as well.

The teacher of skills needs some inducement to grant his services to a pupil. There are at least two simple ways to begin to channel public funds to noncertified teachers. One way would be to institutionalize the skill exchange by creating free skill centers open to the public. Such centers could and should be established in industrialized areas, at least for those skills which are fundamental prerequisites for entering certain apprenticeships—such skills as reading, typing, keeping accounts, foreign languages, computer programming and number manipulation, reading special languages such as that of electrical circuits, manipulation of certain machinery, etc. Another approach would be to give certain groups within the population educational currency good for attendance at skill centers where other clients would have to pay commercial rates.

A much more radical approach would be to create a "bank" for skill exchange. Each citizen would be given a basic credit with which to acquire fundamental skills. Beyond that minimum, further credits would go to those who earned them by teaching, whether they served as models in organized skill centers or did so privately at home or on the playground. Only those who had taught others for an equivalent amount of time would have a claim on the time of more advanced teachers. An entirely new elite would be promoted, an elite of those who earned their education by sharing it.

Should parents have the right to earn skill credit for their children? Since such an arrangement would give further advantage to the privileged classes, it might be offset by granting a larger credit to the underprivileged. The operation of a skill exchange would depend on the existence of agencies which would facilitate the development of directory information and assure its free and inexpensive use. Such an agency might also provide supplementary services of testing and certification and might help to enforce the legislation required to break up and prevent monopolistic practices.

Fundamentally, the freedom of a universal skill exchange must be guaranteed by laws which permit discrimination only on the basis of tested skills and not on the basis of educational pedigree. Such a guarantee inevitably requires public control over tests which may be used to qualify persons for the job market. Otherwise, it would be possible to surreptitiously reintroduce complex batteries of tests at the work place itself which would serve for social selection. Much could be done to make skill-testing objective, e.g., allowing only the operation of specific machines or systems to be tested. Tests of typing (measured according to speed, number of errors, and whether or not the typist can work from dictation), operation of an accounting system or of a hydraulic crane, driving, coding into COBOL, etc., can easily be made objective.

In fact, many of the true skills which are of practical importance can be so tested. And for the purposes of manpower management a test of a current skill level is much more useful than the information that twenty years ago a person satisfied his teacher in a curriculum in which typing, stenography, and accounting were taught. The very need for official skill-testing can, of course, be questioned: I personally believe that freedom from undue hurt to a man's reputation through labeling is better guaranteed by restricting than by forbidding tests of competence.

## Peer-Matching

At their worst, schools gather classmates into the same room and subject them to the same sequence of treatment in math, citizenship, and spelling. At their best, they permit each student to choose one of a limited number of courses. In any case, groups of peers form around the goals of teachers. A desirable educational system would let each person specify the activity for which he sought a peer.

School does offer children an opportunity to escape their homes and meet new friends. But, at the same time, this process indoctrinates children with the idea that they should select their friends from among those with

## 6. Learning Webs

whom they are put together. Providing the young from their earliest age with invitations to meet, evaluate, and seek out others would prepare them for a lifelong interest in seeking new partners for new endeavors.

A good chess player is always glad to find a close match, and one novice to find another. Clubs serve their purpose. People who want to discuss specific books or articles would probably pay to find discussion partners. People who want to play games, go on excursions, build fish tanks, or motorize bicycles will go to considerable lengths to find peers. The reward for their efforts is finding those peers. Good schools try to bring out the common interests of their students registered in the same program. The inverse of school would be an institution which increased the chances that persons who at a given moment shared the same specific interest could meet—no matter what else they had in common.

Skill-teaching does not provide equal benefits for both parties, as does the matching of peers. The teacher of skills, as I have pointed out, must usually be offered some incentive beyond the rewards of teaching. Skill-teaching is a matter of repeating drills over and over and is, in fact, all the more dreary for those pupils who need it most. A skill exchange needs currency or credits or other tangible incentives in order to operate, even if the exchange itself were to generate a currency of its own. A peer-matching system requires no such incentives, but only a communications network.

Tapes, retrieval systems, programmed instruction, and reproduction of shapes and sounds tend to reduce the need for recourse to human teachers of many skills; they increase the efficiency of teachers and the number of skills one can pick up in a lifetime. Parallel to this runs an increased need to meet people interested in enjoying the newly acquired skill. A student who has picked up Greek before her vacation would like to discuss in Greek Cretan politics when she returns. A Mexican in New York wants to find other readers of the paper *Siempre*—or of "*Los Agachados*," the most popular comic book. Somebody else wants to meet peers who, like himself, would like to increase their interest in the work of James Baldwin or of Bolívar.

The operation of a peer-matching network would be simple. The user would identify himself by name and address and describe the activity for which he sought a peer. A computer would send him back the names and addresses of all those who had inserted the same description. It is amazing that such a simple utility has never been used on a broad scale for publicly valued activity.

In its most rudimentary form, communication between client and computer could be established by return mail. In big cities typewriter terminals could provide instantaneous responses. The only way to retrieve a name and address from the computer would be to list an activity for which a peer was sought. People using the system would become known only to their potential peers.

A complement to the computer could be a network of bulletin boards and classified newspaper ads, listing the activities for which the computer could not produce a match. No names would have to be given. Interested readers would then introduce their names into the system. A publicly supported peer-match network might be the only way to guarantee the right of free assembly and to train people in the exercise of this most fundamental civic activity.

The right of free assembly has been politically recognized and culturally accepted. We should now understand that this right is curtailed by laws that make some forms of assembly obligatory. This is especially the case with institutions which conscript according to age group, class, or sex, and which are very time-consuming. The army is one example. School is an even more outrageous one.

To deschool means to abolish the power of one person to oblige another person to attend a meeting. It also means recognizing the right of any person, of any age or sex, to call a meeting. This right has been drastically diminished by the institutionalization of meetings. "Meeting" originally referred to the result of an individual's act of gathering. Now it refers to the institutional product of some agency.

The ability of service institutions to acquire clients has far outgrown the ability of individuals to be heard independently of institutional media, which respond to individuals only if they are salable news. Peer-matching facilities should be available for individuals who want to bring people together as easily as the village bell called the villagers to council. School buildings—of doubtful value for conversion to other uses—could often serve this purpose.

The school system, in fact, may soon face a problem which churches have faced before: what to do with surplus space emptied by the defection of the faithful. Schools are as difficult to sell as temples. One way to provide for their continued use would be to give over the space to people from the neighborhood. Each could state what he would do in the classroom and when, and a bulletin board would bring the available programs to the attention of the inquirers. Access to "class" would be free—or purchased with educational vouchers. The "teacher" could even be paid according to the number of pupils he could attract for any full two-hour period. I can imagine that very young leaders and great educators would be the two types most prominent in such a system. The same approach could be taken toward higher education. Students could be furnished with educational vouchers which entitled them to ten hours' yearly private consultation with the teacher of their choice—and, for the rest of their learning, depend on the library, the peer-matching network, and apprenticeships.

We must, of course, recognize the probability that such public matching devices would be abused for exploitative and immoral purposes, just as the telephone and the mails have been so abused. As with those networks, there must be some protection. I have proposed elsewhere a matching system which would allow only pertinent printed information, plus the name and address of the inquirer, to be used. Such a system would be virtually foolproof against abuse. Other arrangements could allow the addition of any book, film, TV program, or other item quoted from a special catalogue. Concern about the dangers of the system should not make us lose sight of its far greater benefits.

Some who share my concern for free speech and assembly will argue that peer-matching is an artificial means of bringing people together and would not be used by the poor—who need it most. Some people become genuinely agitated when one suggests the setting up of *ad hoc* encounters which are not rooted in the life of a local community. Others react when one suggests using a computer to sort and match client-identified interests. People cannot be drawn together in such an impersonal manner, they say. Common inquiry must be rooted in a history of shared experience at many levels, and must grow out of this experience—the development of neighborhood institutions, for example.

I sympathize with these objections, but I think they miss my point as well as their own. In the first place, the return to neighborhood life as the primary center of creative expression might actually work against the re-establishment of neighborhoods as political units. Centering demands on the neighborhood may, in fact, neglect an important liberating aspect of urban life—the ability of a person to participate simultaneously in several peer groups. Also, there is an important sense in which people who have never lived together in a physical community may occasionally have far more experiences to share than those who have known each other from childhood. The great religions have always recognized the importance of far-off encounters, and the faithful have always found freedom through them; pilgrimage, monasticism, the mutual support of temples and sanctuaries reflect this awareness. Peer-matching could significantly help in making explicit the many potential but suppressed communities of the city.

Local communities are valuable. They are also a vanishing reality as men progressively let service institutions define their circles of social relationship. Milton Kotler in his recent book has shown that the imperialism of "downtown" deprives the neighborhood of its political significance. The protectionist attempt to resurrect the neighborhood as a cultural unit only supports this bureaucratic imperialism. Far from artificially removing men from their local contexts to join abstract groupings, peer-matching should encourage the restoration of local life to cities from which it is now disappearing. A man who recovers his initiative to call his fellows into meaningful conversation may cease to settle for being separated from them by office protocol or suburban etiquette. Having once seen that doing things together depends on deciding to do so, men may even insist that their local communities become more open to creative political exchange.

We must recognize that city life tends to become immensely costly as city-dwellers must be taught to rely for every one of their needs on complex institutional services. It is extremely expensive to keep it even minimally livable. Peer-matching in the city could be a first step toward breaking down the dependence of citizens on bureaucratic civic services.

It would also be an essential step to providing new means of establishing public trust. In a schooled society we have come to rely more and more on the professional judgment of educators on the effect of their own work in order to decide whom we can or cannot trust: we go to the doctor, lawyer, or psychologist because we trust that anybody with the required amount of specialized educational treatment by other colleagues deserves our confidence.

In a deschooled society professionals could no longer claim the trust of their clients on the basis of their curricular pedigree, or ensure their standing by simply referring their clients to other professionals who approved of their schooling. Instead of placing trust in professionals, it should be possible, at any time, for any potential client to consult with other experienced clients of a professional about their satisfaction with him by means of another peer network easily set up by computer, or by a number of other means. Such networks could be seen as public utilities which permitted students to choose their teachers or patients their healers.

## Professional Educators

As citizens have new choices, new chances for learning, their willingness to seek leadership should increase. We may expect that they will experience more deeply both their own independence and their need for guidance. As they are liberated from manipulation by others, they should learn to profit from the discipline others have acquired in a lifetime. Deschooling education should increase—rather than stifle—the search for men with practical wisdom who would be willing to sustain the newcomer in his educational adventure. As masters of their art abandon the claim to be superior informants or skill models, their claim to superior wisdom will begin to ring true.

With an increasing demand for masters, their supply should also increase. As the schoolmaster vanishes, conditions will arise which should bring forth the vocation of the independent educator. This may seem almost a contradiction in terms, so thoroughly have schools and teachers become complementary. Yet this is exactly what the development of the first three educational exchanges would tend to result in—and what would be required to permit their full exploitation—for parents and other "natural educators" need guidance, individual learners need assistance, and the networks need people to operate them.

Parents need guidance in directing their children on the road that leads to responsible educational independence. Learners need experienced leadership when they encounter rough terrain. These two needs are quite distinct: the first is a need for pedagogy, the second for intellectual leadership in all other fields of knowledge. The first calls for knowledge of human learning and of educational resources, the second for wisdom based on experience in any kind of exploration. Both kinds of experience are indispensable for effective educational endeavor. Schools package these functions into one role—and render the independent exercise of any of them if not disreputable at least suspect.

Three types of special educational competence should, in fact, be distinguished: one to create and operate the kinds of educational exchanges or networks outlined here; another to guide students and parents in the use of these networks; and a third to act as *primus inter pares* in undertaking difficult intellectual exploratory journeys. Only the former two can be conceived of as branches of an independent profession: educational administrators and pedagogical counselors. To design and operate the networks I have been describing would not require many people, but it would require people with the most profound understanding of education and administration, in a perspective quite different from and even opposed to that of schools.

While an independent educational profession of this kind would welcome many people whom the schools exclude, it would also exclude many whom the schools qualify. The establishment and operation of educational networks would require some designers and administrators, but not in the numbers or of the type required by the administration of schools. Student discipline, public relations, hiring, supervising, and firing teachers would have neither place nor counterpart in the networks I have been describing. Neither would curriculum-making, textbook-purchasing, the maintenance of grounds and facilities, or the supervision of interscholastic athletic competition. Nor would child custody, lesson-planning, and record-keeping, which now take up so much of the time of teachers, figure in the operation of educational networks. Instead, the operation of learning webs would require some of the skills and attitudes now expected from the staff of a museum, a library, an executive employment agency, or a maître d'hôtel.

Today's educational administrators are concerned with controlling teachers and students to the satisfaction of others—trustees, legislatures, and corporate executives. Network builders and administrators would have to demonstrate genius at keeping themselves, and others, out of people's way, at facilitating encounters among students, skill models, educational leaders, and educational objects. Many persons now attracted to teaching are profoundly authoritarian and would not be able to assume this task: building educational exchanges would mean making it easy for people—especially the young—to pursue goals which might contradict the ideals of the traffic manager who makes the pursuit possible.

If the networks I have described could emerge, the educational path of each student would be his own to follow, and only in retrospect would it take on the features of a recognizable program. The wise student would periodically seek professional advice: assistance to set a new goal, insight into difficulties encountered, choice between possible methods. Even now, most persons would admit that the important services their teachers have rendered them are such advice or counsel, given at a chance meeting or in a tutorial. Pedagogues, in an unschooled world, would also come into their own, and be able to do what frustrated teachers pretend to pursue today.

While network administrators would concentrate primarily on the building and maintenance of roads providing access to resources, the pedagogue would help the student to find the path which for him could lead fastest to his goal. If a student wanted to learn spoken Cantonese from a Chinese neighbor, the pedagogue would be available to judge their proficiency, and to help them select the textbook and methods most suitable to their talents, character, and the time available for study. He could counsel the would-be airplane mechanic on finding the best places for apprenticeship. He could recommend books to somebody who wanted to find challenging peers to discuss African history. Like the network administrator, the pedagogical counselor would conceive of himself as a professional educator. Access to either could be gained by individuals through the use of educational vouchers.

The role of the educational initiator or leader, the master or "true" leader, is somewhat more elusive than that of the professional administrator or the pedagogue. This is so because leadership is itself hard to define. In practice, an individual is a leader if people follow his initiative and become apprentices in his progressive discoveries. Frequently, this involves a prophetic vision of entirely new standards—quite understandable today—in which present "wrong" will turn out to be "right." In a society which would honor the right to call assemblies through peer-matching, the ability to take educational initiative on a specific subject would be as wide as access to learning itself. But, of course, there is a vast difference between the initiative taken by someone to call a fruitful meeting to discuss this essay and the ability of someone to provide leadership in the systematic exploration of its implications.

Leadership also does not depend on being right. As Thomas Kuhn points out, in a period of constantly changing paradigms most of the very distinguished leaders are bound to be proven wrong by the test of hindsight. Intellectual leadership does depend on superior intellectual discipline and imagination and the willingness to associate with others in their exercise. A learner, for example, may think that there is an analogy between the U.S. antislavery movement or the Cuban Revolution and what is happening in Harlem. The educator who is himself a historian can show him how to appreciate the flaws in such an analogy. He may retrace his own steps as a historian. He may invite the learner to participate in his own research. In both cases he will apprentice his pupil in a critical art—which is rare in school—and which money or other favors cannot buy.

The relationship of master and disciple is not restricted to intellectual discipline. It has its counterpart in the arts, in physics, in religion, in psychoanalysis, and in pedagogy. It fits mountain-climbing, silverworking and politics, cabinetmaking and personnel administration. What is common to all true master-pupil relationships is the awareness both share that their relationship is literally priceless and in very different ways a privilege for both.

Charlatans, demagogues, proselytizers, corrupt masters, and simoniacal priests, tricksters, miracle workers, and messiahs have proven capable of assuming leadership roles and thus show the dangers of any dependence of a disciple on the master. Different societies have taken different measures to defend themselves against these counterfeit teachers. Indians relied on caste-lineage, Eastern Jews on the spiritual discipleship of rabbis, high periods of Christianity on an exemplary life of monastic virtue, other periods on hierarchical orders. Our society relies on certification by schools. It is doubtful that this procedure provides a better screening, but if it should be claimed that it does, then the counterclaim can be made that it does so at the cost of making personal discipleship almost vanish.

In practice, there will always be a fuzzy line between the teacher of skills and the educational leaders identified above, and there are no practical reasons why access to some leaders could not be gained by discovering the "master" in the drill teacher who introduces students to his discipline.

On the other hand, what characterizes the true master-disciple relationship is its priceless character. Aristotle speaks of it as a "moral type of friendship, which is not on fixed terms: it makes a gift, or does whatever it does, as to a friend." Thomas Aquinas says of this kind of teaching that inevitably it is an act of love and mercy. This kind of teaching is always a luxury for the teacher and a form of leisure (in Greek, *"schole"*) for him and his pupil: an activity meaningful for both, having no ulterior purpose.

To rely for true intellectual leadership on the desire of gifted people to provide it is obviously necessary even in our society, but it could not be made into a policy now. We must first construct a society in which personal acts themselves reacquire a value higher than that of making things and manipulating people. In such a society exploratory, inventive, creative teaching would logically be counted among the most desirable forms of leisurely "unemployment." But we do not have to wait until the advent of utopia. Even now one of the most important consequences of deschooling and the establishment of peer-matching facilities would be the initiative which "masters" could take to assemble congenial disciples. It would also, as we have seen, provide ample opportunity for potential disciples to share information or to select a master.

Schools are not the only institutions which pervert professions by packaging roles. Hospitals render home care increasingly impossible—and then justify hospitalization as a benefit to the sick. At the same time, the doctor's legitimacy and ability to work come increasingly to depend on his association with a hospital, even though he is still less totally dependent on it than are teachers on schools. The same could be said about courts, which overcrowd their calendars as new transactions acquire legal solemnity, and thus delay justice. Or it could be said about churches, which succeed in making a captive profession out of a free vocation. The result in each case is scarce service at higher cost, and greater income to the less competent members of the profession.

So long as the older professions monopolize superior income and prestige it is difficult to reform them. The profession of the schoolteacher should be easier to reform, and not only because it is of more recent origin. The

## 6. Learning Webs

educational profession now claims a comprehensive monopoly; it claims the exclusive competence to apprentice not only its own novices but those of other professions as well. This overexpansion renders it vulnerable to any profession which would reclaim the right to teach its own apprentices. Schoolteachers are overwhelmingly badly paid and frustrated by the tight control of the school system. The most enterprising and gifted among them would probably find more congenial work, more independence, and even higher incomes by specializing as skill models, network administrators, or guidance specialists.

Finally, the dependence of the registered student on the certified teacher can be broken more easily than his dependence on other professionals —for instance, that of a hospitalized patient on his doctor. If schools ceased to be compulsory, teachers who find their satisfaction in the exercise of pedagogical authority in the classroom would be left only with pupils who were attracted by their style. The disestablishment of our present professional structure could begin with the dropping out of the schoolteacher.

The disestablishment of schools will inevitably happen—and it will happen surprisingly fast. It cannot be retarded very much longer, and it is hardly necessary to promote it vigorously, for this is being done now. What is worthwhile is to try to orient it in a hopeful direction, for it could take place in either of two diametrically opposed ways.

The first would be the expansion of the mandate of the pedagogue and his increasing control over society even outside school. With the best of intentions and simply by expanding the rhetoric now used in school, the present crisis in the schools could provide educators with an excuse to use all the networks of contemporary society to funnel their messages to us—for our own good. Deschooling, which we cannot stop, could mean the advent of a "brave new world" dominated by well-intentioned administrators of programmed instruction.

On the other hand, the growing awareness on the part of governments, as well as of employers, taxpayers, enlightened pedagogues, and school administrators, that graded curricular teaching for certification has become harmful could offer large masses of people an extraordinary opportunity: that of preserving the right of equal access to the tools both of learning and of sharing with others what they know or believe. But this would require that the educational revolution be guided by certain goals:

1. To liberate access to things by abolishing the control which persons and institutions now exercise over their educational values.
2. To liberate the sharing of skills by guaranteeing freedom to teach or exercise them on request.
3. To liberate the critical and creative resources of people by returning to individual persons the ability to call and hold meetings—an ability now increasingly monopolized by institutions which claim to speak for the people.
4. To liberate the individual from the obligation to shape his expectations to the services offered by any established profession—by providing him with the opportunity to draw on the experience of his peers and to entrust himself to the teacher, guide, adviser, or healer of his choice. Inevitably the deschooling of society will blur the distinctions between economics, education, and politics on which the stability of the present world order and the stability of nations now rest.

Our review of educational institutions leads us to a review of our image of man. The creature whom schools need as a client has neither the autonomy nor the motivation to grow on his own. We can recognize universal schooling as the culmination of a Promethean enterprise, and speak about the alternative as a world fit to live in for Epimethean man. While we can specify that the alternative to scholastic funnels is a world made transparent by true communication webs, and while we can specify very concretely how these could function, we can only expect the Epimethean nature of man to re-emerge; we can neither plan nor produce it.

# 7. REBIRTH OF EPIMETHEAN MAN

Our society resembles the ultimate machine which I once saw in a New York toy shop. It was a metal casket which, when you touched a switch, snapped open to reveal a mechanical hand. Chromed fingers reached out for the lid, pulled it down, and locked it from the inside. It was a box; you expected to be able to take something out of it; yet all it contained was a mechanism for closing the cover. This contraption is the opposite of Pandora's "box."

The original Pandora, the All-Giver, was an Earth goddess in prehistoric matriarchal Greece. She let all ills escape from her amphora (*pythos*). But she closed the lid before Hope could escape. The history of modern man begins with the degradation of Pandora's myth and comes to an end in the self-sealing casket. It is the history of the Promethean endeavor to forge institutions in order to corral each of the rampant ills. It is the history of fading hope and rising expectations.

To understand what this means we must rediscover the distinction between hope and expectation. Hope, in its strong sense, means trusting faith in the goodness of nature, while expectation, as I will use it here, means reliance on results which are planned and controlled by man. Hope centers desire on a person from whom we await a gift. Expectation looks forward to satisfaction from a predictable process which will produce what we have the right to claim. The Promethean ethos has now eclipsed hope. Survival of the human race depends on its rediscovery as a social force.

The original Pandora was sent to Earth with a jar which contained all ills; of good things, it contained only hope. Primitive man lived in this world of hope. He relied on the munificence of nature, on the handouts of gods, and on the instincts of his tribe to enable him to subsist. Classical Greeks began to replace hope with expectations. In their version of Pandora she released both evils and goods. They remembered her mainly for the ills she had unleashed. And, most significantly, they forgot that the All-Giver was also the keeper of hope.

The Greeks told the story of two brothers, Prometheus and Epimetheus. The former warned the latter to leave Pandora alone. Instead, he married her. In classical Greece the name "Epimetheus," which means "hindsight," was interpreted to mean "dull" or "dumb." By the time Hesiod retold the story in its classical form, the Greeks had become moral and misogynous patriarchs who panicked at the thought of the first woman. They built a rational and authoritarian society. Men engineered institutions through which they planned to cope with the rampant ills. They became conscious of their power to fashion the world and make it produce services they also learned to expect. They wanted their own needs and the future demands of their children to be shaped by their artifacts. They became lawgivers, architects, and authors, the makers of constitutions, cities, and works of art to serve as examples for their offspring. Primitive man had relied on mythical participation in sacred rites to initiate individuals into the lore of society, but the classical Greeks recognized as true men only those citizens who let themselves be fitted by *paideia* (education) into the institutions their elders had planned.

The developing myth reflects the transition from a world in which dreams were *interpreted* to a world in which oracles were *made*. From immemorial time, the Earth Goddess had been worshiped on the slope of Mount Parnassus, which was the center and navel of the Earth. There, at Delphi (from *delphys*, the womb), slept Gaia, the sister of Chaos and Eros. Her son, Python the dragon, guarded her moonlit and dewy dreams, until Apollo the Sun God, the architect of Troy, rose from the east, slew the dragon, and became the owner of Gaia's cave. His priests took over her temple. They employed a local maiden, sat her on a tripod over Earth's smoking navel, and made her drowsy with fumes. They then rhymed her

## 7. Rebirth of Epimethean Man

ecstatic utterances into hexameters of self-fulfilling prophecies. From all over the Peloponnesus men brought their problems to Apollo's sanctuary. The oracle was consulted on social options, such as measures to be taken to stop a plague or a famine, to choose the right constitution for Sparta or the propitious sites for cities which later became Byzantium and Chalcedon. The never-erring arrow became Apollo's symbol. Everything about him became purposeful and useful.

In the *Republic,* describing the ideal state, Plato already excludes popular music. Only the harp and Apollo's lyre would be permitted in towns because their harmony alone creates "the strain of necessity and the strain of freedom, the strain of the unfortunate and the strain of the fortunate, the strain of courage and the strain of temperance which befit the citizen." City-dwellers panicked before Pan's flute and its power to awaken the instincts. Only "the shepherds may play [Pan's] pipes and they only in the country."

Man assumed responsibility for the laws under which he wanted to live and for the casting of the environment into his own image. Primitive initiation by Mother Earth into mythical life was transformed into the education (*paideia*) of the citizen who would feel at home in the forum.

To the primitive the world was governed by fate, fact, and necessity. By stealing fire from the gods, Prometheus turned facts into problems, called necessity into question, and defied fate. Classical man framed a civilized context for human perspective. He was aware that he could defy fate-nature-environment, but only at his own risk. Contemporary man goes further; he attempts to create the world in his image, to build a totally man-made environment, and then discovers that he can do so only on the condition of constantly remaking himself to fit it. We now must face the fact that man himself is at stake.

Life today in New York produces a very peculiar vision of what is and what can be, and without this vision life in New York is impossible. A child on the streets of New York never touches anything which has not been scientifically developed, engineered, planned, and sold to someone. Even the trees are there because the Parks Department decided to put them there. The jokes the child hears on television have been programmed at a high cost. The refuse with which he plays in the streets of Harlem is made of broken packages planned for somebody else. Even desires and fears are institutionally shaped. Power and violence are organized and managed: the gangs versus the police. Learning itself is defined as the consumption of subject matter, which is the result of researched, planned, and promoted programs. Whatever good there is, is the product of some specialized institution. It would be foolish to demand something which some institution cannot produce. The child of the city cannot expect anything which lies outside the possible development of institutional process. Even his fantasy is prompted to produce science fiction. He can experience the poetic surprise of the unplanned only through his encounter with "dirt," blunder, or failure: the orange peel in the gutter, the puddle in the street, the breakdown of order, program, or machine are the only take-offs for creative fancy. "Goofing off" becomes the only poetry at hand.

Since there is nothing desirable which has not been planned, the city child soon concludes that we will always be able to design an institution for our every want. He takes for granted the power of process to create value. Whether the goal is meeting a mate, integrating a neighborhood, or acquiring reading skills, it will be defined in such a way that its achievement can be engineered. The man who knows that nothing in demand is out of production soon expects that nothing produced can be out of demand. If a moon vehicle can be designed, so can the demand to go to the moon. Not to go where one can go would be subversive. It would unmask as folly the assumption that every satisfied demand entails the discovery of an even greater unsatisfied one. Such insight would stop progress. Not to produce what is possible would expose the law of "rising expectations" as a euphemism for a growing frustration gap, which is the motor of a society built on the coproduction of services and increased demand.

The state of mind of the modern city-dweller appears in the mythical tradition only under the image of Hell: Sisyphus, who for a while had chained Thanatos (death), must roll a heavy stone up the hill to the pinnacle of Hell,

## 7. Rebirth of Epimethean Man

and the stone always slips from his grip just when he is about to reach the top. Tantalus, who was invited by the gods to share their meal, and on that occasion stole their secret of how to prepare all-healing ambrosia, which bestowed immortality, suffers eternal hunger and thirst standing in a river of receding waters, overshadowed by fruit trees with receding branches. A world of ever-rising demands is not just evil—it can be spoken of only as Hell.

Man has developed the frustrating power to demand anything because he cannot visualize anything which an institution cannot do for him. Surrounded by all-powerful tools, man is reduced to a tool of his tools. Each of the institutions meant to exorcise one of the primeval evils has become a fail-safe, self-sealing coffin for man. Man is trapped in the boxes he makes to contain the ills Pandora allowed to escape. The blackout of reality in the smog produced by our tools has enveloped us. Quite suddenly we find ourselves in the darkness of our own trap.

Reality itself has become dependent on human decision. The same President who ordered the ineffective invasion of Cambodia could equally well order the effective use of the atom. The "Hiroshima switch" now can cut the navel of the Earth. Man has acquired the power to make Chaos overwhelm both Eros and Gaia. This new power of man to cut the navel of the Earth is a constant reminder that our institutions not only create their own ends, but also have the power to put an end to themselves and to us. The absurdity of modern institutions is evident in the case of the military. Modern weapons can defend freedom, civilization, and life only by annihilating them. Security in military language means the ability to do away with the Earth.

The absurdity that underlies nonmilitary institutions is no less manifest. There is no switch in them to activate their destructive power, but neither do they need a switch. Their grip is already fastened to the lid of the world. They create needs faster than they can create satisfaction, and in the process of trying to meet the needs they generate, they consume the Earth. This is true for agriculture and manufacturing, and no less for medicine and education. Modern agriculture poisons and exhausts the soil. The "green revolution" can, by means of new seeds, triple the output of an acre—but only with an even greater proportional increase of fertilizers, insecticides, water, and power. Manufacturing of these, as of all other goods, pollutes the oceans and the atmosphere and degrades irreplaceable resources. If combustion continues to increase at present rates, we will soon consume the oxygen of the atmosphere faster than it can be replaced. We have no reason to believe that fission or fusion can replace combustion without equal or higher hazards. Medicine men replace midwives and promise to make man into something else: genetically planned, pharmacologically sweetened, and capable of more protracted sickness. The contemporary ideal is a pan-hygienic world: a world in which all contacts between men, and between men and their world, are the result of foresight and manipulation. School has become the planned process which tools man for a planned world, the principal tool to trap man in man's trap. It is supposed to shape each man to an adequate level for playing a part in this world game. Inexorably we cultivate, treat, produce, and school the world out of existence.

The military institution is evidently absurd. The absurdity of nonmilitary institutions is more difficult to face. It is even more frightening, precisely because it operates inexorably. We know which switch must stay open to avoid an atomic holocaust. No switch detains an ecological Armageddon.

In classical antiquity, man had discovered that the world could be made according to man's plans, and with this insight he perceived that it was inherently precarious, dramatic and comical. Democratic institutions evolved and man was presumed worthy of trust within their framework. Expectations from due process and confidence in human nature kept each other in balance. The traditional professions developed and with them the institutions needed for their exercise.

Surreptitiously, reliance on institutional process has replaced dependence on personal good will. The world has lost its humane dimension and reacquired the factual necessity and fatefulness which were characteristic

## 7. Rebirth of Epimethean Man

of primitive times. But while the chaos of the barbarian was constantly ordered in the name of mysterious, anthropomorphic gods, today only man's planning can be given as a reason for the world being as it is. Man has become the plaything of scientists, engineers, and planners.

We see this logic at work in ourselves and in others. I know a Mexican village through which not more than a dozen cars drive each day. A Mexican was playing dominoes on the new hard-surface road in front of his house—where he had probably played and sat since his youth. A car sped through and killed him. The tourist who reported the event to me was deeply upset, and yet he said: "The man had it coming to him."

At first sight, the tourist's remark is no different from the statement of some primitive bushman reporting the death of a fellow who had collided with a taboo and had therefore died. But the two statements carry opposite meanings. The primitive can blame some tremendous and dumb transcendence, while the tourist is in awe of the inexorable logic of the machine. The primitive does not sense responsibility; the tourist senses it, but denies it. In both the primitive and the tourist the classical mode of drama, the style of tragedy, the logic of personal endeavor and rebellion is absent. The primitive man has not become conscious of it, and the tourist has lost it. The myth of the Bushman and the myth of the American are made of inert, inhuman forces. Neither experiences tragic rebellion. For the Bushman, the event follows the laws of magic; for the American, it follows the laws of science. The event puts him under the spell of the laws of mechanics, which for him govern physical, social, and psychological events.

The mood of 1971 is propitious for a major change of direction in search of a hopeful future. Institutional goals continuously contradict institutional products. The poverty program produces more poor, the war in Asia more Vietcong, technical assistance more underdevelopment. Birth control clinics increase survival rates and boost the population; schools produce more dropouts; and the curb on one kind of pollution usually increases another.

Consumers are faced with the realization that the more they can buy, the more deceptions they must swallow. Until recently it seemed logical that the blame for this pandemic inflation of dysfunctions could be laid either on the limping of scientific discovery behind the technological demands or on the perversity of ethnic, ideological, or class enemies. Both the expectations of a scientific millennium and of a war to end all wars have declined.

For the experienced consumer, there is no way back to a naive reliance on magical technologies. Too many people have had bad experiences with neurotic computers, hospital-bred infections, and jams wherever there is traffic on the road, in the air, or on the phone. Only ten years ago conventional wisdom anticipated a better life based on an increase in scientific discovery. Now scientists frighten children. The moon shots provide a fascinating demonstration that human failure can be almost eliminated among the operators of complex systems—yet this does not allay our fears that the human failure to consume according to instruction might spread out of control.

For the social reformer there is no way back, either, to the assumptions of the forties. The hope has vanished that the problem of justly distributing goods can be sidetracked by creating an abundance of them. The cost of the minimum packages capable of satisfying modern tastes has skyrocketed, and what makes tastes modern is their obsolescence prior even to satisfaction.

The limits of the Earth's resources have become evident. No breakthrough in science or technology could provide every man in the world with the commodities and services which are now available to the poor of rich countries. For instance, it would take the extraction of one hundred times the present amounts of iron, tin, copper, and lead to achieve such a goal, with even the "lightest" alternative technology.

Finally, teachers, doctors, and social workers realize that their distinct professional ministrations have one aspect—at least—in common. They create further demands for the institutional treatments they provide, faster than they can provide service institutions.

Not just some part, but the very logic, of conventional wisdom is becoming suspect. Even the laws of economy seem unconvincing outside the narrow

## 7. Rebirth of Epimethean Man

parameters which apply to the social, geographic area where most of the money is concentrated. Money is, indeed, the cheapest currency, but only in an economy geared to efficiency measured in monetary terms. Both capitalist and Communist countries in their various forms are committed to measuring efficiency in cost-benefit ratios expressed in dollars. Capitalism flaunts a higher standard of living as its claim to superiority. Communism boasts of a higher growth rate as an index of its ultimate triumph. But under either ideology the total cost of increasing efficiency increases geometrically. The largest institutions compete most fiercely for resources which are not listed in any inventory: the air, the ocean, silence, sunlight, and health. They bring the scarcity of these resources to public attention only when they are almost irremediably degraded. Everywhere nature becomes poisonous, society inhumane, and the inner life is invaded and personal vocation smothered.

A society committed to the institutionalization of values identifies the production of goods and services with the demand for such. Education which makes you need the product is included in the price of the product. School is the advertising agency which makes you believe that you need the society as it is. In such a society marginal value has become constantly self-transcendent. It forces the few largest consumers to compete for the power to deplete the earth, to fill their own swelling bellies, to discipline smaller consumers, and to deactivate those who still find satisfaction in making do with what they have. The ethos of nonsatiety is thus at the root of physical depredation, social polarization, and psychological passivity.

When values have been institutionalized in planned and engineered processes, members of modern society believe that the good life consists in having institutions which define the values that both they and their society believe they need. Institutional value can be defined as the level of output of an institution. The corresponding value of man is measured by his ability to consume and degrade these institutional outputs, and thus create a new—even higher—demand. The value of institutionalized man depends on his capacity as an incinerator. To use an image—he has become the idol of his handiworks. Man now defines himself as the furnace which burns up the values produced by his tools. And there is no limit to his capacity. His is the act of Prometheus carried to an extreme.

The exhaustion and pollution of the earth's resources is, above all, the result of a corruption in man's self-image, of a regression in his consciousness. Some would like to speak about a mutation of collective consciousness which leads to a conception of man as an organism dependent not on nature and individuals, but rather on institutions. This institutionalization of substantive values, this belief that a planned process of treatment ultimately gives results desired by the recipient, this consumer ethos, is at the heart of the Promethean fallacy.

Efforts to find a new balance in the global milieu depend on the deinstitutionalization of values.

The suspicion that something is structurally wrong with the vision of *homo faber* is common to a growing minority in capitalist, Communist, and "underdeveloped" countries alike. This suspicion is the shared characteristic of a new elite. To it belong people of all classes, incomes, faiths, and civilizations. They have become wary of the myths of the majority: of scientific utopias, of ideological diabolism, and of the expectation of the distribution of goods and services with some degree of equality. They share with the majority the sense of being trapped. They share with the majority the awareness that most new policies adopted by broad consensus consistently lead to results which are glaringly opposed to their stated aims. Yet whereas the Promethean majority of would-be spacemen still evades the structural issue, the emergent minority is critical of the scientific *deus ex machina,* the ideological panacea, and the hunt for devils and witches. This minority begins to formulate its suspicion that our constant deceptions tie us to contemporary institutions as the chains bound Prometheus to his rock. Hopeful trust and classical irony *(eiro-neia)* must conspire to expose the Promethean fallacy.

Prometheus is usually thought to mean "foresight," or sometimes even "he who makes the North Star progress." He tricked the gods out of their

## 7. Rebirth of Epimethean Man

monopoly of fire, taught men to use it in the forging of iron, became the god of technologists, and wound up in iron chains.

The Pythia of Delphi has now been replaced by a computer which hovers above panels and punch cards. The hexameters of the oracle have given way to sixteen-bit codes of instructions. Man the helmsman has turned the rudder over to the cybernetic machine. The ultimate machine emerges to direct our destinies. Children phantasize flying their spacecrafts away from a crepuscular earth.

From the perspectives of the Man on the Moon, Prometheus could recognize sparkling blue Gaia as the planet of Hope and as the Arc of Mankind. A new sense of the finiteness of the Earth and a new nostalgia now can open man's eyes to the choice of his brother Epimetheus to wed the Earth with Pandora.

At this point the Greek myth turns into hopeful prophecy because it tells us that the son of Prometheus was Deucalion, the Helmsman of the Ark who like Noah outrode the Flood to become the father of a new mankind which he made from the earth with Pyrrha, the daughter of Epimetheus and Pandora. We are gaining insight into the meaning of the Pythos which Pandora brought from the gods as being the inverse of the Box: our Vessel and Ark.

We now need a name for those who value hope above expectations. We need a name for those who love people more than products, those who believe that

> *No people are uninteresting.*
> *Their fate is like the chronicle of planets.*
>
> *Nothing in them is not particular,*
> *and planet is dissimilar from planet.*

We need a name for those who love the earth on which each can meet the other,

> *And if a man lived in obscurity*
> *making his friends in that obscurity,*
> *obscurity is not uninteresting.*

We need a name for those who collaborate with their Promethean brother in the lighting of the fire and the shaping of iron, but who do so to enhance their ability to tend and care and wait upon the other, knowing that

> *to each his world is private,*
> *and in that world one excellent minute.*
> *And in that world one tragic minute.*
> *These are private.*[1]

I suggest that these hopeful brothers and sisters be called Epimethean men.

---

[1] The three quotations are from "People" from the book *Selected Poems* by Yevgeny Yevtushenko. Translated and with Introduction by Robin Milner-Gulland and Peter Levi. Published by Penguin Books, 1962, and reprinted with their permission.

# 世界教育经典名著丛书

★ 遴选了十四位世界著名的教育家、哲学家、心理学家的教育代表作
★ 国内多所高校的十余位权威专家领衔精心译校，翻译皆历时一年以上
★ 多部图书采用了汉英双语的出版形式，可满足读者阅读原著的需求
★ 大量的译者注和精彩的"译者导读"，有助于读者领略名著的思想精髓

《课程与教学的基本原理》
（汉英双语版）
【美】拉尔夫·泰勒 著
罗康 等 译
定价：42.00元

美国教育家泰勒的代表作，被誉为"现代课程理论的'圣经'"。学习课程与教学理论的必读经典。

《去学校化社会》
（汉英双语版）
【美】伊万·伊利奇 著
吴康宁 译
定价：58.00元

当代著名教育思想家伊万·伊利奇在书中炮轰美国教育、现代学校和社会，并绘制了"去学校化社会"的美好图景。著名教育社会学者吴康宁教授倾情翻译并解读这一思想巨著。

《教育的目的》
（汉英双语版）
【英】阿尔弗雷德·诺斯·怀特海 著
靳玉乐 等 译
定价：48.00元

英国哲学家、教育家和数学家怀特海的教育代表作。著名教育学者靳玉乐教授等翻译，译者注释丰富，十分有助于品味经典。

《民主主义与教育》（中文版）
【美】约翰·杜威 著
陶志琼 译
定价：42.00元

《民主主义与教育》（英文版）
【美】约翰·杜威 著
定价：68.00元

美国教育家杜威最有影响力的教育著作。译者历时两年译成，数易其稿，字斟句酌，译文流畅。

《我们如何思维》（汉英双语版）
【美】约翰·杜威 著
杨韶刚 等 译
定价：78.00元

思维训练领域的奠基之作，美国教育哲学家和心理学家杜威的重要代表作。该书曾于1925年被胡适、潘家洵等海内外名流学者列为"青年必读书十部"之一。

《经验与教育》（汉英双语版）
【美】约翰·杜威 著
盛群力 译
定价：38.00元

美国教育家杜威在书中深刻地诠释了"教育即生活""教育即生长""教育即经验的改造"等实用主义教育思想。评论者认为，该书"也许是杜威作品中最简明扼要、最通俗易懂且意义最深刻的一部"。

《童年的秘密》（汉英双语版）
【意】玛利亚·蒙台梭利 著
郑福明 译
定价：78.00元

意大利儿童教育家蒙台梭利所有作品中最有影响力的一部，为我们破解了儿童成长过程中的诸多密码。

《论教育学·系科之争》
【德】伊曼努埃尔·康德 著
杨云飞 邓晓芒 译
邓晓芒 校
定价：58.00元

全面地反映了德国伟大的哲学家和教育家康德的教育思想。我国著名哲学家邓晓芒教授和其弟子杨云飞博士根据德文原著历时一年多精心翻译，并撰写了大量的译者注和精彩的"译者导读"。

《理想国》
【古希腊】柏拉图 著
陶志琼 译
定价：62.00元

古希腊哲学家、教育家柏拉图的代表作，它既是一部"哲学大全"、政治学名篇，也是一部经典的教育著作。译者历时一年多，参考国内外二十余种译本翻译此书，并在书中增加了大量注释。

《爱弥儿》（精选本）
【法】让-雅克·卢梭 著
檀传宝 等 译
定价：48.00元

法国启蒙思想家和教育家卢梭的代表作，一本小说体教育名著。著名教育学者檀传宝教授领衔选译《爱弥儿》全书的精华部分。

**《儿童教育心理学》**
【奥】阿尔弗雷德·阿德勒 著
杨韶刚 译
定价：35.00元

又名《儿童的人格教育》，与弗洛伊德、荣格齐名的心理学大师阿德勒的代表作，帮助教师、家长捕捉儿童的心理敏感期，培养儿童健全的人格。

**《童年的王国：听斯坦纳讲华德福教育》**
【奥】鲁道夫·斯坦纳 著
霍力岩 等 译
定价：38.00元

奥地利哲学家、教育家，华德福教育创始人斯坦纳博士在本书中全面呈现了华德福教育的理念和做法。我国著名幼儿教育专家霍力岩教授领衔翻译。

**《教育漫话·理解能力指导散论》**
【英】约翰·洛克 著
郭元祥 等 译校
定价：48.00元

英国教育家、哲学家洛克的两部教育名著的合集，绅士教育理论的集大成之作。著名教育学者郭元祥教授精心组织翻译。

**《大教学论》（评注版）**
【捷】约翰·阿莫斯·夸美纽斯 著
刘富利 等 译
定价：48.00元

被誉为"现代教育之父"的捷克教育家、哲学家、神学家夸美纽斯的代表作，标志着教学论的诞生。牛津大学教育学者莫里斯·沃尔特·基廷在书中做出了精彩的评论，中文版译者撰写了大量译者注。

**《教育论：智育、德育和体育》（评注版）**
【英】赫伯特·斯宾塞 著
王占魁 译
定价：42.00元

英国教育学家、哲学家和社会学家斯宾塞的代表作，英国和法国的四位教育学家在书中对斯宾塞的教育观点做了独到的点评。

**《教育学讲授纲要》（评注版）**
【德】约翰·弗里德里希·赫尔巴特 著
盛群力 赵卫平 译
定价：50.00元

德国著名教育学家、心理学家和哲学家赫尔巴特的教育代表作，被誉为"真正的教书经"。美国康奈尔大学教授查尔斯·德加谟在书中针对赫尔巴特许多观点的社会现实意义做出了精彩的评注。

¥42.00

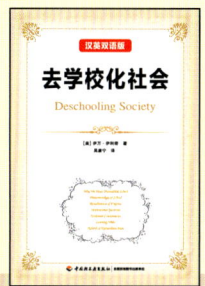

¥58.00

**《课程与教学的基本原理》（汉英双语版）**

【美】拉尔夫·泰勒 著
罗康 等 译

"现代课程理论之父"泰勒的代表作，被誉为"现代课程理论的'圣经'"。高等院校教育专业师生和中小学教师的必读经典。

**《去学校化社会》（汉英双语版）**

【美】伊万·伊利奇 著
吴康宁 译

当代著名教育思想家伊万·伊利奇的代表作。著名教育社会学者吴康宁教授倾情翻译并解读这一思想巨著。

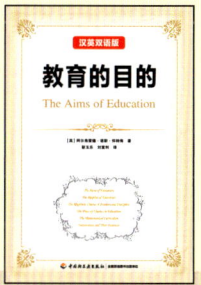

¥48.00

¥58.00

**《教育的目的》（汉英双语版）**

【英】阿尔弗雷德·诺斯·怀特海 著
靳玉乐 等 译

英国哲学家、教育家和数学家怀特海的教育代表作。著名教育学者靳玉乐教授等翻译，译者注释丰富、汉英双语对照，十分有助于品味经典。

**《论教育学·系科之争》**

【德】伊曼努埃尔·康德 著
杨云飞 邓晓芒 译／邓晓芒 校

全面地反映了德国哲学家和教育家康德的教育思想。我国著名哲学家邓晓芒教授和其弟子杨云飞博士根据德文原著历时一年多精心翻译。

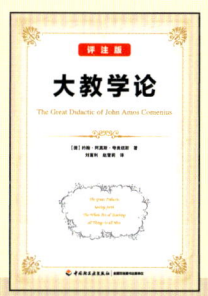

¥48.00

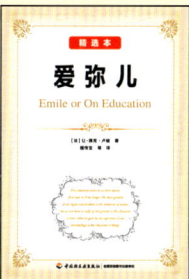

¥48.00

**《大教学论》（评注版）**

【捷】约翰·阿莫斯·夸美纽斯 著
刘富利 等 译

捷克教育家夸美纽斯的代表作，标志着教学论的诞生。牛津大学教育学者莫里斯·沃尔特·基延在书中做出了精彩的评论。

**《爱弥儿》（精选本）**

【法】让-雅克·卢梭 著
檀传宝 等 译

法国启蒙思想家和教育家卢梭的代表作，一本小说体教育名著。著名教育学者檀传宝教授领衔选译《爱弥儿》全书的精华部分。

# "世界教育经典名著丛书"阅读推广计划

尊敬的老师：

您好！感谢您对"万千教育"的关注与支持！

近年来，我们策划出版了"世界教育经典名著丛书"。该丛书包括16部世界著名的教育家、哲学家和心理学家的教育代表作，由国内十余位权威专家精心译校。大量的译者注和精彩的"译者导读"有助于读者领略名著的思想精髓。用纸考究、印刷清晰和软精装使丛书可读宜藏。我们有幸取得了数部著作在中国大陆的独家中文版权和英文版权。

其中《课程与教学的基本原理》《民主主义与教育》《教育的目的》《去学校化社会》《经验与教育》等7种名著采用了**汉英双语**的出版形式，可满足读者阅读原汁原味的经典之需。这些图书也适合作为高校师生专业外语教学文本。

为了让更多的人走近经典，值此"万千教育"编辑部成立20周年之际，我们制订了"世界教育经典名著丛书"阅读推广计划。

如果您对我们出版的经典名著感兴趣，我们将特别为您提供下列服务：

1. **免费样书**。如果您选用上述名著作为教学文本或为了便于您推荐给学生阅读，我们可以免费向您提供教师样书。

2. **优惠折扣**。若您所在院校的学生欲团购上述名著，我们将给予特定的优惠折扣。

欲了解"世界教育经典名著丛书"及阅读推广计划的详情，请扫描右边的二维码。此计划长期有效。

欢迎您与我们联系！

万千教育编辑部

咨询电话：010-65181109
读者邮箱：1012305542@qq.com
万千教育客服微信号：wqjy1998